JOB

BELIEF

A Theological Commentary
on the Bible

GENERAL EDITORS

Amy Plantinga Pauw
William C. Placher†

JOB

STEVEN CHASE

WESTMINSTER
JOHN KNOX PRESS
LOUISVILLE · KENTUCKY

© 2013 Steven Chase

First edition
Published by Westminster John Knox Press
Louisville, Kentucky

13 14 15 16 17 18 19 20 21 22—10 9 8 7 6 5 4 3 2 1

Scripture quotations from the New Revised Standard Version
of the Bible are copyright © 1989 by the Division of Christian Education of the
National Council of the Churches of Christ in the U.S.A. and are used by permission.

Book design by Drew Stevens
Cover design by Lisa Buckley
Cover illustration: © David Chapman/Design Pics/Corbis

Library of Congress Cataloging-in-Publication Data

Chase, Steven.
  Job / Steven Chase. — 1st ed.
    p. cm. — (Belief, a theological commentary on the Bible)
  Includes bibliographical references and index.
  ISBN 978-0-664-23247-4 (alk. paper)
  1. Bible. O.T. Job.—Commentaries. I. Title.
  BS1415.53.C43 2013
  223.'107—dc23

2012036167

Most Westminster John Knox Press books are available at special
quantity discounts when purchased in bulk by corporations, organizations, and special-
interest groups. For more information, please e-mail SpecialSales@wjkbooks.com.

For my daughter, Rachel

Give not thyself up then, to fire, lest it invert thee, deaden thee; as for the time it did me. There is a wisdom that is woe; but there is a woe that is madness. And there is a Catskill eagle in some souls that can alike dive down into the blackest gorges, and soar out of them again and become invisible in the sunny spaces. And even if he forever flies within the gorge, that gorge is in the mountains; so that even in his lowest swoop the mountain eagle is still higher than other birds upon the plain, even though they soar.

HERMAN MELVILLE,
Moby Dick; Or, The Whale, chapter 96, "The Try-Works"

Contents

COMMENTARY

Publisher's Note

William C. Placher worked with Amy Plantinga Pauw as a general editor for this series until his untimely death in November 2008. Bill brought great energy and vision to the series, and was instrumental in defining and articulating its distinctive approach and in securing theologians to write for it. Bill's own commentary for the series was the last thing he wrote, and Westminster John Knox Press dedicates the entire series to his memory with affection and gratitude.

William C. Placher, LaFollette Distinguished Professor in Humanities at Wabash College, spent thirty-four years as one of Wabash College's most popular teachers. A summa cum laude graduate of Wabash in 1970, he earned his master's degree in philosophy in 1974 and his PhD in 1975, both from Yale University. In 2002 the American Academy of Religion honored him with the Excellence in Teaching Award. Placher was also the author of thirteen books, including *A History of Christian Theology*, *The Triune God*, *The Domestication of Transcendence*, *Jesus the Savior*, *Narratives of a Vulnerable God*, and *Unapologetic Theology*. He also edited the volume *Essentials of Christian Theology*, which was named as one of 2004's most outstanding books by both *The Christian Century* and *Christianity Today* magazines.

Series Introduction

Belief: A Theological Commentary on the Bible is a series from Westminster John Knox Press featuring biblical commentaries written by theologians. The writers of this series share Karl Barth's concern that, insofar as their usefulness to pastors goes, most modern commentaries are "no commentary at all, but merely the first step toward a commentary." Historical-critical approaches to Scripture rule out some readings and commend others, but such methods only begin to help theological reflection and the preaching of the Word. By themselves, they do not convey the powerful sense of God's merciful presence that calls Christians to repentance and praise; they do not bring the church fully forward in the life of discipleship. It is to such tasks that theologians are called.

For several generations, however, professional theologians in North America and Europe have not been writing commentaries on the Christian Scriptures. The specialization of professional disciplines and the expectations of theological academies about the kind of writing that theologians should do, as well as many of the directions in which contemporary theology itself has gone, have contributed to this dearth of theological commentaries. This is a relatively new phenomenon; until the last century or two, the church's great theologians also routinely saw themselves as biblical interpreters. The gap between the fields is a loss for both the church and the discipline of theology itself. By inviting forty contemporary theologians to wrestle deeply with particular texts of Scripture, the editors of this series hope not only to provide new theological resources for the church, but also to encourage all theologians to pay more attention to Scripture and the life of the church in their writings.

We are grateful to the Louisville Institute, which provided funding for a consultation in June 2007. We invited theologians, pastors, and biblical scholars to join us in a conversation about what this series could contribute to the life of the church. The time was provocative and the results were rich. Much of the series' shape owes to the insights of these skilled and faithful interpreters, who sought to describe a way to write a commentary that served the theological needs of the church and its pastors with relevance, historical accuracy, and theological depth. The passion of these participants guided us in creating this series and lives on in the volumes.

As theologians, the authors will be interested much less in the matters of form, authorship, historical setting, social context, and philology—the very issues that are often of primary concern to critical biblical scholars. Instead, this series' authors will seek to explain the theological importance of the texts for the church today, using biblical scholarship as needed for such explication but without any attempt to cover all of the topics of the usual modern biblical commentary. This thirty-six-volume series will provide passage-by-passage commentary on all the books of the Protestant biblical canon, with more extensive attention given to passages of particular theological significance.

The authors' chief dialogue will be with the church's creeds, practices, and hymns; with the history of faithful interpretation and use of the Scriptures; with the categories and concepts of theology; and with contemporary culture in both "high" and popular forms. Each volume will begin with a discussion of *why* the church needs this book and why we need it *now*, in order to ground all of the commentary in contemporary relevance. Throughout each volume, text boxes will highlight the voices of ancient and modern interpreters from the global communities of faith, and occasional essays will allow deeper reflection on the key theological concepts of these biblical books.

The authors of this commentary series are theologians of the church who embrace a variety of confessional and theological perspectives. The group of authors assembled for this series represents more diversity of race, ethnicity, and gender than any other commentary series. They approach the larger Christian tradition with a critical respect, seeking to reclaim its riches and at the same time to acknowledge its shortcomings. The authors also aim to make available to readers a wide range of contemporary theological voices from many parts of the world. While it does recover an older genre of writing, this series is not an attempt to retrieve some idealized past. These commentaries have learned from tradition, but they are most importantly commentaries for today. The authors share the conviction that their work will be more contemporary, more faithful, and more radical, to the extent that it is more biblical, honestly wrestling with the texts of the Scriptures.

William C. Placher
Amy Plantinga Pauw

Preface

Writing a theological commentary on the book of Job is a spiritual journey, a journey for which I am very thankful. As a result of this journey and this writing I find that I have fewer things to fear, and many more things to treasure and to love and in which to find hope.

For a place and a community to research and to write this commentary, I would like to thank the Collegeville Institute for Ecumenical and Cultural Research. It is a special place. I would especially like to thank the executive director of the institute, Donald Ottenhoff, and program coordinator Carla Durand and operations manager Elisa Schneider, all three of whom showed unlimited support and compassion. The founder and president of the institute, Kilian McDonnell, OSB, is remembered in so many fond ways it would only embarrass him to begin to name them. I was blessed to have the opportunity to complete the commentary at Studium, a place of refuge for writing, scholarship, and art at Saint Benedict's Monastery. The director of Studium, Ann Marie Biermaier, OSB, exemplified hospitality and kindness. Thanks to all the Sisters at Saint Benedict's Monastery as well for spoken and unspoken support and prayer.

Douglas E. Christie and Jaco Hamman have been exceedingly humane, kind, and caring friends, even from opposite sides of the continent. Blessings to you both.

This book is dedicated to my daughter Rachel, whom I have loved from the moment I set eyes on her. Suffering happens; my hope is that this book might help, as needed, in her own journey as she grows and prospers. She is an ebullient, adventurous, intelligent, and kind spirit that I know will always see a light in the darkness; she will also always project and receive, attend to and even create much less darkness than light. May Job's clarity of truth and relentless integrity take root and grow in you too, Rachel.

Steven Chase

Abbreviations

ACCS	*Job*, Ancient Christian Commentary on Scripture, ed. Manlio Simonetti and Marco Conti
Ambrose	Ambrose, *The Prayer of Job and David*
Aquinas	Thomas Aquinas, *The Literal Exposition on Job*
AV	Authorized (King James) Version
Balentine	Samuel E. Balentine, *Job*
Calvin	John Calvin, *Sermons from Job*
Dhorme	Édouard Dhorme, *Commentary on the Book of Job*
Good	Edwin M. Good, *In Turns of Tempest*
Gordis	Robert Gordis, *The Book of Job*
Gordis, *BGM*	Robert Gordis, *The Book of God and Man*
Gregory	Gregory the Great, *Morals on the Book of Job*
Habel	Norman C. Habel, *The Book of Job*
Hartley	John E. Hartley, *The Book of Job*
JSOTSup	Journal for the Study of the Old Testament: Supplement Series
Maimonides	Moses Maimonides, *The Guide of the Perplexed*
NAB	*The New American Bible*
NEB	*The New English Bible*
NJPS	*Tanakh: The Holy Scriptures: The New JPS Translation*
NIB	*The New Interpreter's Bible*

NRSV   New Revised Standard Version
Newsom   Carol A. Newsom, *The Book of Job*
Perdue   Leo G. Perdue, *Wisdom Literature*
Pope   Marvin H. Pope, *Job*
PTS   Patristische Texte und Studien
Schreiner   Susan E. Schreiner, *Where Shall Wisdom
               Be Found?*
Terrien   Samuel Terrien, *Job: Poet of Existence*

Introduction:
Why Job? Why Now?

Given only three words to describe the book of Job, *suffering* and *why* and *hopeless* would be the most revealing. From the time of the book's composition to today, and at its most fundamentally meaningful levels, the human condition has not altered enough to render those three words either obsolete or no longer resonant to the human condition. It is not a question of *if*, it is a statement of fact that we *will* suffer. With suffering come questions; with questions about suffering and evil often comes a sense of hopelessness. Your spouse is diagnosed with and dies of pancreatic cancer over the course of just one year; a brave woman saves 2,500 children from a Warsaw ghetto—but many, many more die; your daughter disappears and is never heard from again; genocide, rape, and killing continue around the globe; young girls are sold into sexual slavery; another year of floods in Bangladesh and one-quarter of the bone-thin population either drowns or starves; you become unemployed, you lose your self-respect, you lose your house, friends drop away after offering useless advice; false rumors about you cause others to doubt your integrity; a son with severe depression finds a shotgun, and in a moment, he is gone; even "little" things—lost luggage, a minor car crash, a lover grown distant—annoy and cause grief; psychic, emotional, and spiritual trauma become daily companions; you begin to notice and are deeply saddened by ecological loss and degradation. Liturgy has become a chore, prayer a bore. God?

Of course to counter unpleasantness our consumer culture invents an endless series of needs that, if met by this or that latest product or therapy or fantasy, promise instantaneous happiness.

Why do so many read the book of Job? One reason is that not only Christians and Jews, but all who read the book of Job, find deep connection with it. The connection has to do with the reader's own inescapable personal suffering, perennial questioning, and empty, grieving hopelessness. The book of Job does not pull punches: with integrity and honesty it explores head-on the depths and truths of suffering and the related questions of loss, grief, and even, odd for a book of Scripture, divine absence.

Another reason people return to the book of Job again and again is that it is a transcendently beautiful piece of writing. "It is the greatest thing ever written with pen," Thomas Carlyle (a nineteenth-century Scottish essayist and teacher) wrote of Job. "There is nothing, I think, written in the Bible or out of it of equal merit."[1] Job is a piece of literature on the order of *Hamlet*, *The Divine Comedy*, or *Moby Dick*; it is among the greatest literary works the world has produced.

But the primary reason that people turn to the book of Job again and again is that it is a story that all of us can understand, not necessarily on an intellectual level, but on the basis of our own experience.

With literary cunning the book of Job draws us into our own pain, betrayal, grief, loss, heartache, sorrow, death, illness, and incomprehensibility by wounding us precisely at our weakest, most vulnerable point. YHWH's arrows pierce Job, and consequently us, with such uncanny accuracy that each of these illogical shafts wounds us exactly where pain will be most intense, most brutal, most unrelenting.

Is this not how we experience pain and loss and suffering: arrows that strike precisely at the points of our greatest weakness? For instance, an arrow finds our soul and spiritual pain is a swelling cascade of confusion; one is lost with no way before, no way behind, no

---

1. Thomas Carlyle, "The Hero as a Prophet," in *On Heroes, Hero Worship, and the Heroic in History*, ed. Archibald MacMechan (Boston: Ginn, 1901), 55.

guide or means of discernment. Eventually God becomes our foe, an enemy. Our world turns upside down so that events are suspended in slow, agonizing time. With poison in our bones we seek the treasure of the grave over the treasure of diamonds; with hope mocking our heart we dream of digging deep into the earth, even rejoicing in the opening grave, shoveling diamonds away like useless rocks that only block our way to the peace of death. We curse the joy that was the night of our conception and curse the day of our birth. Why did our mothers' knees receive us? All these images of graves and useless gems and prayers cursing conception and birth are, as we will see, from Job's lips. Each represents the wounds of arrows piercing things held most dear.

There is nothing else like the book of Job in the Hebrew or Christian Scriptures. Of all books of Scripture, Job wrestles most vigorously with God. As Johannes Hempel has written, the book of Job "is the struggle for the *last truth* about God."[2] From Job's perspective, this "last truth" may be dripping with ambivalence and shot through with evil. The integrity, if not the victory, of Job's journey is, in its humanness, a universal lament: Why? We practice lament too seldom today. But without lament one becomes only half a person; without lament we struggle only for the last *half truth* about God.

Roy B. Zuck also emphasizes the universal quality of the book of Job, writing,

> Because of its universal appeal and its unequaled literary quality, the Book of Job has drawn *lay persons and scholars* alike over the centuries. For lay believers, this book shows that suffering is common, that friends may misunderstand one's pain.... Scholars are challenged by the Book of Job because of its difficult Hebrew, its outstanding literary architecture, and its numerous problem texts. Its theology, its literary luster, its probing of the world's greatest mystery, its poetic style and beauty—these and other elements give it a fascination beyond description.[3]

2. Johannes Hempel, "The Contents of the Literature," in *Record and Revelation: Essays by the Members of the Society for Old Testament Study*, ed. H. Wheeler Robinson (Oxford: Clarendon, 1938), 73, cited in Balentine, 4.
3. Roy B. Zuck, ed., *Sitting with Job: Selected Studies on the Book of Job* (Grand Rapids: Baker Book House, 1992), 14.

The Composition of Job

"Few biblical books are as complex as Job."[4]

"Reading the book of Job has never been easy."[5]

"God's lyrical reply to Job from the whirlwind has long been a conundrum for biblical interpreters."[6]

"Such a diversity of opinions has prevailed in the learned world concerning the nature and design of the Poem of Job, that the only point in which commentators seem to agree, is the extreme obscurity of the subject."[7]

"The difficulties involved in understanding a text written in natural language may be the result of any one of several factors: complicated or unusual syntax either on the level of the individual sentence or that of the paragraph; use of vocabulary that is unfamiliar to the reader; extensive use of unusual metaphors; an unusually high level of abstraction."[8]

"The many rare words and textual disturbances make the Hebrew text of Job one of the most obscure in the OT."[9]

And so it goes; chosen nearly at random and anything but unique, those quotes represent consensus of readers and interpreters of the book of Job. The book is difficult. This section of the introduction looks at compositional elements that might help us grasp some of the reasons for the difficulties and help us experience and better understand Job's often complex and startling theology.

---

4. Carole R. Fontaine, "Wounded Hero on a Shaman's Quest: Job in the Context of Folk Literature," in *The Voice from the Whirlwind: Interpreting the Book of Job*, ed. Leo G. Perdue and W. Clark Gilpin (Nashville: Abingdon, 1992), 70.

5. Carol A. Newsom, *The Book of Job: A Contest of Moral Imaginations* (Oxford: Oxford University Press, 2003), 3.

6. Norman C. Habel, "In Defense of God the Sage," in Perdue and Gilpin, *Voice from the Whirlwind*, 21.

7. Lawrence L. Besserman, *The Legend of Job in the Middle Ages* (Cambridge, MA: Harvard University Press, 1979), 176.

8. Yair Hoffman, *A Blemished Perfection: The Book of Job in Context* (Sheffield: Sheffield Academic Press, 1996), 177. Hoffman devotes an entire chapter to these obstacles to understanding, "On the Difficult Language in the Book of Job," 176–221.

9. John E. Hartley, *The Book of Job* (Grand Rapids: Eerdmans, 1988), 3.

Composition in this case means the process by which the book attained its present form. As in all aspects of this process, the difficulty of the book of Job also complicates compositional issues such as authorship, date, setting, structure, its relation to other literature, and immense problems with its translation. Throughout this commentary we will work with an assumption of contemporary compositional unity: that is, regardless of the routes by which the book reached its present form, the form and composition of the book as we have it today will guide us as we examine its theological insight and integrity. Northrop Frye has said of the book of Job, "Guesswork about what the poem may originally have been or meant is useless, as it is only the version we know that has had any influence on our literature,"[10] and, we might add, on our theology.

That said, a few compositional elements *can* help to set the theological context.

Composition: Date

The overall complexity of the book of Job contributes to a diversity of opinions as to the date(s) of its authorship and redactive composition. Claims for the date of its composition range from the time of the patriarchs to the postexilic era (nineteenth to fourth century BCE). Most compelling evidence places it somewhere between the seventh and fourth centuries BCE, with the strongest evidence focused on authorship just before the Babylonian holocaust and through the period of the exile (587–538 BCE), with editing and redacting probably taking place shortly after the exile. The book, then, most likely represents reflection on a period of political, cultural, and theological crisis. The poetic dialogues form by far the greater portion of the book of Job, and if these poetic dialogues emerged as a response to the Babylonian crisis, then the other segments of the book fall into place, at least chronologically.

The first and hence oldest composition would have been the prose narrative that is the folktale in Job 1–2 and 42:7–17. This

---

10. Northrop Frye, *Anatomy of Criticism: Four Essays* (Princeton, NJ: Princeton University Press, 1957), 189.

folktale, probably an oral tradition initially, would most likely date from the preexilic period in a wisdom setting that offers a response to undeserved suffering in the context of faithfulness and patience. The major section of poetic dialogue represents and was most likely composed during or shortly after the exile. Two poetic compositions seem to have been added later than the poetic dialogues, being both literary and theological anomalies compared to the larger dialogues. These poetic pieces include a poem on Woman Wisdom (chap. 28) and the poetic monologue of Elihu (chaps. 32–37). A number of scholars date these later additions from the postexilic, Persian period (537–332 BCE).

The book of Job itself gives no direct internal evidence as to location, historical setting, or even the nationality of Job. The land of Uz appears to be an imaginary or mythical place. There is a reference to Job in Ezekiel 14:14, so at least by the time of Ezekiel in the early sixth century BCE, the poetic narrative must have achieved some fame.

Putting this together: the folktale, possibly oral, first came into circulation in the preexilic period, though there is no way to date the tale with any precision. Later, the majority of the poetic dialogue was written by the early sixth century BCE and placed with the folktale. The wisdom and Elihu chapters were then composed by another writer and added to the folktale and poetic dialogue that was the book of Job. Further redaction may have occurred after the addition of these later two sections. Thus overall, the best guess is that the book of Job was composed over a period of time sometime between the sixth (or possibly seventh) and fourth centuries BCE.

Theologically, even with this long period of possible authorship and editing, what remains of significance is that the book of Job was composed during a period of social, cultural, and personal crisis, upheaval, and moral and theological bewilderment.

Composition: Authorship

Given the wide discrepancy in the dating of the book of Job, it should not be surprising that questions of authorship are also impossible to answer with any certainty. Literary, genre, and theological comparisons with other texts within Hebrew Scriptures, within Hebrew wisdom writings, or a within a variety of non-Hebrew literature do little other than place the book of Job in a possible "family of origin." Such comparisons do nothing to pinpoint individuals, or even sects, that might have been responsible for the writing and redacting.

A few scholars believe the book had one author, but most believe that there was more than one. Some believe one editor put the book together in its present form, others, that there was more than one. All of these are conjectures.

Nonetheless, from both internal and external literary evidence, we can speculate with some accuracy about what the author knew. The writer was probably among the ancient sages whose work was attested in Proverbs and Ecclesiastes. If so the author would have been primarily interested in right conduct, a disciplined way of life with the assumption that faithful adherence to the teaching would bring prosperity and a long life (see Prov. 4; this assumption, of course, is what Job found not to be the case). Such sages, like Job, had deep religious commitment based on a high ethical monotheism. They taught that the fear of YHWH is the beginning of wisdom (Prov. 1:7; 9:10; Job 28:28a) and that departing from evil is understanding (Job 28:28b). These sages also had a keen interest in literature of other countries. They served as court counselors, scribes, teachers, and administrators throughout ancient Israel and in foreign cities. This accounts for their knowledge of diverse geography, customs, and literature as these are expressed in Job.

The author of Job fits this characterization well.[11] The writer is skilled in the use of proverbs, rhetorical questions, and enigmatic riddles. Of the poet and the poem, Samuel Terrien adds that, "The poem of Job has usually been approached either as a book of edification or as a tract of skepticism. Some have seen in it merely a discussion of innocent suffering and a plea for patience under duress. . . . Still others have praised it as a monument of revolt against the tyranny of dogma. . . . This classic Hebrew poetry offers a challenge

---

11. This sentence to the end of the section is based on Hartley, *Book of Job*, 15–17.

to the modern mind for it views life without illusion, but not with despair. It punctures traditional beliefs in God, but not in faith. It sees the futility of death, but not of creation.... It resolves the irony of doubt by depicting human life as an active contemplation.... The Joban poet foreshadows the theology of the agony of God, by which human agony is shared and borne."[12]

Other qualities of the author(s) can be gleaned from the book of Job itself. The author had a deep knowledge of nature, both animals and plants. The writer presents a series of animal portraits from the mouth of YHWH that is beautifully rendered, displaying knowledge of the ways of wild animals. The poet was familiar with many precious gems, using, for instance, five different words for gold. The poet describes the development of the human embryo with some delicacy and knowledge. The poet was familiar with weather patterns and constellations, and displays in poetry his soulful contemplation of the beauty, wonders, and diversity of the created order. The poet is informed about ancient mining practices, giving the most detailed passage on those practices preserved in Hebrew. The poet is knowledgeable about hunting, using six different descriptions of animal traps. The author was informed about other countries, particularly Egypt; it is possible that the Egyptian Book of the Dead had some influence on the construction of Job's oath of innocence (chap. 31).

The author's knowledge of patriarchal history is reflected in his ability to set his work in the patriarchal period, seen particularly in the use of archaic names for God and in judging character by adherence to patriarchal standards of ethics. The author was intensely interested in spiritual matters. Evidence for this includes Eliphaz's encounter with a spirit, the most detailed account in ancient Israel of a nonprophetic encounter with a numinous being, and the poet's allusion, alone in the Hebrew Bible, to the myth of the primordial man (15:7–8).

Job's hoped-for litigation or trial with God concerning innocent suffering is one of the primary concerns of the book of Job: Why

12. Samuel Terrien, *Job: Poet of Existence* (New York: The Bobbs-Merrill Company, Inc., 1957), 15–16, 247.

does the just person suffer? What is the correlation between sin and suffering? Why do the wicked prosper?

Finally, the friends represent common masks to biblical faith—ideology, orthodoxy, conventional wisdom, heroic idealism—and are intent on foreseeing what God will do in order to preserve their *theologies*; Job wants to find a way to take off the masks and to have God take off God's mask in order to preserve a *relationship*.

Composition: Literary

The book of Job is difficult to understand yet unsurpassingly beautiful literature.

What we have is the received text of the Masoretic tradition, a text containing three important aspects: the consonantal text, the vowel paintings, and the marginalia. The consonantal text reflects centuries of copying from the autographs down to the Middle Ages, when the textual tradition was fixed by scholars whom the Jewish tradition calls Masoretes. Translators of the Hebrew Masoretic Text of Job must make guesses and emendations, refer to the Septuagint and Aramaic versions of Job, and often rely on grace and a creative imagination. Even some of the very best translations leave out verses or entire chapters as too corrupt (in the Hebrew) to translate accurately. Idiomatic phrases, inadequate vocabulary (for instance, there are five different words for lion), expressions without equivalents (the *satan*, for instance), allusions to tradition, and figures of speech plague the most practiced translators. These along with more detailed problems in the poetry make positively accurate translation almost impossible.

See "Further Reflections: Masoretic Text and Canon" for more detailed discussion of transmission of the book of Job, the Masoretic Text, and difficulties of translation that help explain why one scholar has written: "It is a mark of creative genius that this author rarely appropriates literary forms or genres in their ideal form. Rather, they are adapted, modified, and transformed to meet particular artistic and theological ends."[13]

13. Norman C. Habel, *The Book of Job: A Commentary*, Old Testament Library (Philadelphia: Westminster, 1985), 42.

Theology

Suffering. Why? Hope! "What is it," asks Jack Miles, "that makes God godlike? What is it that makes the protagonist of the Bible so weirdly compelling, so repellent, and so attractive at once?" Speaking later of the end of the book of Job, Miles writes, "The climax is a climax for God himself and not just for Job or for the reader. After Job, God knows his own ambiguity as he has never known it before . . . yet the pervasive mood, as this extraordinary book ends, is not one of redemption, but reprieve."[14] "Ambiguity" may not be the best word for what God knows at the end of Job, but it is clear that over the course of the book, God's personality changes, radically, and more than once.

Focusing on this transformational God of Job, we can return to the three words that begin this introduction and from them begin to formulate a theology that flows through the book of Job. First, the theology of Job is based on universal experiences, not rational systems for neatly answering ambiguous questions. Joban theology is thus existential or spiritual theology in the sense that it is really best understood or assimilated not in some rational, systematic way, but in how we live and make meaning out of our own lives.

Methodologically, the theology of Job is set in the form of questions and questioning. The more one reads Job, the more one sees that the answer to any of these questions is always another question. Theologically, answers may help us to move forward, but whenever we let ourselves find shelter or get stuck in an answer, we fail to do justice to the book of Job as a "struggle for the *last truth* about God." Fundamentally, the book of Job is a series of conversations; the reality of true conversations involving both listening and communication is never answers but rather an invitational stance toward uncertainty that leads ever deeper into the all-encompassing journey of "why?"

Second, suffering, especially innocent suffering, is the theological root of the book of Job. We can say that metaphorically Job is a tree of suffering. From its root every other theological question grows in a

14. Jack Miles, *God: A Biography* (New York: Alfred A. Knopf, 1995), 327, 328.

wholly organic way. An opening theological question thus might be: what is authentic faith for the blameless and upright when they lose everything that is precious to them, as God admits, "for no reason" (Job 2:3)? Trunks and branches spread from the question of why the righteous suffer, which leads in turn to a host of related questions: What is the relationship between suffering and sin? Is there really any "innocent" suffering? Is there only one explanation for suffering? Is suffering beneficial? How is one best to endure adversity? And the ancient question that leads to wisdom: how does one suffer well? Leaves sprouting from the branches of these questions bring the tree alive: why is it that the upright suffer while the wicked often prosper? Fruits of this tree might be the questions surrounding divine providence and the nature of the afterlife. The irony of the tree of suffering that Job experiences is that it grows in a climate of loss, physical pain, death.

Is there a purpose in suffering? This question has haunted both Jewish and Christian readers from ancient times. Gregory the Great's vast *Morals on the Book of Job*, perhaps the greatest ancient commentary on the book of Job, attempts to understand the pedagogical purpose of suffering. Thomas Aquinas, another commentator on Job, finds purpose in suffering for the betterment of humanity: "Job has been tested through adversity not so that his virtue might appear before God, but so that it might be manifested to men."[15] John Calvin, who comments on Job in sermons and is thus often focused on particular and practical concerns of the congregation, writes of a number of possible reasons for suffering: "The scriptures, in many places plainly and clearly state that God, for various reasons, tests the faithful by adversities. At one time God tries them in order to train them to patience; at another to subdue the sinful affections of the flesh; at another to cleanse; sometimes to humble them; sometimes to make them an example to others; and at other times to stir them up to the contemplation of the celestial life."[16]

For many of the commentators, suffering teaches us something about the self as well as about God. Thus the doctrine of God comes

---

15. Thomas Aquinas, *The Literal Exposition on Job* 23:10, 302–3, 135.
16. Calvin, 33:418, cited in Susan E. Schreiner, *Where Shall Wisdom Be Found? Calvin's Exegesis of Job from Medieval and Modern Perspectives* (Chicago: University of Chicago Press, 1994), 103.

into play in Job. Is God responsible for evil? What is God's relation to evil? Isaiah 45:7 says, "I form light and create darkness, I make weal and create woe; I the LORD do all these things." Did God create evil? Within the book of Job, one of the Gods that shows up in the story, the God present in the narrative for, by far, the longest section of the book, is a hidden God. Throughout the poetic dialogues God does not speak and is, in effect, absent. Job calls out for this God to appear but the God does not, and Job (and the reader) must ask, why? This hiddenness is itself a question of divine transcendence, while questions of revelation and theophany within the narrative raise further questions about divine immanence or presence. Creation highlights the role of revelation in Job: the book is brilliantly illuminated with subjects from the created universe, from stars to worms, from gems to horses. The theophany in the whirlwind is a surprise; it is also another example of beautiful writing, and again raises theological questions unique to the rest of Scripture.

Does God change? In the prologue, the *satan* incites a presumably sovereign God to afflict Job with unimaginable suffering "for no reason" (2:3). During the poetic dialogues with the friends, a supposedly compassionate God remains distant and silent and hidden, leaving us to wonder if God cares about those who cry to the heavens for relief. In the whirlwind speeches, God speaks with such self-conscious pride and at such monopolizing length about so many things that seem, at first blush, to be irrelevant to Job's plight, we are left to wonder if mere creatures like Job matter to the Creator at all. In the epilogue, the God who condemns the friends and restores Job seems more fickle than just, more arbitrary than predictable.[17]

Just as we need to ask questions about the doctrine of God in Job, so do we need to explore the issue of theological anthropology. How do the multiple portrayals of Job (patient and defiant) and the friends (comforters and accusers) affect the divine-human relationship and the issue of suffering? Why does God not answer one in a thousand questions Job asks (9:3)? "What are human beings, . . .

---

17. Many commentators develop their own descriptions of the divine personalities that emerge in Job. These are based on Samuel E. Balentine, *Job*, Smyth & Helwys Bible Commentary (Macon, GA: Smyth & Helwys, 2006), 30–31.

that you [God] set your mind on them" (7:17)? Why , as written in the Psalms (8:5a), are human beings "a little lower than the Gods"? Does that height simply make them a better target for the arrows of suffering? Why is humanity fashioned "like clay" only to return to "dust" (10:9)? "Can a mortal be of use to God" (22:2)? Why are we born to trouble and suffering (5:7)? Why does God not just leave Job (and humanity) alone (7:19)?

Other theological issues growing from this tree of suffering include theodicy, divine justice and divine power, providence, the afterlife, what it means to be wise and what it means to be wicked, the possibility of a mediator or arbitrator between Job and God (which many have read as a christological question), original sin, and the nature of prayer, innocence, guilt, faith, and hope. The issues and questions raised in the book of Job are encountered by persons throughout the world.

In the book of Job the tree of questions rooted in suffering grows, is pruned, and grows again, seemingly without end. The cultural philosopher George Steiner has written, "We have long been, I believe we still are, guests of creation. We owe to our host the courtesy of questioning."[18] *The courtesy of questioning.* The book of Job, if its implications truly were understood, would seem blasphemous to many religious people. But the

> [Dialogue between Satan and God]
>
> [Satan speaks] "There was a certain man in the land of Uz whose name was Job."
>
> "We remember him."
>
> "We had a wager of sorts," said Satan. "It was some time ago. . . .
>
> "Did I lose or win? The issue was obscured by discussion. How those men did talk! You intervened. There was no decision."
>
> "You lost, Satan," said a great Being of Light. . . .
>
> Satan rested his dark face on his hand, and looked down between his knees through the pellucid floor to that little eddying in the ether which makes our world. "Job," he said, "lives still."
>
> Then after an interval: "The whole earth is now—Job."
>
> H. G. Wells, *The Undying Fire: A Contemporary Novel* (New York: Macmillan, 1919), 8–9.

---

18. George Steiner, *Grammars of Creation* (New Haven, CT: Yale University Press, 2001), 338.

questions, the questions that are never able to trap an answer, keep the book alive and true; they keep the honesty and truth of the tree of suffering growing: we owe our host "the courtesy of questioning." Several commentators on Job say simply that it is impossible to translate. Perhaps the problems with translation are more related to the pain and sorrow and grief and running sores about which we have yet to learn what it means, through the courtesy of questioning, to play the *perfect* (or even human) *host to suffering*.

1:1–2:13

Prologue:
Affliction, Friendship, Silence

In no book of the Bible other than Job do the conjectures of theology develop out of existential questioning in the midst of such unrelenting suffering. Wisdom, innocence, guilt, suffering, sin, creation, the nature and person of God, the place of evil in the cosmos, and scores of other theological issues normally argued and discussed as if detached from human life weave in and out of the Joban narrative, in each case with a raw inescapable example from which any reader with integrity cannot look away. Job himself is the object of suffering. But each of the characters in the narrative brings personal experience to a theological category or doctrine. Even God is given character, a personality out of which theological meaning is illuminated through unmediated experience of the sacred and divine presence. The theology of the book of Job that wraps itself around the reader like a conversation often makes us uncomfortable; even more, it forces the reader to question core convictions about God, self, and others. Job brims with theological meaning, but far from smoothing the rough edges or giving "system" or "construct" to theology, in the midst of Joban suffering theology is twisted and warped, deconstructed and broken—and often not satisfactorily put back together.

From chapter 1, Job's life is portrayed as a model of theological righteousness: Job is blameless and without sin; he is upright, a man of complete integrity; he fears God, which in the Hebrew tradition is the first and most important stage of wisdom (Ps. 111:10; Prov. 9:10); and of course he turns away from evil. His early days are full—a sign that he is steeped in God's favor: he has sons and

But if a man wishes to search out wisdom, let him not seek it in the abyss, like the philosophers who think that they can know its depths by their own initiative and their own ability. And let him not seek it in the sea—for indeed where there is tempest and windstorm, there wisdom cannot be—but let him seek it there where there is tranquility of heart and the peace that is beyond understanding.

Ambrose, "The Prayer of Holy Job," in *Seven Exegetical Works*, 2.5.23, trans. Michael P. McHugh (Washington, DC: Catholic University of America Press, 1972), 367.

daughters, a loving wife, servants, and wealth, including sheep, camels, oxen, and donkeys.

Finally, he is the "greatest of all the people of the east" (Job 1:3), meaning, since the east was itself associated with wisdom, that he is also the wisest of men in a culture where wisdom was equated with what we would call moral theology. The book of Job is a *wisdom* book that asks, "Where shall wisdom [theology] be found?" (28:12).

Prologue: Framing the Narrative

The prologue to the book of Job is probably an ancient moral tale that, along with the epilogue, brackets the much longer poetic dialogue. The prologue also hints at and foreshadows most of the major Joban themes. At first the prologue seems insignificant, no more than a rock jetty that protrudes, with its simple beacon, only a little, hesitant way into Ambrose's "tempest and windstorm" of Job's trials. But in reality it is a rocky promontory, an ancient abutment that, as the reader will come to know, keeps Job from the "tranquility of heart and the peace that is beyond understanding" that Ambrose insists are essential foundations to wisdom.

Perhaps there is a lighthouse on this storm-tossed jetty, but it casts an eerie kind of light. In his translation of Job, Raymond P. Scheindlin comments that Job "touches the limits of literature and perhaps transcends them" and suggests that we read Job not because it provides "answers to our questions, consolation for our grief, or redress for our anger, but because it expresses our questions, grief, and anger with such force."[1] They express such force in part thanks to the simple, ancient folktale prologue attached to the beginning of the poem. Even in its insecure light it reminds us that it refuses to accept anything short of justice, righteousness, and truth, even when answers to our questions are nowhere in sight.

We should early on clear up one misconception about the person of Job. Despite James 5:11, as we move from prologue to poetic dialogue we will see the famous "patient Job" for what it is: a myth. Job is anything but patient or enduring. In just one illustrative instance, Job is driven to wish he were dead: "Let the day perish in which I was born, and the night that said, 'A man-child is conceived.' Let that day be darkness!" (3:3–4a). Patient Job is not.

Setting the Story

Suffering is obviously the major theme running throughout the book of Job, with wisdom accommodated to theological doctrine the seeming goal. But the experience of suffering is at best a questionable soil in which to plant seeds of theology, expecting a crop of wisdom. Suffering is gritty and untidy, poor soil for theology or for wisdom. And yet theology that is grounded in the spiritual practice of reading Scripture does, even in the case of Job, somehow accommodate itself to the messiness of suffering. In the process of that reading we will find a few blossoms, a few new fruits of wisdom.

Experience leading to theological speculation and questioning fills the book of Job: we find discussion of guilt, justice, and retribution, implications for the doctrine of God and divine unknowability, theological anthropology, innocent suffering, hints of Christology, shadows of Edenic beginnings, the inexplicable origin of and presence of evil, suffering as spiritual journey and as moral pedagogy, questions about the nature of faith and hope, the very purpose of life, the dilemma of death, the fecundity of creation and the madness of destruction, doctrines of providence, revelation, election,

1. Raymond P. Scheindlin, *The Book of Job: Translation, Introduction, and Notes* (New York: W. W. Norton & Co., 1998), 26.

the "face" of justice and righteousness, the nature of wisdom and wisdom of nature. And we will see that Job is a book that, rather than answering theological questions and thereby putting them to rest, keeps them alive.

Job's Piety in the Prologue Chapters

The writer/redactor of Job is scrupulous, at least in the prologue, in his depiction of Job's unequaled piety. Job rises early to offer burnt offerings, just in case his children may have sinned and cursed God. After his first set of calamities, he mourns in deep grief, but still falls on the ground and worships God (1:20). Even more emphatic is the description of Job's piety, repeated three times in exactly the same words: Job is, according to the narrator, "blameless [*tam*] and upright [*yashar*], one who feared God and turned away from evil" (1:1, 8; 2:3). Not satisfied with this picture of Job, God adds to these words at 2:3 that even after the first calamities, Job "still persists in his integrity [*tummah*]," a word that will be important as the book progresses (2:9; 27:5; 31:6). In the mind of God in the prologue, Job is perfect, complete, finished, moral, and above all a man unequaled in righteousness. Before his own fall Job is not unlike Adam in the garden of Eden: the greatest of all men in wisdom and wealth, righteousness and blessing.

Job Does Not Sin: Things Still Fall Apart

Then, heaven takes note of this man of the earth and things begin to fall apart. Job is innocent and pure, yet suffering begins to overtake him. As the scenes of the prologue move in rhythm between earth and heaven, things not only begin to fall apart, they become ambiguous, ironic, paradoxical. God the omniscient, the righteous, the holy, appears to lack integrity; Job the wise, the just, the upright, and the perfectly moral is thrown from the garden of Uz into absolute chaos and suffering (Adam was condemned to a lifetime of making a living with his hands; Job's hands are useless, covered in sores and scabs and pus). Job the innocent, Job who in all this "did not sin or charge God with wrongdoing" (1:22), becomes Job whose "suffering was very great" (2:13). Piled one atop the other in a single day, a kind of reverse day of creation, Job loses his oxen, his donkeys, his sheep, his cattle, and all but three of his servants, to the double indignities of human enemies and then fire from heaven. Following immediately and worst of all, he then loses all of his beloved children, seven sons and three daughters. In a bit of a reprieve, God and the *satan* get back together. But the result is a new pact between the two from which Job's body becomes covered with loathsome, putrid sores.

The first losses break his heart and soul; these later losses put his body to waste. To make matters worse, from Job's perspective, all that has happened to him seems to have come from nowhere.

Franz Kafka's book *The Trial* is a twentieth-century retelling of the book of Job. Kafka captures something of Job's disorientation, bafflement, and confusion as Job's moral universe loses every significant point of reference. Like Job, Kafka's protagonist, K., can no longer find the way back to his former innocence or secular piety: given K.'s suffering and misfortune, the very concept of acquittal itself becomes useless and absurd.

Job too is entering a world of contradictions. After the first series of catastrophes Job "arose, tore his robe, shaved his head, fell on the ground and worshiped" (1:20). His wife urged him to "curse God,

> [K.'s attorney speaks] "There are three possibilities [for acquittal], that is, definitive acquittal, ostensible acquittal, and indefinite postponement. Definite acquittal is of course the best, but I haven't the slightest influence on that kind of verdict. As far as I know, there is no single person who could influence the verdict of definitive acquittal. The only deciding factor seems to be the innocence of the accused. Since you're innocent, of course it would be possible for you to ground your case on your innocence alone. But then you would require neither my help nor help from anyone."
>
> [K. speaks] "It seems to me that you're contradicting yourself."
>
> Franz Kafka, *The Trial*, trans. Willa and Edwin Muir (New York: Alfred A. Knopf, 1948), 192.

and die" (2:9). After the sores appeared, Job "took a potsherd with which to scrape himself, and sat among the ashes" or dung-heap (2:8), places of degradation and social ostracism.

Job's body is covered with "loathsome sores" (*shehin ra*). *Shehin ra* is a general Hebrew term for skin disease that can be translated in a number of ways: "running sores" (NEB); "severe inflammation" (NJPS); "severe boils" (NAB); "sickening eruptions."[2] This is the same man whom God had declared "blameless and upright . . . who fears God and turns away from evil. [Who] still persists in his integrity" (2:3), a "man who did not sin or charge God with wrongdoing" (1:22), a man who "did not sin with his lips" (2:10). This same man ends the prologue as a pathetic and broken bundle of confusion.

Most of the Christian tradition has persistently and adamantly denied innocent suffering. The logical conclusion of denying innocent suffering would be that since Job is suffering he must not be innocent; he must have sinned and sinned greatly. This is exactly what the friends' position comes to be. But God has affirmed Job's righteousness in no uncertain terms. Something is very wrong.

FURTHER REFLECTIONS
Innocent Suffering

It is clear in the prologue that Job suffers innocently. Furthermore, throughout the book, Job reminds his friends and his God that he is innocent, that from his perspective his suffering is unjust. The problem of innocent suffering is a perennial question in both theological and spiritual reflection. It is easy to find instances of innocent suffering today. For instance, according to the Evangelical Lutheran Church in America, of the world's current population of 6.7 billion people, 963 million people go to sleep hungry each night. In the developing world, "16,000 children die from hunger or preventable diseases such as diarrhea, acute respiratory infections, or malaria. Malnutrition is associated with over half of those deaths.

2. Ibid., 57.

That is equal to 1 child every 5.4 seconds."[3] Sometimes though, these numbers are numbing, and they buffer us from the enormity of the suffering. To remind us of the injustice and turmoil of innocent suffering, it is helpful to sift through concrete examples, without inconceivable numbers as buffers. For instance, in his book *The Third Reich at War*, Richard J. Evans describes an instance of *early* brutality (before the concentration camps were built and the brutality increased) in the Second World War:

> The SS officer in charge, August Häfner, later reported that, after objecting that his own men, many of whom had children themselves, could not reasonably be asked to carry out the shootings, he obtained permission to get Ukrainian militiamen to do the deed instead. The children's "wailing," he recalled, "was indescribable. I shall never forget the scene throughout my life. I find it very hard to bear. I particularly remember a small fair-haired girl who took me by the hand. She too was shot later ... Many children were hit four or five times before they died."[4]

But as John E. Thiel writes, Job's story actually offers the minority stance on the existence of innocent suffering that counters the majority tradition's denial.[5] What? The majority position in the Hebrew and Christian Scriptures and tradition denies the reality of innocent suffering? Well ... yes! The book of Job is a counterexample to the majority opinion in both Christian Scripture and Christian tradition that people who suffer are not innocent.

The French poet Charles Baudelaire was informed that Christianity for the most part denied innocent suffering. He responded simply, "then your God is my Satan," turned around, and walked away. Again, the book of Job presents a minority view on the issue of suffering—that is, that the innocent *do* suffer. Unlike Baudelaire, Job stays and fights; he refuses to accept this majority denial.

---

3. Statistics on children and hunger from "World Hunger Facts," Evangelical Lutheran Church of America, http://www.elca.org/Our-Faith-In-Action/Responding-to-the-World/ELCA-World-Hunger/Resources/Hunger-Facts.aspx.
4. Richard J. Evans, *The Third Reich at War* (New York: Penguin, 2009), 230.
5. John E. Thiel, *God, Evil, and Innocent Suffering: A Theological Reflection* (New York: Crossroad, 2002), 20, 59.

How did the denial of innocent suffering become the majority stance in the Christian tradition? The major premodern strategies for denying innocent suffering are intended to protect the goodness, power, and wisdom of God (that is, if God is really all good or all powerful or all wise and there is suffering in the world, it could not be due to God, it must be due to an evil outside of God or the guilt of the sufferer). These premodern strategies are (1) the classical Jewish doctrine of the covenant: blessing and curse based on human behavior; this is also the root of the doctrine of retribution in which the righteous prosper and the wicked are judged; and (2) the classical Christian doctrine of original sin wherein, since all are born in sin, all suffering is justified on the basis of inherent, pervasive sin in all humanity. The doctrine of original sin does not appear among the beliefs of the earliest Christians or in Scripture. There is no mention of original sin in the New Testament, nor is there any conceptualization in its pages that matches later church doctrine. Paul does say that sin is inescapable, but never that it is inherited at birth. The doctrine begins with Augustine.

For a discussion of this denial and how innocent suffering is often linked to original sin, see "Further Reflections: Original Sin," pp. 163–67.

God and the Satan

Though the earliest readers of the book of Job, and even recent readers,[6] claim to be more concerned with Job's reaction to suffering than with God's responsibility, the contemporary reader cannot help but be dismayed by both. At a meeting of the "heavenly beings" (1:6; 2:1, *ben ha'elohim*, literally "the sons of God"[7]) the *satan* initiates Job's suffering with the explicit consent of God. The consent is given on the basis of a wager between God and the *satan* over how Job will react to the loss of his many blessings: will Job continue to

6. Cf. Robert Gordis, *The Book of Job: Commentary, New Translation, and Special Studies* (New York: Jewish Theological Seminary of America, 1978), 2.
7. In the book of Job, the names of God are about evenly divided between Shaddai, Elohim, and YHWH.

worship God even when heavily cursed? This seems to strike God in a peculiar way. The prologue makes clear that what happens to Job *is* God's responsibility. Indeed, God comes across as startlingly disarming, selfishly motivated, impetuously distracted, persistently boastful, uncertain and needy, quick to destroy life to prove a point important to a fragile ego, easily challenged, quick to test the most pious and faithful of servants, willing to change the rules of creation in midgame, and strikingly efficient at washing his hands of responsibility or blame.

In the heavenly council God gives an assessment of Job, not only calling him his "servant" and thus placing him alongside Abraham (Gen. 26:24), Moses (Exod. 14:31), and David (2 Sam. 7:5), but ranking him possibly even beyond these with the description "there is no one like him on earth" (1:8).[8] The *satan* does not challenge God's appraisal of Job, but rather shifts the question to Job's motivation. He suggests that Job's loyalty is contingent: "Does Job fear God for nothing? . . . You have blessed the work of his hands. . . . But stretch out your hand now, and touch all that he has, and he will curse you to your face" (1:9, 10, 11). God does not hesitate for a moment to approve this plan, and Job eventually finds himself on a dung-heap on the outskirts of Uz. At first the *satan* is wrong: "In all this Job did not sin or charge God with wrongdoing" (1:22), and so within the heavenly court we find the *satan* trying again. Wise, the *satan* waits for that moment when God gloats, in essence saying, "See, Job is cursed and yet he

> A pawn in a contest about which he knew nothing, the beneficiary of "friendly" advice he refused to accept, the target of suffering he could not understand, and a victim in a universe that threatened to overwhelm him, Job has been a man for all ages. Ever since the biblical era, the legend of Job has been part of the collective memory of the West and one of the defining myths of our civilization. . . . [Job's story] has forced its readers to wrestle with the most painful realities of human existence.
>
> Schreiner, *Where Shall Wisdom Be Found?* 11.

---

8. Cf. Samuel E. Balentine, *Job*, Smyth & Helwys Bible Commentary (Macon, GA: Smyth & Helwys, 2006), 52.

continues to bless me; he does love me in good times and in bad."
God is so pleased with himself and Job's response that God is willing
to up the ante: at the *satan's* suggestion, God is willing to add to Job's
affliction of heart and soul an affliction (short of death) of the body.
Once again, the *satan* is wrong . . . for the time being. The narrator
again informs the reader that "in all this Job did not sin with his lips"
(2:10). Ironically, in the very next chapter, Job's lips will explode in
a cascade of cursing and lament.

FURTHER REFLECTIONS
The Satan

The Hebrew word for the member of the heavenly court usually
translated into English as *Satan* is *hassatan*. To translate this "heavenly being" as *Satan* leds to misleading associations of the *satan*
with the devil or Satan of later Christian theology. In Job *hassatan*
has not yet taken on either Jewish or Christian attributes usually
associated with Satan, the eternal enemy of both God and humanity. It is simply a noun, a title, just one of the council of "heavenly
beings" that assemble before God; readers will do well to banish
from their minds the more common images of Satan when reading
the prologue to Job. The word is actually composed of two words,
the definite article *ha,* meaning "the," and *satan,* meaning most literally "adversary" or "accuser." The definite article is present in every
occurrence of the word in Job and indicates that the word is not a
personal name, but a title descriptive of a function or responsibility. Here in Job the *satan's* function and responsibility is apparently
keeping an eye on the earth on God's behalf and reporting back
on people's conduct. Of the "heavenly beings" who present themselves before God, the *satan* is singled out as the prosecutor who
cynically denies that humans are capable of disinterested righteousness or love of God. The *satan* serves in a function similar to
a prosecuting attorney who can bring charges against another in
a court. The *satan* is not God's opponent, but rather an advocate
surveying human behavior and reporting on persons living in truth
with faith and love.

Job's Friends and Comforters

Three friends of Job from different lands hear of his "troubles" and agree to meet "together to go and console [*nud*] and comfort [*naham*] him" (2:11b). The use of *nud* gives the added intentions of going "to show grief," "to comfort," and "to show compassion and sorrow," while *naham* can also mean "to console" or "to show sorrow." The names of the friends are all drawn from the Pentateuch (unlike "Job," further highlighting the fact that Job is a Gentile). As the three cycles of dialogue begin, the friends will continue to converse with Job in the same order in which they are named initially in 2:11: Eliphaz the Temanite, Bildad the Shuhite, and Zophar the Naamathite. A fourth friend, Elihu, appears in chapters 32–37, where, rather than enter into a dialogue with Job, he berates Job in a one-sided soliloquy.

The friends' visit is obviously pastoral in intent, but as the story progresses, comfort and consolation is exactly what the friends do *not* provide. They argue with, accuse, and berate Job.

As the friends approach, they at first do not recognize Job because he is so altered physically as well as morally and spiritually. When they finally do recognize him, they join Job, sitting on the ground (the dung-heap outside the city) for seven days and seven nights in complete silence, in which "no one spoke a word" (2:13). Most commentators note that the seven days and seven nights conform to traditional Hebrew rites of mourning (Lam. 2:10; Isa. 3:26; Ezek. 8:14), including mourning the dead (Gen. 50:10; 1 Sam. 31:13). Thus, though the friends have come to console and comfort, they perform, even in the prologue, a ritual for the dead. Symbolically, rather than following through with the pastoral objective of helping their friend to move on with his life, they participate in a ritual of ending with overtones of death.

And so the prologue itself ends, having moved from a "man who was the greatest of all the people of the east" (1:3) to a man unrecognizable to his friends and, in studied understatement, a man whose "suffering was very great" (2:13).

But there is more to this silence than ritual mourning. The friends initially do get something right: the silence of their listening *is* a form

> For the innocent sufferer, is blessing God really the only legitimate response to faith? Or is cursing God also within the limits of a faithful encounter between an innocent sufferer and God?
>
> Balentine, *Job*, 39.

of consolation. In contemplative silence there is recognition that, yes, a kind of death has occurred; something of Job has died. The friends listen with Job in silence to a new path developing in Job's spiritual journey. The new path is the way of suffering, and for seven days they listen and share in the journey. It is likely that initially in this silence they all hear something of their own perceptions of God dying in Job as well. In these spiritual senses transformative rebirth is possible only through death of the self. The silence is a kind of womb; the new birth of Job—and of God—begins in chapter 3 and comes to some form of shared transformation only in chapter 42, the final chapter, where both Job and Job's God finally display a transformative renewal of cautious hope.

In the book of Job, heaven and earth collide, and all these theological questions—most without obvious resolution and *none* attributable to any *patience* in Job—are experienced by Job. They are experienced as friendship in the midst of the unkind, hope in the midst of ambiguity, the search for trust in the midst of innocent suffering, while God for the most part remains inscrutable, if not hidden. The writer of Job creates a heaven and an earth that seem to be fully accessible only through the lens of suffering.

3:1–26

Job's Lament: A Death-Wish Poem

"God damn the day I was born!" (3:3).[1]

With these words at the beginning of a wondrously beautiful, nearly transcendent piece of poetry that only serves to heighten the agony of Job's lament, Job ends his seven days and seven nights of silence. Transitioning to poetic form from the prose narrative of chapters 1 and 2, he will take the light of the day and the darkness of the night as new images, transposing them into a haunting reversal of the creation stories of Genesis 1 and 2. In the process he will cry out for a new kind of silence: the silence of the deadened womb in which, in effect, he asks, "Was Nothing born from the womb of Mother-Nothing?" Through these images Job damns the day of his birth and cries out for death. The writer of the book of Job gives us poetry calibrated to the depths and injustice of Job's own suffering, a screaming kind of poetry transformed back into silence by Job's invocation of his own birth's death.

Paradoxical? Yes! But so is innocent suffering, especially innocent suffering instigated, initiated, and even intensified by YHWH, a God who will not show his face, a God who kills seven sons and three unmarried daughters, and then from both the reader's and Job's perspective remains silent, appearing to hide. Through forty excruciating chapters Job pleads and prays, cries out and tries to find reason for his fate; throughout, God is silent.

---

1. Translation of Job 3:3 by Stephen Mitchell, *The Book of Job* (New York: HarperCollins, 2002), 13.

Job never disputes God's existence or God's power, but here in chapter 3 he begins what will become a sustained, poetic dispute over God's justice, God's use of power, and God's ways. As one commentator writes, this dramatic poem as a whole is "of extraordinary richness and vitality, powerful in imagery, often difficult in language, bold in thought, that confronts the question of the justice of God's dealings with men."[2] Here in chapter 3, however, the dispute over justice has not officially begun: at this stage Job is not arguing, he is cursing and lamenting, he is in a state of raw emotion, too raw to bring forth a rational argument; he is expressing a total disillusion with life, with light, with day. His only wish is for the leveling, numbing unconsciousness of death, where finally "the wicked cease from troubling, and . . . the weary are at rest" (3:17). He seeks the grave as another person seeks hidden treasure in the earth (vv. 21–22).

This is a new Job. We have seen a good and prosperous man tried by every affliction and misfortune who, in spite of everything, has borne all misfortunes patiently. Now, out of the silence, from the same lips by which Job did not sin (2:10), "Job opened his mouth and cursed the day of his birth" (3:1)—or as Stephen Mitchell translates, Job explodes, "God damn the day I was born!" This is not an ambiguous curse as in chapters 1 and 2; here Job does not use the word *barak*, which may mean either "bless" or "curse." With unambiguous voice, he opens his mouth to "curse" (*qalal*) the day he was born and the night he was conceived. He wishes he had been aborted, stillborn, rather than have this life he is given: "I am not at ease, nor am I quiet; I have no rest; but trouble comes" (3:26).

Job 3:1–10

The Living Dead

With the imprecation "Let the day perish in which I was born, and the night that said, 'A man-child is conceived'" (3:3), Job curses both the day of his birth and the night of his conception; the images and

---

2. David Daiches, "God Under Attack," in *The Book of Job*, ed. Harold Bloom (New York: Chelsea House, 1988), 39.

juxtapositions of day and night, and birth and death, will resonate throughout the poem. An immediate question given the wager between God and the *satan* in chapters 1 and 2 that crops up here and throughout chapter 3 is, do Job's words constitute cursing God? The reader is left to decide: Job curses the creation but not the Creator, he curses providence but not the divine Will, he curses life but not Being itself. And if he does not curse God directly, he does call on other gods (in this case Sea and Leviathan) to end his misery: those "who curse the Sea, those who are skilled to rouse up Leviathan" (3:8) turn light to darkness because they "did not shut the doors of my mother's womb" (3:10). So enraged by pain and loss, so senseless to all but suffering, he grasps at magic, incantation, spells, summoning other gods to call up those skilled at provoking chaos, ruin, darkness, and death.

The poetic frenzy calling down ruin, darkness, and death begins with Job's curse of the day he was born in verses 4–5 and of the night of his conception in verses 6–7. But since his "treasure" (see v. 21) is death, the curse darkens the day and wipes pleasure from the night. Translation of verses 4–5 is hampered by lack of English words for darkness; to darken the day, Job the theurgist calls down *hoshek* (darkness), *tsalmaveth* (death's shadow), *ananah* (thick or ominous cloud), *kimrir* (blackness of the day, or Pope's "eclipse"), and *ofel* (the "sinister darkness" of v. 6; "thick darkness," NRSV). These are all fierce forces of oblivion intended to negate his birth.

With verses 6–7 the cry for destruction continues. Job curses that night of pleasure that resulted in his conception. In verse 7 he demands "that night [of conception] be barren," the cries of pleasure removed. He covers the darkness of the night with an even greater darkness, the *ofel* or "sinister darkness" used in verse 6. The Joban poet then shifts back to cursing the light of day and once again

The Heart asks Pleasure—
   first—
And then—Excuse from Pain—
And then—those little
   Anodynes
That deaden suffering—

And then—to go to sleep—
And then—if it should be
The will of its Inquisitor
The privilege to die—

Emily Dickinson, *The Complete Poems of Emily Dickinson*, ed. Thomas H. Johnson, #536 (Boston: Little, Brown, 1960), 262.

wishing that the day, especially the day of his birth, become dark, that is, dead. In these short verses Job has used an agitated invocation to those skilled in rousing up Leviathan to help him wipe clean from the calendar the day of his birth and the night of the sexual congress in which he was conceived. He even chants an invocation that his mother be barren and prays that his own eyes be kept from seeing the "eyelids of the dawn" (v. 9). The poetry thus works at a much deeper level than death: a living being prays to become a specter never having been born.

Job 3:11–26

The Lament

Lament psalms are common, and elsewhere in Scripture we find individuals, nations, even creation lamenting. In Ecclesiastes (see Eccl. 6 for an example with images that echo those in Job) it is suggested that, given the toil, trouble, and vanity of life, one might as well be dead or even "stillborn" (a wish of Job's, 3:16; see Eccl. 6:3). But Ecclesiastes offers its teachings as a lesson in wisdom, a lesson in how to live with at least some equanimity in an otherwise meaningless world. It does not, as does Job, confront us with a person with whom we have come to identify, a person whose lament is so hopeless and dark that he actually begs, not for another lesson in wisdom, but for death as a means of escape. Nowhere else in the Scriptures do we find such a personal lament as Job's, without hope, that is, an invocation of death as complete self-oblivion.

In keeping with the poetic reversal and deconstruction of this deeply textured lament poem, these laments for peace in death in verse 13 are juxtaposed against the imagery of lament over birth in verse 12, where Job asks, "Why were there knees to receive me, or breasts for me to suck?" A touching irony emerges from these verses that causes us to further identify with Job's experience. "Breasts to suck" normally do put infants to sleep, just as Job wishes for himself; but this twists what are perhaps some of our most basic instincts for life and turns them toward death.

Job places before us a total negation of beginnings—both

creation's and his own—and then begins a longing, nostalgic look at Sheol, the Hebrew afterworld. For Job, Sheol is a leveling place, a place where the stillborn rest, where kings and counselors and princes lie together while the works of their hands on earth fall into ruin (vv. 14–15), where the wicked cease troubling others and the weary can find their rest (v. 17), where prisoners no longer hear their taskmaster (v. 18), where the small and the great lie down together, where slaves are free of their masters (v. 19). Job's Sheol is the great leveler of princes and kings, of slaves and masters; from Job's present perspective Sheol is that place where all are equally free—in death. The ironic intensity of the poem reaches its climax when Job compares "those who long for death" to those who "dig . . . for hidden treasures" (v. 21): both "rejoice . . . when they find the grave" (v. 22). Those who long for death find the peace of the grave; those who dig for treasure find a great repository of wealth. Death is Job's treasure.

Throughout chapter 3 Job walks a thin line between the two sides of the wager set up by the *satan* and accepted by God: whether or not Job would curse God. In chapters 1 and 2 Job did not curse God. Here we cannot be so sure. Job reverses the process of creation—"Let there be darkness!" Job says, and in his words we hear a parody of YHWH's speaking creation into being with

> Job describes not life but its cessation, the absence of possession and poverty, power and oppression. Nothing remains but sleep, rest, freedom from exertion, and the ubiquitous darkness.
>
> Good, *In Turns of Tempest*, 207.

"Let there be light!" He pleads for and dreams of death as an antidote to life. Are these curses upon the God of life? If Job's treasure is the grave, what kind of blessing is that? But Job has entered a world without meaning, a life of misery, an existence without compassion: at this point Job has moved to a point beyond simple blessing and cursing. Pure suffering withers the urge toward any kind of piety. Pure suffering reconfigures the meaning of blessing: a bit of bread, a cup of water are blessings. And if neither bread nor water come, one searches for more simple bread and water until, finally, only to alleviate the hunger and slake the thirst, fantasies of oblivion become one's blessing.

> ...nothing comes from
> nothing,
> The darkness from the
> darkness. Pain comes from
> the darkness
> And we call it wisdom. It is
> pain.
>
> Randall Jarrell, "90 North," lines 31–33
> in *Randall Jarrell: The Complete Poems*
> (New York: Farrar, Straus & Giroux,
> 1969), 113–14.

The Holocaust of World War II saw the suffering and death of millions of Jews, Gypsies, homosexuals, Bolsheviks and non-Aryans. What was blessing and cursing to them when God went into hiding? As readers of chapter 3 of Job we know the inception and evolution of Job's suffering: it is YHWH God, and in a sense Job does not need liberation from God; God initiated misery but is now simply *Deus absconditus*. God is no longer the problem or the answer: Job speaks the truth to God's face while God is ripping out Job's heart. Still, God hides, is gone.

In his unrelenting misery, his physical suffering, his debilitating fear, in further suffering in the form of his dread (*pahad*) of suffering itself, Job's lament perhaps in some way recognizes some form of constraint: he longs for death but does not kill himself. There is always some constraint—usually inexplicable—holding one back from suicide in the midst of an otherwise unbearable pain; there is constraint, that is, until there is constraint no longer, and then suicide *is* the only escape from suffering. Why does Job not commit suicide? There is some constraint but it appears not to be God: hidden, God is only the mystery. One simply does not know what compels Job not to die by his own hand.

FURTHER REFLECTIONS
Theodicy

Ever since suffering entered the world, men and women have asked, why? This is not so much the question "what was the cause of this?" but rather a protest against some profound injustice or lack of logic in the world. One branch of thought (and it is a rational project) that has tried to answer the senselessness of suffering is known as *theodicy*. The word literally means "justifying God." The point of theodicy is to try, rationally, to defend a supposedly all-loving God against the lamentable whys in the world. Terry Eagleton writes, "The greatest artistic project of this kind [a theodicy] in British literary culture is John Milton's mighty epic *Paradise Lost,* in which the poet seeks to 'justify the ways of God to men' by accounting for why humanity is in such a wretched state.... For some readers, however, the poet's pious attempts to exonerate the Almighty simply result in damning him even deeper. Trying to justify God by providing him with elaborate arguments in his own defence, as the poem does, is bound to bring him down to our own level. Gods are not supposed to argue, any more than princes or judges are."[3]

Though there is certainly enough arguing in Job, the book of Job is *not* a theodicy. Many have claimed that it is a theodicy, but it is not an attempt to explain the ways of God to man. Theodicy is a post-Enlightenment approach that simply would not have entered the minds of any of the book's characters. If there are any answers to be found in Job, they are not of the rational variety; they are of the ethical or moral order accessed by the imagination. Even in early commentators such as Gregory the Great we find that his "defense of God's actions remains a minor theme in the *Moralia* because he does not see theodicy as the main issue raised by inexplicable suffering."[4]

In fact, only Enlightenment writers seem to use theodicy as a way of explaining suffering. Modern and postmodern writers mostly construe the enterprise as preposterous at best. In his book *The Evils of Theodicy*, Terrence W. Tilley (a speech-act theorist) maintains that Job warns against the possibility of providing a theodicy. The book rejects any expectation of what Paul Ricoeur called the "systematic totalization" a theodicy requires. Job warns against silencing the sufferer's voice, even the curses and accusations. One of the effects of theodicy is silencing the sufferer, and as Tilley points out with characteristic vigor, "to silence a suffering voice may be

---

3. Terry Eagleton, *On Evil* (New Haven, CT: Yale University Press, 2010), 132.
4. Susan E. Schreiner, *Where Shall Wisdom Be Found? Calvin's Exegesis of Job from Medieval and Modern Perspectives* (Chicago: University of Chicago Press, 1994), 48.

to participate in one of the most despicable practices theodicists (or anyone else) can perform. . . . Silencing sufferers is part of the 'foolishness of theodicy [which] has led us to search for meaning in suffering.'"[5]

The book of Job is not a theodicy. Job is certainly not silenced. Job does not search for meaning in suffering in the rational sense, but rather for justice for innocent suffering in the legal and moral sense. Job's friends may be theodicists; Job certainly is not.

Perhaps the most astonishing statement of all in this beautiful poem of chapter 3 comes at verse 25: "Truly the thing that I fear comes upon me, and what I dread befalls me." Can it be that Job has in fact maintained his piety and worship out of fear of punishment, as the *satan* had suggested? Or if Job's piety grows out of "dread" and his worship is an attempt to ward off what he "feared," is the *satan* at least partly right? Even more troubling, in this verse Job is not just expressing fear (*yirah*) in the sense of obligation and responsibility, but something even deeper; he is expressing dread (*pahad*) of possible results of not leading a "pious" life.[6] Religious persons in this sense are often, to one degree or another, "Jobs," attempting to fulfill pious obligations to fend off terrible results. In some instances such piety even comes to mean what it is to be religious.

But again the wonderful ambiguity of the poet prevails: here in chapter 3 at a high point in his suffering, Job speaks of the "hedge" (v. 23, *suk*; NRSV "fence"; see also 1:10) that God has built around him and asks, "Why is light given to one who cannot see the way?" (3:23a). The way is hidden, humanity is "fenced in" by God. Still, light is given even to those who suffer. What is the purpose? Why the light of hope when men and women are in effect imprisoned and the way of escape, let alone the way of healing, is hidden? Is this any kind of hope, or does it produce emotions more equivalent to the "terror" and "fear" Job has been describing? In the imprisoned,

5. Nel Noddings, *Women and Evil* (Berkeley and Los Angeles: University of California Press, 1989), 26, cited in Terrence W. Tilley, *The Evils of Theodicy* (Eugene, OR: Wipf & Stock, 2000), 110.
6. Cf. Edwin M. Good, *In Turns of Tempest: A Reading of Job with a Translation* (Stanford, CA: Stanford University Press, 1990), 207–8.

hidden circumstances Job describes, hope and legitimate piety grounded in love of God seem unlikely, even dishonest. The "hedge" God has built around Job has nothing to do with Job's having sinned; again, that he is without sin is made clear in chapters 1 and 2. But the friends will later suggest that Job's situation, a part of which is this divinely constructed "hedge," *is* the result of his sin. Job will continue to deny throughout the book that his suffering is in any sense grounded in sin or guilt. The very ambiguity of the "hedge" raises questions of the meaning of faith, hope, and love in a world "hedged in" by sin, a world in which the way to escape sin is hidden, yet a world in which something—but not enough—of the light of God shines through the cracks. These questions and the arguments Job raises move us into issues of Christology and Christian redemption, theological categories outside the scope of this book. What we can say at this point, which is by no means an answer, is that Job can expect neither escape nor salvation.

In the final verse of this chapter Job seems simply to let go. He has moved from the highest pitch of emotion, "God damn the day," to exhaustion. He can only repeat what he longs for but cannot find: ease, quiet, and rest. These do not come; only turmoil and trouble (*rogez*) arrive. These are his treasures, his fortune.

4:1–14:22

First Poetic Dialogue Cycle

4:1–5:27

Eliphaz's First Response to Job:
"Now a word came to me"

Job breaks the week of silence with a deep lament, speaking mostly of and to himself. But his friends have been listening, and his readers have been listening too. Chapter 4 of the book of Job opens the response: the friends' listening now evolves into three great cycles of dialogues between Job and his friends. In each cycle Eliphaz, most likely the oldest, is the first to speak. Eliphaz begins by "advising" Job, but the advice seems misguided: it does not address the trouble Job is facing or the concerns that Job has already expressed. Eliphaz has his own agenda and he "comforts" Job according to that agenda, not according to what Job has experienced or spoken.

To this point we have every reason to believe that the friends empathize with Job's suffering and intend their long journey and seven long days of mourning to be followed by consolation and comfort addressed with wisdom to Job's needs. Though some commentators perceive consistent effort on the part of Eliphaz to find the fault not in Job but in his helpless situation, the vast majority conclude not only that Eliphaz never addresses the very real suffering that Job exhibits and describes, but that Eliphaz's words are filled with intentional double meanings that not only do not comfort Job but are alternately inconsistent, ambiguous, contradictory, illogical, unkind, unfeeling, and tactless, and have the overall effect of trivializing Job's suffering.[1] This ambiguity may add to the depth and beauty of the poetry, but it does little to console or comfort Job.

This first speech of Eliphaz touches on three fundamental doctrines that weave throughout the book. Each focuses on the relationships between God, humanity, and suffering. Again the theology causes each of the friends to mishear Job, but it does allow the reader to wrestle with theological issues in complex ways as we listen in on the exposition of a doctrine and how that exposition can be so terribly misunderstood, even used as "moral ammunition" against another.

> I have of late—but wherefore I know not—lost all my mirth, forgone all custom of exercise, and indeed it goes so heavily with my disposition that this goodly frame, the earth, seems to me a sterile promontory, this most excellent canopy, the air, look you, this brave o'erhanging firmament, this majestical roof fretted with golden fire, why, it appears no other thing to me than a foul and pestilent congregation of vapours. What a piece of work is man . . . and yet, to me, what is this quintessence of dust?
>
> William Shakespeare, *Hamlet*, act 2, scene 2, lines 291–98.

The three theological perspectives initiated by Eliphaz in these chapters are (1) the fate of the righteous and the wicked, (2) the idea that humans are naturally born to suffering (different from the doctrine of original sin), and (3) that suffering is a discipline that has within it positive moral content.

4:1–6 *A Polite Entry and Words of Consolation . . . Or Are They?*

Before the theology, Eliphaz begins with ambiguous, ironic words that at first seem kind and consoling, yet early on show impatience. "If one ventures a word with you, will you be offended?" (4:2a, polite) is followed immediately by "But who can keep from speaking?" (v.

---

1. Cf. Kemper Fullerton, "Double Entendre in the First Speech of Eliphaz," in *Journal of Biblical Literature* 49 (1930): 320–74, and Edwin M. Good, *In Turns of Tempest: A Reading of Job with a Translation* (Stanford, CA: Stanford University Press, 1990), 208–13, who bases his work on Fullerton's.

2b, impatient). Throughout the Old Testament, deeds of mercy are seen as signs of righteousness. Diplomatically, Eliphaz begins by pointing out Job's righteousness and his many deeds of mercy: Job has "instructed many," "strengthened the weak," "supported those who were stumbling," "made firm the feeble knees" (vv. 3–4). The irony is that Eliphaz is feigning mercy to Job and thus, according to his own logic, is accumulating and proving his own righteousness. The seeming kindness has little to do with Job and everything to do with Eliphaz. Honest readers will recognize this trait of Eliphaz as not so different from their own self-serving narcissism.

In the final verse of this section (v. 6), Eliphaz offers his first stock, orthodox response: "Is not your fear of God your confidence, and the integrity of your ways your hope?" This too does little to comfort Job. Overall Eliphaz shows his reliance on spiritually inappropriate canards rather than empathy. Eliphaz's questioning of Job's piety subtly points to his own righteous piety. He also speaks out of a black-and-white moral universe: fear of God brings reassurance; integrity and righteousness bring hope. As one commentator writes, "Eliphaz's primary concern is not to explain why the righteous suffer, which is clearly the problem that Job presents, but rather to argue that the wicked are certainly punished."[2]

4:7–11 Eliphaz's Response to Suffering I:
Fate of the Righteous and the Wicked

After appealing to Job's confidence, integrity, and hope, Eliphaz states in simple terms the ancient concept of justice that will surface so often in the book of Job:

> Think now, who that was innocent ever perished?
>   Or where were the upright cut off?
> As I have seen, those who plow iniquity
>   and sow trouble reap the same.
>
>   (vv. 7–8)

---

2. Samuel E. Balentine, *Job*, Smyth & Helwys Bible Commentary (Macon, GA: Smyth & Helwys, 2006), 107.

Put simply, Eliphaz is recounting the doctrine of retributive justice: the righteous are blessed and the sinful punished (with the correlative implication—later applied to Job—that one who is punished or suffering must have "plowed iniquity" and one who is healthy and blessed must be "innocent"). Whether Eliphaz's claim is true or not, it is painfully clear that he has only heard what he wants to hear from Job: to this point Job has said *nothing* in judgment of divine justice; it is helpful to recall here Job's last words before Eliphaz speaks:

> I have no rest, no peace;
> What has come is agony.[3]

This is not a fine point of theology, nor is Job concerned here with morality or justice; his point is that he is suffering. Having traveled from afar, having sat with Job in silence for seven days and seven nights, having heard Job's lament, Eliphaz wants to deliver a moral sermon to an innocent and upright man who asks only for comfort. Cut off from everything that gives meaning to his life, Job, rather than consolation for his real pain, hears from Eliphaz only of the "breath [*neshamah*] of God" by which the sinful "perish" and the "blast [*ruach*; lit., "wind, spirit"] of God's anger" (4:9) that consumes, with the implication that it is Job who will be consumed and punished.

And, in any case, how important is such a change [the disappearance of punishment by torture as public spectacle], when compared with the great institutional transformations, the formulation of explicit, general codes and unified rules of procedure; with the almost universal adoption of the jury system, the definition of the essentially corrective character of the penalty and the tendency, which has become increasingly marked since the nineteenth century, to adapt punishment to the individual offender? . . . Punishment, then, will tend to become the most hidden part of the penal process.

Michel Foucault, *Discipline and Punishment: The Birth of the Prison*, trans. Alan Sheridan (New York: Vintage Books, 1995), 8, 9.

---

3. Translation from David Daiches, "God Under Attack" in Harold Bloom, ed., *The Book of Job* (New York: Chelsea House, 1988), 41.

FURTHER REFLECTIONS
Retributive Justice

The doctrine of divine retributive justice is easy enough to state: the righteous will be blessed and the evil will be punished by God in this life; and conversely and put in conditional terms, if one is blessed he or she must be righteous, and if one is punished he or she must be evil. This doctrine, also known as the Deuteronomic Code, will be applied to Job by all of the friends in a variety of ways; Job is also so steeped in this doctrine that he will often doubt himself, taking to heart the idea that his suffering might be rooted in some personal sin, however small. One of the greatest obstacles to Job's recovery is his own struggle with this doctrine or code, a struggle that he has not only with the friends, but more importantly with God. Much of Job's healing comes only as he is able to release this doctrine's imperious grip on him.

Though Eliphaz's words to Job in 4:7–11 seem harsh and are not the pastoral comfort Job craves, they do represent Hebrew orthodoxy of the period (and are sustained as orthodoxy or at the very least internalized as true to this day by many Hebrews and Christians). The images of sowing and reaping (v. 8) remind us of a similar natural law in the New Testament: "You reap whatever you sow" (Gal. 6:7). As a natural law, what Eliphaz says is indisputable: one does not harvest corn after sowing thornbushes. As a moral law it is not always the case; this is what the characters of the book of Job are struggling with. Nonetheless, this initial exchange sets the stage for the debates to follow between Job and his friends and the one-way argument from Job to God. Using different strategies, varying arguments, and significant illustrations from creation, Job draws on his own experience to argue for the inadequacy or fallacy of this doctrine of retributive justice. At the same time the friends will argue, on the basis of this doctrine, that God's governance of the world is always just.

The idea that God repays virtue with reward and vice with punishment is a theology found in each section of the Hebrew canon: Torah, Prophets, and Writings. Each appropriates the idea of divine retribution as an essential part of the argument that the world is morally coherent and assured by God's governance. In the Torah, Deuteronomy places the retribution principle within the context of covenant, insisting that blessing and cursing is God's way of sustaining moral coherence in partnership with Israel:

> See, I have set before you today life and prosperity, death and adversity. If you obey the commandments of the LORD your God that I am commanding you today, by loving the LORD your God, walking in [God's] ways, and observing his commandments ... then you shall live and become numerous, and the LORD your God will bless you. . . . But if your heart turns away and you do not hear ... I declare to you today that you shall perish. (Deut. 30:15–18)[4]

The Prophets appeal to covenantal sanctions in announcing that God has punished Israel because its disobedience violates the partnership with God and jeopardizes the moral foundations of creation (cf. Hos. 4:1–3; Amos 4:1–3, 6–13; Mic. 3:9–12).

The Writings articulate the principle of retribution with different voices. Nevertheless, the assumption that God secures the world's moral order by dispensing fair and equitable justice to the righteous and wicked remains axiomatic. A classic example is Psalm 1:

> Happy are those
> who do not follow the advice of the wicked,
> . . . .
> but their delight is in the law of the LORD,
> and on his law they meditate day and night.
> They are like trees
> planted by streams of water,
> which yield their fruit in its season,
> and their leaves do not wither.
> In all that they do, they prosper.
>
> The wicked are not so,
> but are like chaff that the wind drives away.

---

4. On the Joban poet's intention to undercut the Deuteronomistic theory, see Lawrence L. Besserman, *The Legend of Job in the Middle Ages* (Cambridge, MA: Harvard University Press, 1979), 11–25 and 180 n. 18.

....

for the Lord watches over the way of the righteous,
but the way of the wicked will perish.

(Ps. 1:1–4, 6)

To get a better understanding of Deuteronomic theory, it is
helpful to look at two models of Old Testament divine-human relationship. J. Gerald Janzen speaks of two "default positions" in the
divine-human relationship that mark two periods in Israel's history
with God and two segments in the Bible's narrative of that history.
The first is the period of Israel's ancestors in Genesis 12–50, beginning with Abraham and Sarah (which Janzen calls the Abrahamic
period). The second period is inaugurated by the covenant-making
ceremonies under Moses at Mount Sinai (which Janzen calls the
Mosaic paradigm). The two divine-human relationships had the following characteristics:

1. Abrahamic: kinship, based on structure of family or clan
   relationships
   — God: "Shaddai"
   — God as divine father of clan; responsible for cosmic/human
      blessing
   — Based on organic relationships arising through birth
   — Implicit values and claims through honoring blood ties in
      acts of:
         an ethic of generosity
         loyalty, kindness, altruism, justice, love

2. Mosaic: covenant, based on structure and dynamic of political
   relations
   — From time of Exodus and Sinai
   — God: "Yawheh"
   — God as Israel's Lord and King
   — Arising from political relationships, population density,
      complex social relations
   — God:
         Delivers people from Egypt and oppressive laws

Establishes new, just laws, observance of which is
life-sustaining
Establishes explicit acts of covenantal choice and
commitment
— Becomes prominent paradigm throughout rest of OT

Over centuries, the Mosaic paradigm became the substitute for the older kinship language.[5] The logic of the Mosaic law began to shape Israel's way of life and its ethos to the point that a crisis in covenant relations could be dealt with only with a legalistic ethos. The real flaw in the system, however, was the tendency to revert to the kinship model in time of crisis. Frank Moore Cross has written, "As the social groups become larger, kinship ties become increasingly dysfunctional as the basis for the larger group; but kinship terminology seems to become *more used* to express the new bond that ties the larger group together."[6] Janzen later asks, "But what happens when the language of kin relations becomes merely formal rhetoric, mere window-dressing on the actuality of political covenant relations? What happens when the secondary model [Mosiac] becomes in fact primary, when for all practical purposes, the customized default setting becomes the original default setting?"[7] The logic of the law becomes so deeply ingrained in their hearts that people, forgetting other nonmoralistic dimensions of the tradition, come to interpret their experience in strictly equivalent terms, so that every good thing that happens is interpreted as a sign of divine approval and reward, and every bad thing that happens is taken as evidence of divine disapproval and punishment. The book of Job shows at painful length what can happen.

Interpreting the ethical teachings originally applied to Israel, the friends begin to apply them to Job the individual. Although the friends' counsel is more unfeeling and pietistic than comforting,

---

5. On the two "default positions" in Hebrew divine-human relationships, cf. J. Gerald Janzen, *At the Scent of Water: The Ground of Hope in the Book of Job* (Grand Rapids: Eerdmans, 2009), 17–29.

6. Frank Moore Cross, *From Epic to Canon: History and Literature in Ancient Israel* (Baltimore: Johns Hopkins University Press, 1998), 7.

7. Janzen, *Scent of Water*, 49.

there is no doubt that they are faithful proponents of traditional, Deuteronomic ethical teaching (cf. Eliphaz, 4:5–9 ; Bildad, 8:3–4; and Zophar, 11:13, 15, 20).

Ironically, Job too is working within the legalistic parameters of the theology of distributive justice: the problem for Job is that his own experience does not coincide with the doctrine and he is not willing to ignore or sublimate his experience. On the basis of that experience he can only conclude that God dispenses reward and punishment without regard to personal conduct: "It is all one; therefore I say, he destroys both the blameless and the wicked" (9:22).

But the friends keep the questions alive: is there a direct correspondence between a person's conduct and a person's fate? Why do the righteous suffer?

4:12–5:7 Eliphaz's Response to Suffering II: A Night Vision, Humans Are Born to Trouble

As if an appeal to the doctrine of retribution were not enough for an innocent man in the depths of suffering, Eliphaz has even more tactless, orthodox, moral advice for Job. To add to his lack of compassion, Eliphaz distills the new claim from a dream: he has had a vision of a terrifying spirit who delivers a personal, authoritative, terrifying warning.

In the strange vision that came to him in the night, a spirit passed before Eliphaz, invoking dread and trembling and leaving him shaking in his bones (4:14). The vision is silent (words and silence are important throughout the book of Job), and then a word (*debar*) comes stealthily to Eliphaz. The "spirit glided past my face" (v. 15), Eliphaz says. The manner of Eliphaz's speech "is designed to heighten the numinous and mysterious, but also eerie, bizarre, and spooky quality of his spiritual vision,"[8] which allows Eliphaz to claim a privileged revelation that gives him special insight (4:12–5:7), which he is happy to pass on to Job. The content of the message given to Eliphaz is stated in v. 17:

8. John E. Hartley, *The Book of Job* (Grand Rapids: Eerdmans, 1988), 112.

Can mortals be righteous before God?
Can human beings be pure before their Maker?

With authority of the spirit, Eliphaz now redirects the argument, implying that none can be righteous and pure. If that is the case, perhaps the doctrine of divine retribution is wrong. None can be righteous or pure before God, yet according to the doctrine of retribution, only the righteous or pure will be blessed.

Which are we to believe? Probably neither, either, and both. It takes the added authority of the spirit, but Eliphaz sets in motion a strand of the debates between friends and Job that will continue throughout the rest of the book: who can be pure and righteous before God, and thus who can be blessed (or in Christian theological terms, who can be righteous before the Lord, who can be redeemed on the basis of purity alone)? The question is never really answered with any degree of assurance in the book of Job, leaving some commentators, including Carl Jung in his book *Answer to Job*, with the insight that Job *necessitates* the response from God that we see as Jesus Christ.

But perhaps what is really important at this point is that comfort and consolation are not happening, regardless of who is right and who is wrong. Eliphaz, through his theology, is telling Job to "get over it," remaining as he will throughout the rest of the book extremely tactless, offering meaningless arguments to

> In the present case Eliphaz wants to suggest, in my opinion, that Job has often spoken such words either, perhaps, to drive others to jealousy or with a different intention. You that ask such questions, see whom you resemble. Indeed, if Eliphaz has spoken so in these circumstances without obtaining forgiveness, it will be the same for us. Our situation will be even worse, because we have views similar to those of Eliphaz. And we have the advantage of the proofs the facts provide. We have been allowed to see the real reasons for the misfortunes that happened to Job. Yet we are just like those who believe they found a reason to blame him and to attack him without waiting for the evidence of the facts.
>
> John Chrysostom, *Commentary on Job* 4:12, PTS 35:64, in ACCS, 24.

prove a secondary point that can only remind Job of his own misfortune (see 4:20–21; 5:3–4, 5–7).

5:17–27 Eliphaz's Response to Suffering III:
The Discipline of Suffering

Eliphaz's third response to Job is foreign neither to the orthodoxy of the Old Testament, New Testament, or Christian spirituality. Eliphaz tells Job, in effect, that his suffering is good for him, it is a "discipline [*musar*] of the Almighty" (5:17a), and therefore in the midst of suffering Job ought to be praising God: there is divine pedagogy in suffering and Job should be happy about it. Such praise will bring restitution, beatitude, and peace. According to Eliphaz, God is good, even if God has brought on suffering, because suffering is a testing, a purging, a "reproof" (v. 17, *yakah*) like that of a teacher toward a student (cf. Prov. 3:11–12; Ps. 118:18; Heb. 12:5–11). If the "reproof of discipline" is passed, if the pedagogy of suffering is also formational, all will end well for Job. He ought, therefore, to submit even to his present suffering happily, Eliphaz suggests: "Happy [*asher*] is the one whom God reproves; therefore do not despise the discipline of the Almighty" (v. 17). God's discipline may initiate wounds (v. 18, *mahats*) and inflict injury (v. 18, *yadov*), but so be it. As one commentator explains Eliphaz's ethical response to suffering at this point, "One who needs correcting is reproved in order that he might repent and find forgiveness. . . . *Misfortune is God's rod of discipline*; it reveals his loving care for humanity."[9]

Eliphaz convinces himself of this position because, while God is the great disciplinarian, God is also the great healer: "For he wounds, but he binds up; he strikes, but his hands heal" (v. 18). Job ought to show less remorse and fear (in fact he ought, according to Eliphaz, to be praising God) and more recognition of God's presence. Eliphaz tries to illustrate his position with the purging power of destructive plagues: famine and war (from both of which God will "redeem you from death," v. 20), the scourging fire,[10] destruction, and wild animals. Many of these negative images are exactly

9. Ibid., 125, emphasis added.
10. Robert Gordis, *The Book of Job: Commentary, New Translation, and Special Studies* (New York: Jewish Theological Seminary of America, 1978), 59.

what Job is enduring and serve only to deepen Job's wounds.

Finally Eliphaz compounds the impact of his insensitive advice by holding out a carrot to Job, a reward that is not an eschatological hope but in Eliphaz's mind the earthly result of a virtuous life. He says that if Job will heed his advice, Job will at least be "in league with the stones of the field, and the wild animals shall be at peace with you" (5:23). What Elipahaz means by this and what underlies all Eliphaz's advice is the conviction that God

> [Sir Eliphaz, speaking to Job] I want you to get my view that if an enterprise, even though it is fair and honest-seeming ... begins to crumble and wilt, it means that somehow, somewhere you must have been putting the wrong sort of clay into it. It means not that God is wrong and going back on you, but that you are wrong.
>
> H. G. Wells, *The Undying Fire* (New York: Macmillan, 1919), 73.

is willing and able to reverse Job's plight if Job will only admit his unrighteous behavior. John Hartley writes concerning this verse, "Whoever trusts in God's power is . . . free from fear. . . . His relationship with God is actualized in his being in harmony with nature, as guaranteed by a covenant with the stones and the beasts of the field."[11] The problem for Job at this point is that, given his experience of divine retribution and intense suffering, given that he can apparently never be righteous or pure before his Maker, and given the idea that suffering as a moral discipline for which he should be grateful is an insult and trivializes his suffering, what is there of God that he can trust? As Job claims, even the stones and the beasts have abandoned him.

6:1–7:21

Job's First Response to Eliphaz: "My suffering is without end"

In his first response to his "comforters," Job defends his opening curse and lament of chapter 3 and continues a meditation on death. In an indictment of his friends, he addresses them directly and

11. Hartley, *Job*, 127.

charges them with failing to live up to their responsibilities toward him (chap. 6). Job then brings a second lament with petitions, now directly addressing God, that blames God for his suffering and for the suffering of humankind in general (chap. 7). In chapter 3 Job's hope, if it could be called that (it is more precisely a curse), is an irrational or magical hope: that he had never been born, that the day of his birth and night of his conception be eradicated from the calendar of months and years, or that, if born, he would have been stillborn, born dead. Here, especially in chapter 7, Job continues to focus on death as the only answer to his suffering, but with a slight shift: he wishes he were dead now (not that he had never been born) because through death his suffering would end. With this shift Job does experience a moment of "hope," hope that he will die: "I loathe my life" (7:16). Job moans, "O that I might have my request, and that God would grant my desire; that it would please God to crush me, that he would let loose his hand and cut me off! This would be my consolation" (6:8–10a). But—and this emphatically—we must not imagine that Job holds any illusions about the afterlife; his "consolation" is not that in death he will be with real friends, that he will be redeemed, that he will have his place among the angels, or even that he will find peace for an anguished conscience. Job's conception of Sheol, of death, is absolute. Sheol is that which is not; it is nothingness: "As the cloud fades and vanishes, so [are] those who go down to Sheol" (7:9). All that go there in death are equal, but he has contemplated this void, this vanishing, this emptiness, where beggar and king are cohorts, and he has decided that he prefers Sheol to the life he has been forced to experience, and in this possibility of death he finds a withered hope. This is a dark decision, but it is different from that of chapter 3, and with this decision, as we will see, Job's perception of and relationship with God is changing as well.

Chapter 6 *Job's "Friends"*

The final words of Eliphaz's speech in chapter 5 say, in essence: "You are going to be all right, Job." This friend has not seen Job honestly, without fear, or through the eyes of compassion. Given Job's unrestrained lament in chapter 3 on the meaninglessness of suffering and his emphatic curse on the day he was born and on the night he was conceived—his explicit wish that he were dead—it is not surprising that Job is in no mood to accept Eliphaz's orthodox platitudes of pietistic "comfort." Job responds by continuing his lament and by ignoring Eliphaz, comparing the friend's words to wadis that in Syria and Palestine run like torrents during the rainy season but dry up during the hot, dry months of summer when they are needed the most. Eliphaz's words are dry and useless. Nothing Eliphaz has said is of any help to Job in his misery. The task of the friend is to "sympathize" (*nud*) and "comfort" (*hesed*, show "kindness"; cf. Job 2:11; 6:14). But as Habel comments, "Eliphaz's reaction to Job's plight is taken by Job as evidence that the friends have repudiated their role as comforters. Thus within the narrative the friends now no longer function in their original capacity, but assume the role of 'wise' disputants or 'hagglers,' as Job designates them (6:27)."[12] Once again beautiful poetry and juxtaposition of images and metaphors only serve to heighten the reality of Job's suffering and death wish.

> People who meet with sorrows normally want those present to know the severity of the troubles besetting them. . . . What he [Job] means is something like this: you [Eliphaz] profess sound values in somebody else's troubles, and while standing at a distance from my calamities you offer encouragement with complete serenity. . . . What should have won me mercy is the basis for my being hated and condemned and I am unable to win mercy no matter what I say.
>
> John Chrysostom, *Commentaries on the Sages*, vol. 1, *Commentary on Job*, trans. Robert Charles Hill (Brookline, MA: Holy Cross Orthodox Press, 2006), 97–98.

Job's friends choose to see sin and thus withhold forgiveness; as Chrysostom writes, they bring no mercy.

Theologically, the despairing one needs *hesed*, loyalty, in times of crisis, an inner rapport of deep concern that outlasts external breaches of faith. This Job has not received. Job sees this loss of faith in his friends and states his belief in the most radical terms: "Those who withhold kindness from a friend forsake the fear [*yirah*] of the

12. Norman C. Habel, *The Book of Job: A Commentary*, Old Testament Library (Philadelphia: Westminster, 1985), 141.

Almighty" (6:14). "Fear" in this sense approximates the idea of religion or traditional faith, and Eliphaz has suggested to Job that "fear" of God should be Job's confidence and strength. Job contends that a true friend would not negotiate friendship on the basis of conforming to religion or traditional faith or the fear of God. Instead, as a sufferer, attacked by God, the Archer, Job needs more than traditional theology to sustain him.[13] Job pleads with his friends that affection, when authentic, should "not regard the theological position of the person it embraces. Indeed true love will not stop at heresy but will cherish even the heretic."[14] What Job is asking for is something we all need and crave: unconditional cherishing.

Is Job Sane?

The shifting metaphors in Job's speech throughout chapters 6 and 7 are difficult to follow and raise the question of whether an otherwise brilliant poet has turned sloppy, or whether the jumbled language is an intentional portrayal of Job deranged by suffering. The "wild," "mixed," and even "mad" speech of Job that some see in these two chapters, if not the words of a madman, do characterize suffering as a spur to thinking boldly, outside expected norms, and perhaps "a man may not be held responsible for what he does in anguish."[15] The most likely explanation of the language of these chapters is that the poet is in complete control of metaphor and language, as he has been throughout, and he now portrays an anguished mind beginning to lose control. Just a few of the seemingly insane leaps of Job's words include the metaphor of weighing (6:2–3) that is followed immediately by an unrelated military image of attack by poisoned arrows (v. 4); an image of inedible food (vv. 5–7) has some coherence with the poison in verse 4, but is succeeded by a dual image of crushing and cutting (v. 9), neither of which seems related to food; strength (vv. 11–12) is put in terms of rock and of bronze, two images related to one another, but not to anything else in these chapters; an extended simile of the drying up of water-carrying wadis (vv. 14–20) gives way (vv. 22–27) to terms of legal and extralegal dealing; the speech

---

13. Cf. Habel, *Job*, 148.
14. Ibid., 56.
15. Marvin Pope, *Job* (Garden City, NY: Doubleday, 1965), 60.

then returns to eating (v. 30), but then abruptly shifts (7:1) to day labor, drifts into inheritance (v. 3), then into a mixed metaphor of tossing and turning while trying to sleep (v. 4), to the image of skin disease (v. 5), and then to weaving (v. 6).[16] "Therefore my words have been rash" (6:3), Job says, and indeed they are, intentionally so. The poet's grotesque subtlety portrays disorientation, suffering, and anguish by reflecting them in disjointed and bizarre language and metaphor. Yair Hoffman comments, "Conventional literary and linguistic tools were unsuitable to express [these viewpoints]. Hence, he [the poet] was forced to create innovative means of expression suitable to the nature of the positions which he expressed."[17] That is, suitable to the troubled mind and soul of Job himself.

Chapter 7 *"Joy in pain unsparing"*

Still meditating on death, the lamentation of chapter 7 opens with a more universal lament, moving beyond the suffering of the righteous to the hard lot, toil, and labor of human beings in general (v. 1; cf. Gen. 3:17–19). Job, now addressing God directly, compares humanity's lot to a hireling or "laborer" (*sakir*) hired for a day's work, who longs for wages at the end of the day, and to the "slave" (*'ebed*) whose only hope is shade from the intense heat of the afternoon (7:2). Job once again observes that human existence is servitude and human life futility, that humanity generally shares his own predicament. But there is a difference: the day laborer hopes for his wages, the slave hopes for shade; Job's only hope is for death. Unlike chapter 3, where Job fanaticizes the impossible—cosmic nothingness and de-creation—Job now begs for something realizable: an end to his life. "I loathe my life" (7:16), he lashes out, I am allotted only "emptiness" (*shav*, 7:3), only meaninglessness and futility and suffering. Death is his hope.

The anguish driving Job is both nocturnal and diurnal: the nightly twisting and turning leaves him exhausted for the day, in which he must once again face the unspeakable, the dark night. "My

---

16. Cf. Good, *In Turns of Tempest*, 213–14.
17. Yair Hoffman, *A Blemished Perfection: The Book of Job in Context* (Sheffield: Sheffield Academic Press, 1996), 222.

I am groaning under the miseries of a diseased nervous System; a System of all others the most essential to our happiness—or the most productive of our Misery . . . Lord, what is Man! Today, in the luxuriance of health, exulting in the enjoyment of existence; In a few days, perhaps a few hours, loaded with conscious painful being, counting the tardy pace of the lingering moments, by the repercussions of anguish, & refusing or denied a Comforter.—Day follows night, and night comes after day, only to curse him with life which gives him no pleasure.

Robert Burns, letter 374, December 3, 1789, in *The Letters of Robert Burns*, vol. 1, *1780–1789*, 2nd ed., ed. G. Ross Roy (Oxford: Oxford University Press, 1990), 456–57.

flesh is clothed with worms and dirt; my skin hardens, then breaks out again" (7:5). Multiple physical and psychological complications of Job's illness can also be named.[18] As if the pain itself were not enough, Job is "clothed" (v. 5) with traditional symbols of mortality and death: the worm (*rimmah*) and the dust (*afar*), which together appear to symbolize the grave. With such clothing Job is attired in death itself.

Clothed in worms and dust, hoping for death, Job moves from shocked denial and fantasy in chapter 3 to anger, confusion, rage, and accusation. In the midst of this shift Job also begins to develop a new relationship with God. The relationship is at this point in every respect negative, yet it is a connection not seen in chapter 3 and much more deeply felt and realized than in chapters 1 and 2. Job expresses this better than anyone: "Indeed, I shall not restrain my mouth: I shall speak in the anguish of my spirit [*ruach*], I shall complain in the bitterness of my soul [*nefesh*]" (7:11, trans. Hartley). What he speaks and complains of is God. He is anguished and bitter but also, though he may not consciously realize it, at prayer. It is not the genteel prayer he offered for his children in chapter 1,

---

18. Suggestions of diseases from which Job is suffering have included leprosy, erythema, smallpox, eczema, and malignant ulcers. Symptoms mentioned in the book are inflamed eruptions (2:7), intolerable itching (2:8), disfigured appearance (2:12), maggots in the ulcers (7:5), terrifying dreams (7:14), fetid breath (19:17), emaciated body (19:20), erosion of the bones (30:17), blackening and peeling off of the skin (30:30). The "loathsome sores" (2:7) carry the additional connotations of boils, severe inflammation, running sores, and skin eruptions. Regardless of the nature of the malady, the salient point is that it was inflicted directly to the body by the *satan* with God's approval.

but it is nonetheless prayer in its ferocious, ready-for-battle kind of anger, prayer as prayer, even in fervent anger, at least acknowledges divinity. It is a prayer of accusation brilliantly arranged to imply arbitrary order in chaos, to serve as images and summaries of his fate. He demands of God, why do you "set a guard [*mishmar*, "muzzle"] over me?" (7:12); he directly accuses God, "You scare me with dreams and terrify me with visions" (v. 14). In anger he reminds God of his own insignificance, that his days are no more than a "breath" (v. 16). When you look toward me, Job says, "I will be gone" (v. 8), I am no more than "a cloud [that] fades and vanishes" (v. 9). In a time when place gave identity and definition to individuals and peoples, Job speaks to God of the placelessness that now defines him and the dead, "nor do their places know them any more" (v. 10a). So, he prays, "Let me alone!" (v. 16).

> It is difficult to put into words what I suffered—the longing that seemed to be tearing my heart out by the roots, the dreadful sense of being alone in an empty universe, the agonies that thrilled through me as if the blood were running ice-cold in my veins, the disgust with living, the impossibility of dying. Shakespeare himself never described this torture; but he counts it, in Hamlet, among the terrible of all the evils of existence.
>
> Hector Berlioz, *The Memoirs of Hector Berlioz*, trans. David Cairns (St. Albans: Granada, 1970), 142.

"Will you not look away from me for a while, let me alone?" (7:19). "If I sin, what do I do to you?" (v. 20). In contrast, in Psalm 8 the author takes pride and comfort in the idea that God is mindful of humanity:

> When I look at your heavens, the work of your fingers,
> the moon and the stars that you have established;
> what are human beings that you are mindful of them,
> mortals that you care for them?
>
> (Ps. 8:3–4)

This is directly parodied by Job:
> What are human beings, that you make so much of them,
> that you set your mind on them,

visit them every morning,
test them every moment?

(Job 7:17–18)

As David Daiches writes, Job is "being hounded by a Hound of Heaven." Even if he has sinned, Job says, how can that affect or make any difference to God? Daiches continues, commenting on another of Job's prayerful cries in 7:20: "'What difference does it make to you, Man Watcher?' That terrible phrase, 'man watcher,' spat out in fury, completes the reversal of the Psalmist's view."[19]

FURTHER REFLECTIONS
Providence

The word *providence* is from the Latin *pro*, meaning before or in front of, and *videre*, meaning to see or to perceive; thus *providence* is literally "to see in front of" or "to see what is to come." Job begins in chapters 6 and 7 to "see" forward into his predicament and to move from lament that pleads for deliverance from suffering through death to direct accusations against the divine power, order, justice, and goodness of providence that he believes is responsible for his suffering. Job makes it clear that Shaddai is the source of his overwhelming anguish: the "arrows of Shaddai stick fast in me, my spirit drinks their poison, God's terrors are arrayed against me" (6:4, trans. Hartley). The providence that Job's friends define in terms of retributive justice is, for Job, only the source of anguish, and he pleads to be left out of any divine providential scheme: "What's a man, that you magnify him so, set your mind on him, visit him every morning, test him every night" (7:16–18, trans. Good). To the extent that divine providence partakes of the will of the divine vision, Job at this point wants nothing to do with it.

The great twelfth-century Jewish philosopher Maimonides wrote about Job in his *Guide of the Perplexed* and outlined five theories of

---

19. Daiches, "God Under Attack," 44.

providence from previous schools, all of which have their advocate at various times in Job:

1. The view of Epicurus that there is no providence because there is no God; all that happens is mere chance.
2. Aristotle's view that God exercises providence, but only over those things that are stable and permanent. Thus there is general providence over various species, but not over their individual members (such as you or I or Job), who are unprotected from harmful chance events.
3. The Ash'arite school of Islamic theology that sees providence as the exercise of the divine will, which one cannot understand or question. Therefore God may cause the righteous to suffer and the wicked to prosper for no discernible reason.
4. The Mu'tazilite school of Islamic theology which believes that all God's actions in the world are dictated by wisdom. If righteous people suffer it is because God is testing them, with the opportunity to gain greater reward in the world to come.
5. An earlier Jewish perspective already discussed, according to which the principle of God's relationship to the world is justice. Providence is thus "consequent on the individual's deserts, according to his actions." Thus good comes to those who do good deeds, and suffering is punishment for sin.[20]

Not only does divine providence become a major theme, "to see" becomes a major metaphor: in verses 7–8 alone the words *eye* or *see* or *behold* are used no fewer than six times; the string of verbs depicting God's attention to humanity in verses 17–18 (exalt, visit, test, attend to) are variations of divine watching. Of course Job begs God to "look away" (v. 19), to quit looking until, finally, in the midst of all this divine providence, Job taunts God with another visual image: "you will seek me, but I shall not be" (v. 21).

Susan E. Schreiner is an astute interpreter of three major premodern commentaries on the book of Job, those by Gregory the Great,

---

20. Moses Maimonides, *The Guide of the Perplexed* 3:17–18, 51. See also Robert Eisen, *The Book of Job in Medieval Jewish Philosophy* (Oxford: Oxford University Press, 2004), 45–48.

Thomas Aquinas, and John Calvin. In one essay, Schreiner writes: "In the sixteenth century, both Catholic and Protestant exegetes found in the book of Job an opportunity to analyze the difficult issues of suffering and providence. These commentators inherited two exegetical traditions.... In the allegorical tradition, influenced primarily by Gregory the Great, the book of Job became the occasion for discussing, among other topics, the beneficial nature of affliction. In the literal tradition, formulated by Thomas Aquinas, the story of Job was interpreted as a debate about the nature of divine providence."[21] Calvin combines both these themes and adds other important elements that come into focus in the book of Job. For Aquinas, the primary issue relating to providence is immortality. Both Aquinas and Calvin agree, reading back into Job, that if one is limited to "that which appears from experience" it is indisputable that the wicked prosper and the good suffer.[22] Thus to restrict providence to the earthly life means accusing God of injustice, and so both see the book of Job as necessarily focused on providence, history, and immortality as interlocking categories (immortality being that time and space where the just conclusion of providence is executed).

Though his doctrine of immortality is developed, what is pertinent for Calvin is his in-depth exploration of the incomprehensibility of providence when viewed within history and nature. It is this exploration that forces Calvin into a doctrine of immortality, but more importantly a conclusion in which he defines Job's suffering in terms of the hiddenness of God. Job's spiritual torment, for Calvin, is attributable only to divine incomprehensibility, and this issue of suffering leads Calvin to discuss the incomprehensibility of providence itself, whether in this life or any afterlife. As Schreiner writes, "In [Calvin's] attempt to understand Job's anguish, Calvin struggles with a recurring tension between God's visibility and hiddenness, revelation and silence, knowability and incomprehensibility."[23] Thus

---

21. Susan E. Schreiner, "'Why Do the Wicked Live?': Job and David in Calvin's Sermons on Job," in *The Voice from the Whirlwind: Interpreting the Book of Job*, ed. Leo G. Perdue and W. Clark Gilpin (Nashville: Abingdon Press, 1992), 129.

22. Cf. Thomas Aquinas, *The Literal Exposition on Job* 21:26–27, 287.

23. Schreiner, "Why Do the Wicked Live?" 135.

for Calvin, it is out of chaos itself that Job ascertains something of the incomprehensible, divine, providential control by God of the earthly realm. This takes place for Calvin in the second whirlwind theophany as YHWH describes Leviathan and Behemoth. This beastly glimpse of chaos in creation and God's control over it provides for Calvin sufficient reason for trusting that God will always act in continuity with power, goodness, and wisdom. This may be sufficient for Calvin, but in the end I do not think it is sufficient for Job, nor certainly for modern and postmodern readers trying to wrestle with suffering and providence.

In contemporary theology, the God of process theology, in order to disentangle the good God from the responsibility for evil, suggests that the almightiness of God (omnipotence) rather than the justice of God be qualified and diminished. The result, supposedly, is that the problem of evil in its relation to God is resolved by denying God's absolute power in favor of God's role as the principal of moral order. This is an interesting take on providence and the nature of suffering, but it is very un-Joban. It is precisely the problematic, changeable *process* of omnipotence overpowering any divine justice that haunts and keeps Job under the almighty eye. For instance, there are many modes of relationship sequentially or providentially arranged, but complete disconnection, as Job experiences them, is not one of them. God's omnipotence (as providence) does place everything that occurs in Job's life under the divine will, but throughout the book of Job this omnipotence is sequentially unrelated to or disconnected from divine justice.

As incomprehensible as the ongoing relation between Job and God may be, a form of providential co-creation may, even today, allow for some hidden co-creation between the reader and Job in which healing between and within the reader and Job and God is even now providentialy active. If this is the case Job, in a sense, calls God's providential bluff only to experience providence as the very thing that is killing him: "I had heard of you by the hearing of the ear, but now my eye sees you" (42:5). Job is seeing God seeing Job in return. The "seeing" is Job's torture. Still, if 42:5 represents a new form of providence, it is a providence in which Job and his god are co-creators in an admittedly new moral order.

In the final verse of chapter 7, Job refers back to his suffering as a descent into Sheol (vv. 9–10), and the reference to God "seeking" Job encapsulates the extended surveillance and providence imagery of the chapter (vv. 7–8, 17–18, 19). In a book of ironies, the irony evident in the choice of the verb "seek" (*shahar*) at the end of chapter 7 to depict God's search for his victim is evident: "It usually implies a sense of eager and diligent seeking of worshipers eagerly seeking God. Job reverses this normal usage and speaks of God seeking human beings as victims."[24] Finally, in another ironic reconfiguration of divine providence that normally affirms God's presence, the torment God visits on Job does one thing very well: it denies God's absence.

8:1–22
Bildad's First Response to Job: "Repent!"

8:1–7 *Bildad's Justice*

Having repeated the salient points made by Eliphaz (in chaps. 4 and 5), Bildad wastes little time making clear his only doctrinal position in this chapter. The position is not new to the book; indeed it represents a calcification of a point already clearly made: God's ways are just (8:3), and without exception the righteous are blessed and the wicked are punished. For Bildad, any apparent exceptions are momentary or illusory: justice will win out in this lifetime. Bildad's is a premodern position, what we might call an old-time religion in which he puts forth his own evidence based on tradition and the teaching of the ancestors (vv. 8–10). For Bildad even the ways of nature adhere to this position (vv. 11–19). Here in chapter 8 Bildad gives the clearest and most forthright depiction of divine, retributive justice in the book of Job. There is no ambiguity in Bildad's universe: some people are righteous, others are wicked, the righteous are blessed, and the wicked are punished. End of story.

This cannot be much comfort to Job. Bildad opens with a sarcastic remark responding to Job's complaint that the friends blow like

---

24. Habel, *Job*, 157.

empty wind at his words (6:26); Bildad responds by calling Job's words a "great wind" (8:2). Ignoring Job's real complaint, Bildad mouths his own position, framing it in a rhetorical question and insensitively relying on Job's dead children as example and proof of his position:

> Does El bend justice,
> Shaddai bend the right?
> If your sons have sinned against him,
> he has sent them off in custody of their guilt.
> (8:3–4, trans. Good)

David Clines has pointed out that the "if" is not hypothetical. Thus, using Bildad's logic, the evidence of evil *is* the sons' death, and their horrendous death in turn is evidence of their sin and guilt. Put plainly, for Bildad Job's children died because they deserved to. He may intend to be truthful, if not kind, but his tongue is rough and his deepest sympathy (if it is that) rebounds as harsh criticism.[25] For

---

The Fathers' interpretation of Bildad's position is, in general, unfavorable. Even though they can discern a certain amount of correctness in his assertions (Chrysostom, Julian of Eclanum), they cannot help noticing his narrow views (Ephrem) and worldly mentality (Didymus), which places human happiness on a level with material goods and riches. . . . [Olympiodorus writes, in *Commentary on Job* 8:5–7:] "Bildad says, 'I suggest you pray to the Lord with all your devotion and diligence. Everything else should come after your prayers.' This is what 'be early' means. And if you are true and empty of any deceit and falseness, God will give you back a condition of life and status worthy of a righteous person. You will enjoy an abundance of goods as great as you possessed earlier. Notice however how Bildad demonstrates in this part of his discourse of praise his belief that the happiness of the righteous is found in the material goods of worldly life."

ACCS, 44, 45.

---

25. David J. A. Clines, "The Arguments of Job's Three Friends," in *Art and Meaning: Rhetoric in Biblical Literature*, ed. D. J. A. Clines, D. M. Gunn, and A. J. Houser, JSOTSup 19 (Sheffield: Sheffield Academic Press, 1982), 206. Clines also points out that the friends differ among themselves, not only in personality but also in viewpoint, and writes, "If they all have the same point to make, the book is indeed long-winded and flabby" (209).

Bildad, the power of the deity who rules the cosmos is intimately linked to justice as it is observed and served on earth. In order to maintain divine power, justice, and beneficence, Bildad supports a doctrine of providence in which the coherence of divine justice and divine power are mutually supportive. In verse 3, Bildad proposes that whatever the deity does is just: God in God's power controls all, and all that God does is just. That Job's children suffered untimely deaths is in itself sufficient evidence that they deserved death: the power of death is no different from the justice of death, regardless of innocence or even seemingly just behavior.[26] Console? We can almost feel Bildad's theology of providence, power, and justice as a sword slowly thrust into Job's already knotted gut.

A consequence of Bildad's equation of justice with divine power is that he can tell Job in complete seriousness and with absolute certainty that even though Job is suffering, he is experiencing divine mercy: he is at least alive and therefore must have sinned less than his children, who are dead. It is difficult to imagine a less comforting or more insensitive response to Job's plight. Nonetheless, Bildad means it as a source of hope: the balance of human and divine justice is still on Job's side—Job is "pure and upright" (v. 6)—and God never "perverts [*avath*, meaning also "twist, bend, make crooked"] justice" (v. 3). Therefore, according to Bildad's sense of justice, Job should "seek [*shihar*] God and make supplication to the Almighty" (v. 5). Seeking God is a form of wisdom, and pleading with Shaddai for mercy is a form of prayer. Both indicate righteousness and will thus, for Bildad, be answered and rewarded.

Heightening the impression that Bildad's words are themselves "a great wind" (v. 2), the Joban poet gives ironic play to this word *shihar*, which is the same verb Job used in 7:21 warning that if God were to "seek" him, God would—implying, in part, because of divine *in*justice—find that "I shall not be." In suggesting that Job "seek" God as God will "seek" Job, based on Job's earlier speech the poet implies that were Job to seek justice in the way Bildad describes, God—or at least God's justice—also "shall not be." Bildad does not recognize the contradiction between God's unbending justice and

26. Cf. Good, *In Turns of Tempest*, 218.

his proposed solution of Job's contrition; if Bildad has been listening to Job, he has certainly not caught the irony in the "seeking" he proposes.

8:8–10 *Bildad's Appeal to Tradition*

Given Bildad's doctrinal stance, it is not surprising that he first tries to validate his position through appeal to "bygone generations," to the "ancestors" and orthodox tradition rather than experience. "Our days on earth are but a shadow," Bildad says (8:9), and so we do not personally have the accumulated wisdom to see divine justice clearly. But the accumulation of wisdom from the tradition can "teach you and tell you and utter words out of their understanding" (v. 10). Bildad refers here to the more orthodox Deuteronomic tradition that represents the majority stance on suffering and divine justice over against the minority stance that Job is developing. In Bildad's mind Job is challenging the wisdom of the forefathers, which was traditionally given more credence than mere personal experience. For Bildad, in order for Job to recover righteousness and blessing he must cease challenging, on the basis of his own experience, the wisdom of the doctrines handed down through the generations of the tradition.

8:11–22 *Bildad's Appeal to Creation and Conclusion*

In an excellent book on Wisdom literature in the Old Testament, Leo G. Perdue writes that "even a cursory reading of the wisdom texts [he has in mind here the wisdom texts of Proverbs, Job, and Qoheleth] indicates that they have at their theological core the theme of creation."[27] In accord with this wisdom tradition, Bildad next moves to images of creation to illustrate his "wisdom" concerning divine justice and ultimately providence. Three illustrations are used. The first is a papyrus plant, which with abundant water and sun will grow rapidly to a height of eight to ten feet. A useful plant, it

---

27. Leo G. Perdue, *Wisdom Literature: A Theological History* (Louisville, KY: Westminster John Knox, 2007), 3.

can be woven and used to make baskets, mats, parchment, and swift, small boats. Though also beautiful, its chief characteristic is caught in the word "flourish," *ga'a*, which can also mean "thrive," "grow tall," or "be exalted or proud." But though the plant grows straight and tall and at a great rate, if deprived of water it can wither and die in a single night. Bildad uses the image of the dying and dead papyrus, comparing it to "the paths of all who forget God; the hope of the godless shall perish" (v. 13), not flourish. The metaphor clearly is directed at Job: Job's water is "hope" (*tiqvah*) but Job's hope is dry and so Job is "perishing" (*abad*).

The second image illustrates the fragile basis of a godless person's trust. Such a person's confidence is "gossamer, a spider's house" (v. 14), frail beyond anything else in creation. Those who grab at the gossamer of a spider's web grasp nothing. Bildad warns Job that there is no security against divine justice any stronger than this fragile web for any untrusting person—such as Job.

The creation image in verses 16–19 is more obscure and has led to a variety of interpretations. The difficulty comes in the apparent discrepancy between verses 18 and 19. Does the tearing out of the plant (v. 18) cause it to die, or is it able to withstand this attack and grow into a new beautiful plant (v. 19)? Most interpreters consider verse 18 a continuation of the fate of the wicked.[28] Following this, Bildad seems to offer a note of hope: "Those who hate you will be clothed with shame, and the tent of the wicked will be no more" (v. 22). But "tent" subtly recalls the image of the "house" that fell on Job's children, whom Bildad has already condemned as sinners through the logic of his orthodox doctrine. Thus Bildad holds out hope, then withdraws it almost in the same breath. In saying that the tent of the wicked will "be no [*ayin*] more," Bildad echoes Job from 7:21: "You will seek me, but I will be no [*ayin*] more." As Edwin M. Good writes, "In a neat rhetorical touch, Bildad ends his speech with the same word as Job in his prior one. But what sort of comfort

---

28. Hartley, *Job*, 161–63, lists G. Fohrer as the main proponent of this position, and A. Hakam and Gordis as proponents of a second position which argues that the plant is the description of the righteous in contrast to the wicked, in which case the righteous plant thrives, is uprooted by evil, but is able to "re-root" itself in righteousness through its original blessing.

is it? The 'tent of the wicked' becomes the analogue of the suffering of Job."[29]

Bildad has no doubt that the simple law of retributive justice prevails. Based on that law, as he tells Job, if he were pure and upright he would not now be suffering. Tradition, nature, and—as Bildad claims—his own eyes all show this law's truth. Bildad has not yet reached the point where he pulls out the neat balance point of the same law: Job must be complicit in evil based on his obvious suffering. That will come later. He does not seem to know yet whether to focus on Job's suffering and obvious sin, or to hold out a scrap of hope for some redemption if Job would only turn back to God. In either case, Bildad ends by trying to stuff the chaotic misery of Job's suffering into a neat box. But the lid has been opened: Job is innocent and he is suffering. Bildad's box is useless and his friendship questionable.

FURTHER REFLECTIONS
Divine Justice

Bildad's "vision" of divine justice is based on what he knows from tradition (history) and what he can observe in nature. The contemporary theologian Langdon Gilkey writes:

> The Hebrew tradition (excluding Job and Qoheleth), represented by the speeches of Job's friends, asserted that the God of power and of order also established and upholds moral justice in history: The good are rewarded and the evil punished. . . . We note two important presuppositions of this traditional argument. First, God plans, wills, and effects all that happens in history, down to the least detail. Hence evil events in a person's life do not merely happen but are divine acts and thus a divine punishment for that person's sin. Second, it is assumed, as a correlate, that history, the sequence of human events in time, is morally intelligible. The good are rewarded and the wicked punished, and this spectacle

---

29. Good, *In Turns of Tempest*, 221.

of moral justice is plainly visible to any unbiased eye that
surveys history's course.[30]

The first assumption speaks of the effective and active omnipotence of God, the second of the moral intelligibility of history (or creation). In a radical turn from this philosophy and morality, the author
of Job presents us with movement away from the "certainty" of
moral justice *discernible and visible* in history, creation, or tradition.
The poet carefully portrays Job not on the basis of nature, history, or
moral intelligibility but on the basis of his own *personal experience*,
on the integrity of his own experience and what that tells him about
moral justice.[31]

Premodern exegetes of Job proposed a different perspective
on the operative quality and effect of suffering and moral justice.
Ambrose, for instance, proposed two themes focused on the salutary nature of suffering. The first is the theme, echoing Paul, that
sees strength and asceticism "made perfect in weakness" and suffering, which leads in turn to spiritual fortitude. One is formed into an
"athlete of Christ" in order that the person "might be fashioned by
temptations and attain to the crown of a greater glory."[32] A second
theme is the identification between suffering and freedom, especially freedom leading to spiritual wisdom. Ambrose suggests that
afflictions endured by Job are governed by references to insight,
discernment, knowledge, and good judgment. Thus Ambrose links
suffering to moral strength and spiritual understanding rather than
sin, evil, or divine punishment.

Medieval and Reformation exegetes of Job added a new dimension outside history or creation; the dimension is still ordered
according to divine providence and justice but is based on immortality. There are hints in the book of Job of immortality, but hints
only. Though these hints are vague, interpreters such as Thomas

---

30. Langdon Gilkey, "Power, Order, Justice, and Redemption," in Leo G. Perdue and W. Clark
    Gilpin, eds., *The Voice from the Whirlwind: Interpreting the Book of Job* (Nashville: Abingdon,
    1992), 162.
31. Ibid., 163.
32. Ambrose, "The Prayer of Job and David," in *Seven Exegetical Works*, 327–67 (Washington,
    DC: Catholic University of America Press, 1972), 2.1.2, 353.

Aquinas read the book of Job through this lens of immortality. According to Aquinas, Job alone of all the human characters in the book had a concept of immortality. Aquinas explains that both Job and his friends believed in providence and saw in the orderly course of nature evidence for the existence of God's governance and justice, but he gets at the real weakness of Bildad and his friends' vision of divine justice by pointing out that justice is not always present in history or creation alone.[33] Since Job's friends restrict providence to the earthly life, they were fundamentally wrong in their perception of providence and justice and so also wrong in their conclusions about Job. As Susan E. Schreiner writes, in Aquinas, "the existence of the afterlife functions as an extension of history so that God can exercise justice after death. . . . [Aquinas's] real concern is to show that a belief in providence without the supporting doctrine of immortality results in a false perception about the true natue of human history."[34] History according to Aquinas, disordered as it is, does not of itself provide sufficient proof of such justice.

Altogether, in this we have moved far from Bildad's doctrine of the righteous rewarded and wicked punished. What can we really know about divine justice? Jerome and Gregory the Great see the salutary effects of suffering, suffering forming a spiritual athlete for Christ. Aquinas and Calvin can only begin to talk about providence and divine justice in the context of immortality and the doctrine of the afterlife. And Calvin finds in Job's suffering not proof of sin, but real spiritual torment justifiable only in the context of a hidden, incomprehensible God.[35]

Using modern perspectives on suffering and divine justice, Langdon Gilkey, on the other hand, looks to process theology and the theology of divine suffering from neo-orthodox theology, to Tillich, and especially to Moltmann in order to suggest two additional themes that influence current thought concerning divine justice and what we can know of it. Both are based on the book of Job, and

---

33. Aquinas, 8.3, 157–58.

34. Schreiner, *Where Shall Wisdom Be Found?* 76.

35. On the hiddenness of God in Calvin, see B. A. Gerrish, "To the Unknown God," in *The Old Protestantism and the New: Essays on the Reformation Heritage* (Chicago: University of Chicago Press, 1984), 131–49.

Gilkey implies that all can be traced back to Joban themes. The first is that "the question of *what* sort of relation might obtain between the will of God and the course of history remains an unanswered query in modern Christian and Jewish thought . . . and at least one of the presuppositions of the Joban dialogue, namely that God directly causes to happen all that happens, is no longer with us."[36] Another challenge begun by Job is that suffering has no positive relation of any sort to the divine will. Despite the prominence of this view in Deuteronomic understanding of history and common Christian understanding, one can see this view challenged beginning with Job and moving through later commentators. The later of Gilkey's themes also relies on the implicit presence of grace in suffering. He writes, "God does not so much judge, repudiate, condemn, or destroy evil, as God transforms it, embraces it, participates in it, and overcomes it," through love and grace. He adds, "hints of grace as transcendent to law, to the distinction between good and evil, righteousness and unrighteousness, are surely present in Job. The important point in our discussion is that of the principle of grace."[37]

Job himself, as we have seen, represents a minority stance within Scripture, a stance and a perceptual vision that embraces and incorporates the visions of his friends, yet begins to transcend that ancient vision of cosmological, divine control of every detail of life. Incomprehensible and absent, the Joban God of the dialogues is in fact transcendent and finally beyond any detail of life, especially with regard to justice. On the other hand Gilkey's "hints of grace" also "hint" divine immanence, mostly immanant suffering as it's "justice" invades human history. In a sense, Job is a modern and postmodern sufferer: modern as he elicits *divine* suffering, postmodern in his existential, personal experience of suffering as a fragmenting process that has the capacity to deconstruct and reconstruct personal identities in a co-creative process simultaneously with a God at once transcendent and hidden while at the same time *agapic* and immanent.

---

36. Gilkey, "Power, Order, Justice, and Redemption," 169. For Gilkey's comprehensive discussion on the relation between providence and justice, see 159–71.
37. Ibid., 167.

9:1–10:22

Job's First Response to Bildad:
A Darkness at the Heart of God

Job now discovers darkness at the heart of God, yet he continues to rely on his own heart to speak with integrity and truth. In doing so Job confronts God out of a faith tested and wracked by suffering, constricted by dread more than liberated by hope, and able to see only divine injustice out of his own experience of darkness. He recognizes the totalizing "no" that is the true answer to Eliphaz's earlier question: "Can mortals be righteous before God?" (4:17a). But his own repetition of the question: "How can a mortal be just before God?" (9:2b) is more ambiguous: it is a question, not an assertion; it will lead Job to question God's own heart and righteousness. Yet in all this, Job's unrelenting attention to his God is in itself prayer that gives witness to the possibility of a new kind of faith even in the midst of suffering, even as he dwells in God's own heart of darkness.

As he begins to grasp something of the mystery that is suffering, Job still keeps his focus directly on God as the originating cause and source of the incomprehensibility of suffering. Job keeps locked on his target: he places YHWH in his sights and he will not turn away. Any image of seeing God or entering into divine presence would be useless at this point: useless because hopeless, and hopeless because Job himself is now without hope. But Job will not relent, he will not turn away: YHWH is his heart of darkness, his enemy. Out of the divine silence Job begins to suspect that there may be something dark at the heart of God.

The speech of chapters 9 and 10 is even more complex than Job's last. However, most commentators recognize a logic in Job's seemingly twisted and unrelated metaphors that signals a new direction in Job's thinking. The complexity of his speech "arises from Job's intertwining a remarkable multiplicity of images around a central thread of argument. That argument, which we have not seen fully elaborated before, turns on the language of law and legal procedure—a theme that will occupy Job more and more as the dialogue proceeds."[38] Slowly, Job begins to seize on the idea of challenging God in a court of law; he believes that only in a trial, fairly conceived and run taking into account history, nature, and tradition, will he find the justice his integrity demands.

This is a radical position reflecting Job's despair and inner agitation, which initially he is quick to abandon. But it is a position to which he will return. Ironically, perhaps tragically, the new "central thread of argument" also coincides with Job's increasingly agitated frame of mind. The very idea of challenging God in a court of law may indicate remnants of trust in divine justice, but at the same time it reflects impossible, fanciful thinking, a grandiose self-concept. The vehicle of Job's aggressive movement toward God is the genre of lamentation, which can be responsible for cathartic hope even as it sustains the dread of hopeless grief. Lamentation, however, seems also to be responsible for each new and evolving insight that will inevitably return again and again to the truth of the experience of his heart, even if his heart is dust and ashes and dread, a hopeless grief, a hopeless faith. For a moment in the confusion, Job even catches a glimpse of a kind of christological ladder, a mediator. But even this initial intuition is only another harsh prelude to yet one more disappointment and lamentation (9:32–35).

9:1–35 *Divine Power and Justice in a Court of Law*

Unlike Job's earliest lament (chap. 3) and his first speech (chaps. 6–7) it is clear that in chapters 9 and 10, rational or not, Job is moving in the direction of the viability of litigation against God. In turning to the language of litigation Job offers two prolonged critiques of God's justice in response to Eliphaz (9:1–13, cf. 4:17–21) and to Bildad (9:14–24, cf. 8:3). He opens with a phrase nearly identical to Eliphaz's question "Can mortals be righteous [*tsaddiq*] before God?" (4:17). Job asks, "How can a mortal be just [*tsaddiq*] before God?" (9:2).[39] Job agrees with Eliphaz that it is impossible to be

---

38. Good, *In Turns of Tempest*, 221.

39. As reflected in the various translations of *yitsddaq*, Job and Eliphaz talk both to and past each other: *yitsddaq* carries a surplus of meanings. Cf. Pope: "how can a man be acquitted"; Good and Hartley: "innocent"; Habel: "cannot win a suit against"; Balentine prefers REB: "no one can win his case against God" (9:2).

tsaddiq before God. But Eliphaz implies that humanity cannot be *tsaddiq* (righteous) before God on moral and religious grounds. Job, on the other hand, interprets *tsaddiq* to mean "innocent" in a legal sense; thus Job's question is whether mortals can be morally or legally innocent before God. Job's question also carries the accusation that one cannot be innocent because God changes rules even in the middle of the game, skewing the law in God's favor to conform to God's changing will.

Job's primary obstacles to a successful trial are terrifying divine power and what he sees as questionable divine justice. In a classic psalm of praise, it is God "who alone works great wonders, . . . who by understanding made the heavens, . . . who spread out the earth on the waters, . . . who made the great lights" (Ps. 136:4–7). But in Job's mouth, God removes mountains in anger (9:5), "shakes the earth out of its place" (v. 6), has the power to command the sun not to rise, and "seals up the stars" (v. 7). For Job the heaven's wisdom of the Psalms becomes the chaotic power one would expect from the *enemies* of creation: Leviathan, Sea, Death, Tiamet.

Divine power, from Job's perspective, is chaotic and irrational, and the poetic imagery mimics it: Job moves instantly from God's destructive power to God's inscrutable wisdom, reminiscent of the language of Second Isaiah (Isa. 40:22; 42:5; 44:24): God, Job now says, "stretched out the heavens and trampled the waves of the Sea" (9:8; Yam), implying the triumph of fertile order over the disorder of oceanic chaos. After talking about God sealing up the stars, Job now talks about the Creator of the constellations (v. 9) "who does great things beyond understanding, and

> To seek for some lasting security is futile. To undo our very ancient and very stuck habitual patterns of mind requires that we begin to turn around some of our most basic assumptions. Believing in a solid, separate self, continuing to seek pleasure and avoid pain, thinking that someone "out there" is to blame for our pain—one has to get totally fed up with these ways of thinking. One has to give up hope that this way of thinking will bring us satisfaction. Suffering begins to dissolve when we can question the belief or the hope that there's anywhere to hide.
>
> Pema Chödrön, *When Things Fall Apart: Heart Advice for Difficult Times* (Boston: Shambhala Classics, 2000), 39.

marvelous things without number" (v. 10). Job covers all the bases: not only does he turn the genre of doxology of praise to the Creator into a bitter set of grievances about God, Job simultaneously recognizes God's wisdom, justice, and power to do good. Here Joban logic parodies the either/or thinking of his friends by changing the dialectic to a negative both/and kind of logic in which Job recognizes all avenues of escapes from his suffering as traps and mazes leading nowhere but back to suffering.

"I am blameless; I do not know myself; I loathe my life"

Job's experience of power and justice leads him to believe that the God he will encounter seeks his destruction (9:17–18). God crushes him with the force of a whirlwind (*searah*; the same "whirlwind" of 38:1), leaving him both breathless and condemned. In one moment he is "innocent" (v. 20a), the next "blameless" (vv. 20b, 21a), the next he does not know himself, the next he once again hates his life. He is losing himself: "I am blameless; I do not know myself; I loathe my life" (v. 21). This is a sentence reflecting a kind of mad luminosity uttered before Freud, before Baudelaire, before Nietzsche, before the notion of melancholy, before the medieval noonday demon, acedia. It is a confession regarding evil and righteousness reflecting a lamentable reality. Yet how can one be "blameless" if one does not know oneself? Coupled with blamelessness and lack of self-knowledge, to loathe his life is at worst a claim of the worst kind of mental disorder and at best the antithesis of a core principle of Western philosophy, theology, and piety: "know thyself."

A survivor of the Nazi Holocaust, Elie Wiesel spent his life after World War II writing of the darkness of war and destruction that had fallen on the twentieth century. A Jew, he gravitated naturally and most often to issues of the relation between power and justice, their use and misuse. In one of his plays, *The Trial of God*, set in Shamgorod, Russia, in 1649, Wiesel transposes the book of Job to a small Jewish village that is about to be destroyed in a pogrom against the Jews. The play is set in an inn among the few remaining residents of the town who refuse to flee. The residents decide that, given the recent massacres and the destruction they know is soon to befall them as well, they, like Job, will put God on trial. The innkeeper, a "bearish" man named Berish, is the Joban figure who readily accepts the role of prosecutor. At one point, one of the witnesses for God suggests divine mercy as a mitigating factor in suffering and as a possible bridge between divine power and justice. Berish replies:

> God is merciless, don't you know that? How long will you remain His blind slaves? I no longer rely on Him; I'd rather rely on the drunkenness of the priest. . . . How do you expect me to speak unless you want me to lie? God is God, and I am only an innkeeper. But He will not prevent me from letting my anger explode! He will not succeed in stifling my truth—and neither will you.[40]

Chapter 10 of Job picks up on the image of Creator playing loose with creation. The comparison in chapter 10 is to a mother: would a mother play with power and justice in this way with her child? Job both appeals to and accuses his Creator: "Your hands fashioned and made me; and now you turn and destroy me. Remember that you fashioned me like clay; and will you turn me to dust again? Did you not pour me out like milk and curdle me like cheese? . . . You have granted me life and steadfast love, and your care has preserved my spirit. Yet these things you hid in your heart; I know that this was your purpose" (10:8–10, 12–13). God creates and destroys, gives and withholds love, and the meaning of both gift and horror are hidden in God's heart; how am I to know who I am if I cannot know you, and what of you can I know that you continue to hide in your heart?

Job repeats again: "I loathe my life." And why should he not? What is there to love about capriciousness, a personality that will not reveal itself, and worse, wanton abuse of power disregarding justice? William Shakespeare writes, famously, in *King Lear*, "As flies to wanton boys are we to the gods; They kill us for their sport."[41] Job says, "If I sin, you watch me" (10:14a); "Bold as a lion you hunt me; you repeat your exploits against me" (10:16). Being a creature

---

40. Elie Wiesel, *The Trial of God: A Play in Three Acts*, trans. Marion Wiesel (New York: Random House, 1979), 42.
41. William Shakespeare, *King Lear*, 4.1.36–37.

of the Creator reduced to loathing life itself, both Berish and Job alternate between righteous rage and stagnant, lethargic capitulation. At the same time Job knows that the things that are important to God are not available to humans, "these things you hid in your heart" (10:13a). Like Berish, Job moves from a capitulating shell of a man on the dung-heap to the man tearing off the masks of God whose face is hidden. In this sense, Berish speaks for Job: "I Berish, Jewish innkeeper at Shamgorod—accuse Him of hostility, cruelty and indifference . . . He is . . . He is . . . guilty. Yes, guilty!"[42]

> **What's madness but nobility of soul**
> **At odds with circumstance?**
>
> Theodore Roethke, "In a Dark Time," lines 7–8, in *The Collected Poems of Theodore Roethke* (Garden City, NY: Doubleday, 1966), 231.

10:1–22 *A Darkness at the Heart of God*

Chapter 10 returns to an accusatory lament against God for withholding forgiveness, for continued innocent suffering, but also a lament that continues the litigation theme of chapter 9 and, with it, a continued condemnation of God. Much of the imagery of lament in chapter 10 we have seen before. The birth metaphor that presents God as lord of the womb and responsible for conception, birth, and nurture is especially prominent, as it was throughout the lament of chapter 3 (see 10:8–12 for creation imagery and vv. 18–20 for birth and womb imagery). As in Job's earlier laments, he questions why God should pay such careful attention to humans, why God's "eye" should be on humanity day and night; Job begs to be left alone from such ceaseless, eternal scrutiny (see especially vv. 14–17, summed up in the vivid phrase in v. 16a, "Bold as a lion you hunt me").

But the Joban author is never satisfied with simple replication. The writer's mastery of the craft is such that, should we come across an image, metaphor, or turn of phrase that sounds familiar, we ought immediately to be alerted that the author, rather than being repetitious, is adding a layer of nuance that not only reinterprets the original, but in most cases sets the stage for another layer of meaning still to come.

42. Wiesel, *Trial of God*, 125.

A few examples illustrate the mastery of technique and subtle nuancing of the Joban author. In the first, the birth, womb, conception, and nurturing metaphors of chapter 10 bring chapter 3 to mind. But beyond the return of these metaphors, the poet of Job gives the birth metaphor "an astonishing reversal of meaning. The traditional goal of an accusatory lament is to turn God's face toward the sufferer for the purpose of redemption (cf. Ps. 139:13–18), but Job destabilizes this metaphor, which is central for the strophe and thus its tradition, by indicating that the divine intent in his creation is to destroy, not to nurture, his offspring and him."[43]

The second image, in verses 8–11, metaphorically portrays God as a potter clothing humanity with skin and flesh and knitting bone and sinew together. With artistic skill, God has shaped Job in the womb and bestowed on him both life and the gift of love. In this image of God the potter creating a human vessel, one would expect the gift of divine breath to follow (as in Gen. 2:7). Instead, Job uses the pottery image to describe how he is formed and shaped, but finally returned, breathless, to the dust from which he was made.

Everything around Job is falling apart. He at least has the honesty to stay close to his heart, to stand in his own reality. In chapter 10, we encounter Job's experience of God's heart, it is where one encounters hidden deceit, destruction, betrayal, and darkness.

A third illustration of the mastery and nuance, not to mention boldness of vision, of the Joban poet follows from the first two. We have seen it before, but the reader by now expects that the original meaning is about to become more subtle or more complex or both. Job concludes the speech by returning to the language of chapter 3. His return to lament and the language of chapter 3 is a return to the possibility that death may be his only way of escaping torment. He understands only too clearly that death is a land of no return (10:21a), but he has exhausted his options. The darkness at the heart of God is upon him. And while the longing for death of chapter 3 is a cry for a de-creation of the night of his conception and the day of his birth, in chapter 10 Job's cry for death comes through a series of images of darkness that even in Hebrew crush the light of Job's life. The English language does not have the elasticity to hold such a

43. Perdue, *Wisdom Literature*, 108.

> No worst, there is none.
>   Pitched past pitch of grief,
> More pangs will, schooled at
>   forepangs, wilder wring.
> Comforter, where, where is
>   your comforting?
> Mary, mother of us, where is
>   your relief?
> My cries heave, herds-long;
>   huddle in a main, a chief
> Woe, world-sorrow; on an age-
>   old anvil wince and sing—
> Then lull, then leave off. Fury
>   had shrieked 'No ling-
> ering!'
>
> Gerard Manley Hopkins, "No Worst,
> There Is None," in *The Poetical Works
> of Gerard Manley Hopkins*, ed. Norman
> Mackenzie (Oxford: Oxford University
> Press, 1990), 182.

death cry. First, Job invites God out of his life, to leave him alone: "Are not the days of my life few? Let me alone, that I may find a little comfort" (v. 20). Then comes Job's dark death cry:

Let me alone that I might find a
    little comfort
before I go, never to return,
to the land of darkness[44] and deep
    shadowed darkness,[45]
the land of ominous gloom[46] and
    obscurity[47] and death's shadow[48]
    and chaos without order,[49]
where light glows like a sinister-
dark shade.[50]
        (Job 10:20b–21a, NRSV;
            21b–22, au. trans.)

Where the Hebrew is at least ablossom in "darkness," the English is tepid tea.

FURTHER REFLECTIONS
Power and Justice on Trial

The trial motif is one of the major unifying themes in the book of Job. The opening words of Job's speech in chapter 9 begin Job's extended meditation on bringing God to trial as a way to release him from suffering, or at least to vindicate the truth of his righteousness:

44. *hoshek*; "gloom" NRSV; *hoshek* once covered the primal waters (Gen. 1:2).
45. *tsalmaveth*; "deep darkness" NRSV.
46. *ofel*; "gloom" NRSV.
47. *efah*; not translated in NRSV.
48. *tsalmaveth*; not translated in NRSV.
49. *lo sedarim*; "chaos" NRSV.
50. *ofel*; "darkness" NRSV.

"Indeed I know that this is so; but how can a mortal be just before God?" (9:2). The sentence alludes to Eliphaz's question at 4:17: "Can mortals be righteous before God?"

Later in the speech of chapters 9–10 Job expresses agreement on the face of it with Eliphaz. Humanity cannot be found righteous before God, not because every person is necessarily sinful, but because "If one wished to contend [*rib*] with him, one could not answer him once in a thousand" (9:3). In this key sentence, the poet inserts one of the many nuanced meanings for "contend" (*rib*). Elsewhere *rib* can mean "quarrel" or, as a technical term for a legal procedure, "dispute." The iconography of Job often shows a Job cinching up his belt, ready to do battle with God. The syntax is ambiguous with regard to prepositions and pronouns. Yair Hoffman illustrates four possibilities raised by syntactical ambiguity, using only "contend" as the translation for *rib* in 9:3:

If he/He wished to contend with him/Him, he/He cannot answer him/ Him

1. If a man wished to contend with God, God cannot answer to man.
2. If a man wished to contend with God, man cannot answer to God.
3. If God wished to contend with man, man cannot answer to God.
4. If God wished to contend with man, God cannot answer to man.[51]

What at first might seem merely technical syntactical issues becomes, if we allow the poet credit for fully using the choice of words in 9:3, the core of Job's anguishing but unrelenting efforts to understand and come to terms with his situation, his suffering, and his God.

The motif of Job's quest for a *fair* trial, with God as the defendant and Job the prosecutor, unfolds throughout the rest of the book of Job. It may be, however, that for the writer of the book of Job, power and justice—the very components of a viable, fair court

---

51. This material and much of the material on the trial motif in Scripture is from Hoffman, *Blemished Perfection*, 42–71. On trial motif see also Habel, *Job*, 178–201.

system—are themselves on trial. To go to trial with God, as Job wishes to do in chapters 9 and 10, Job must negotiate the impossible currents of divine power and divine justice; Job experiences this power and justice as capricious, complex, and nuanced qualities that wreak havoc on Job's life. They are not divine power and justice complementary to the traditional piety of Job's friends.

Instead, Job is getting to know a different God, a God whose power and justice and wisdom are a hall of mirrors: God is powerful, though destructive; God is just in creation, though arbitrary in the order of justice on a day-to-day basis; God is wise, though also capable of hiding the ways of divine wisdom. Job begins to be caught up in his experience of a near Alice in Wonderland balance between power and justice. Having begun the discussion of the relation between justice and power through a discussion of creation in chapter 3, in these chapters Job draws a connection between the Creator's power and justice and the creation's experience of that power and justice: the connections are out of balance. As Job's speech grows ever more hysterical, on the surface nearly mad, he tries to sort out his innocence from the capricious nature of God:

> If it is a contest of strength, he is the strong one!
> If it is a matter of justice, who can summon him?
> Though I am innocent, my own mouth would condemn me;
> though I am blameless [*tam*], he would prove me perverse.
> I am blameless [*tam*]; I do not know myself;
> I loathe my life.
> It is all one; therefore I say,
> he destroys both the blameless [*tam*] and the wicked.
>
> (9:19–22)

For detailed analysis of the trial metaphor as it unfolds throughout the book, see "Further Reflections: Job's Trial Strategy," pp. 232–34.

In his speech in these chapters, Job continues to speak from the heart, from his experience, not on the basis of theology, not on the basis of tradition, not on the basis of history or creation. Simply put, he will not ignore what his experience shows to be true. Job's integrity is such that we begin to see a man in whom faith and the experiences of the heart complement one another, even though in doing so Job is slowly losing himself.

11:1–20
Zophar's First Response to Job:
"Forget your misery . . . There is hope!"

Zophar, the last friend in this first cycle of dialogues, is the first to accuse Job of sin or wickedness directly. He does this solely on the evidence of Job's current predicament, deducing from the doctrine of retributive justice that, since Job is suffering, he is guilty. Period. Zophar's deduction represents the logical reversal of the Deuteronomic theory put in conditional form: the wicked are punished; if Job is suffering (being punished), then he is wicked and has sinned.

This doctrine will remain a major point of reference and theological understanding throughout the rest of the book. Both this issue and the meaning of suffering focus on the integrity and action of God in the world; both then contribute to building up and defining a doctrine of God. Job's "complaint" is suffering, but the basis of his growing interest in initiating a trial with God is his growing sense that this doctrine of retributive justice has very little to do with justice and even less to do with his suffering.

The previous speeches of the two other friends contain hints that in applying the retributive doctrine to Job's situation, they would have to conclude that he has sinned. Zophar is the third of the three friends to use the theory to interpret Job's situation. The friends will become angry with Job and more insistent that, based on the obvious evidence—his suffering—he must be guilty of sin or unrighteousness. Zophar begins this as he accuses Job in no uncertain terms: "Should your babble [*bad*] put others to silence, and when you mock [*lag*], shall no one shame [*kalam*] you?" (11:3). Babble (*bad*) is more precisely "lie," hence Job's lies will keep Zophar silent no more, Job's mocking is legitimate grounds for Zophar to shame (even humiliate) Job.

Oh wretch! To whom life and death are alike impossible! Most miserable at present in this, that being thus miserable I have my senses continued to me only that I may look forward to the worst. It is certain at least, that I have them for no other purpose, and but very imperfectly even for this. My thoughts are like loose dry sand, which the closer it is grasped slips the sooner away.

William Cowper, letter to Lady Hesketh, January 22, 1796, in *Letters of William Cowper*, ed. W. Benham (London: Macmillan, 1914), 310.

Job has become more adamant in his defense of his blamelessness, though with ongoing suffering and unsympathetic friends arrayed against him, he is also becoming more agitated, afraid, and, at times, incoherent as he tries to express and understand what is happening to him. The anxiety, fear, and incoherence will only increase.

Zophar shames Job: "Do not let wickedness reside in your tents" (11:14b). The implication? Wickedness resides in Job's tents.

Unlike Eliphaz, Zophar does not appeal to a mystical, visual experience, and unlike Bildad, he does not recall the traditions of forebears or the revelatory witness of creation. Rather, Zophor reasons deductively from the propositions set forth in the Deuteronomic theory, filling his speech with motifs drawn from legal, wisdom, hymnic, and theological traditions. In three sections—an accusation against Job (vv. 1–4), God's wisdom (vv. 5–12), and a call to repentance (vv. 13–20)—Zophar tries to persuade Job to quit his wordy, wild statements, to repent, and thus to return to the security he has known. Zophar sees himself, of course, as strikingly unencumbered with issues of sin or wickedness.

The fact that no friend to this point has directly accused him of sin is small comfort to Job. Zophar's more pointed attack brings even less consolation. In trying to impress Job with the awesomeness of divine wisdom, Zophar tries to teach Job that God's ways are too profound for human understanding. For Zophar, Job is wrong to speak of the need or possibility of a trial. Indeed in Job's case God is showing mercy by not punishing him even more; Zophar audaciously states: "God exacts of you less than your guilt deserves" (v. 6c). Zophar and Job perceive the world in ways that never intersect: it is as if one says "justice" as the other hears "wickedness."

Accusations, Divine Wisdom, and a Call to Repentance

Zophar wastes no time in denouncing Job's insistence on guiltlessness and arrogant boasting as well as misquoting Job to Zophar's advantage. In his own vision Zophar equates verbosity (and Job is a verbose man) with guilt: in his mind a man of "a multitude of words" (v. 2a; literally, "a man of lips") ought not to go unanswered; such a wordy, babbling man cannot possibly be righteous (*tsaddiq*) (v. 2b). In asking if Job thinks his "babble" (*bad*, meaning also "empty, idle talk") will "put others to silence," Zophar is referring to an ancient tradition of argument in which the winner reduces the loser to silence. But even by these rules, the fact that both Zophar and Job are still talking indicates the argument is far from over (notice the silence of Job in the context of God's argument against him from the whirlwind).

Zophar's claim to quote Job—"For you say, 'My conduct is pure, and I am clean in God's sight'" (v. 4)—is best summed up by Edwin Good: "It is difficult to find in Job's mouth anything that Zophar attributes to him. 'I am perfect' (9:21) comes closest to it."[52] Zophar caricatures Job's view in an attempt to make him look even more absurd. Job in fact never says, "My conduct is pure." The word for conduct or doctrine also implies beliefs received through the tradition of the fathers. Job never argues from the position of the tradition, only from his experience, and Job never claims his conduct or doctrine is pure; indeed his conduct has been disturbed and his understanding of his suffering is anything but clear or pure. Similarly, Job never says, "I am clean [*bar*] in God's sight" (11:4b; another Zophar claim). The Hebrew *bar* refers to that which shines, and in that sense that which is clean, pure, and spotless. It also describes moral purity, as in "pure of heart" (Pss. 24:4; 73:1). But while Job does hold to his innocence, rather than *bar* he uses the word *tam* ("blameless"; 9:20–21), a word that means personal integrity more than spotless purity.[53] This is important because it is particularly Job's integrity (even more than purity) that helps him stand his ground and that is the basis of his insistence that his suffering cannot be the result of sin.

---

52. Good, *In Turns of Tempest*, 230.
53. Cf. Hartley, *Job*, 194–95.

> So that we should look not for wisdom created, but Wisdom creating. . . . We, then, who on Wisdom's coming were found ungodly, what title of good practice have we given, whereby we might obtain to receive that Wisdom? "The price of this Wisdom man knoweth not," because whoso is separated from brute animals by the understanding faculty of reason, understands that he is not saved by his own merits, knows and sees that he had not given any thing of good practice that he might come to faith. For it is as it were to give a price for the obtaining of Wisdom, to anticipate the coming to the knowledge of God by the merchandize of one's conduct.
>
> Gregory the Great, *Morals on the Book of Job*, 18.61, Job 28:12–15, p. 362; 62, pp. 363–64.

Zophar does wish that God would speak to Job, putting the possibility of God's speech to Job in terms of divine "wisdom" which "is many-sided" (vv. 6, 7–12), implying that it is too "many-sided" for Job or anyone else to grasp wholly. Ironically, as Zophar speaks of divine wisdom and human limitation, he implies that he, Zophar, is privy to this same wisdom about which Job can only "babble." Divine wisdom is described as greater than the four dimensions (including heaven) of creation: it is higher than the heavens, deeper than Sheol, longer than the earth, and broader than the sea (vv. 8–9). God as Wisdom judges and imprisons the worthless, those filled with iniquity, and the stupid (vv. 10–12). Thus to have full insight into God, one must know the center of the divine being as well as the outermost limits of divine influence. But again Zophar seems to trap himself in his own impossibilities as he claims to know the dimensions of wisdom, the content of wisdom, the workings of wisdom, and the power and justice of wisdom. We can picture Job reaching down to scratch a scab with a shard of pottery, shaking his head and wondering at the narrow audacity of a friend who describes wisdom in transcendent terms yet claims to know the intimate, immanent dynamics of wisdom and, with utmost piety, of course, is willing to share that knowledge with Job!

Once again, Zophar's proposal is insensitive and unhelpful. Redirect your heart, pray, repent of your sin, put your sin aside (vv. 13–14). He has no idea what the sin could be, but his solution remains simple: remove it, move away from it, cast it out of your tents. Zophar offers neither discernment, spiritual direction, reasonable advice, or insight about how to put his poorly thought-out proposals into practice. The theology works simply for Zophar: Job is wicked but he could easily repent of the sin, walk away from it, find some hope, and believe in the promises of a good outcome. Zophar speaks platitudes as wooden as his doctrine: you will be secure, you will not fear, you will forget your misery, your life will brighten, indeed it will be brighter than the noonday sun and darkness will be like the morning (an ironic metaphor, given Job has wished for the day to go dark and the night-darkness to be erased from the calendar of days), you will have confidence, hope, protection, rest, safety, and many will come to you for advice (vv. 15–19).

None of the friends have seen Job's heart, have really listened, have dared rhetorically or spiritually to absorb Job's tragedy in silence, a silence directed toward understanding.

Zophar feels he must end on a more ominous note, and so returns to end his speech with one last reminder of the fate of the wicked: their eyes will fail, their way will be lost, and their only hope will be to breathe their last breath and die (v. 20). Metaphorically, Job's eyes have already failed. Literally, he has lost his way. And he has wished aloud, more than once, that he could in fact take a last breath, exhale, and die.

How can Zophar and Job be so diametrically opposed on issues of sin and iniquity, punishment and curse, righteousness and purity, and blessing and reward? All three of Job's friends have now answered Job on the basis of this theological tradition, and none have spoken to him of his experience: the loss of his livelihood, the loss of his children, the onset of his horrendous illness, the loss of his reputation and goodwill. The friends continue to be deaf to Job's real issues in favor of a vengeful and incriminating interpretation of tradition, theory, and history. And they will continue to do so with a decreasing sympathy for Job's suffering, grief, mourning, fear, confusion, and dread.

12:1–14:22

Job's First Response to Zophar:
Truth of Creation . . . Truth of Hopelessness

Flawed By Integrity: Risking Hope for Connection with God

Set at the conclusion of the first round of speeches by all three friends, chapters 12–14 present Job struggling to reconcile his own experience while in the midst of crushing isolation, poverty, emotional pain, near death. Arrayed against him are all things that once gave comfort and consolation: tradition, history, covenant, providence, creation, justice, hope, moral integrity, truth, his God. The contents of these three chapters are complex and intricate; they will pit Job's integrity against the possibility of hope. Yet through all these trials Job remains in conversation with God, in a disarrayed prayer of agony. The poetry is gorgeous. Norman C. Habel has written that Job's third speech "offers an artistic culmination to the first cycle of discourses. . . . reflected in a colorful progression of nature analogies juxtaposed with traditional axioms about mortals and a brilliant dialectic between pessimistic orthodox tradition and a bold new theme of hope."[54]

But this theme is snatched away from Job over and over. Hopelessness following hope is a part of his divinely inspired malady. The constant rebound between hope and hopelessness in turn situates Job's connection with God: Job's encounter with God takes place on a very dark and trackless plain, within a boundless plain fit only for alienation and aimless wandering.

Aimless wandering, but not capitulation. As Paul Ricoeur has pointed out, an ethical comprehension of God begins to dissolve over the course of a prolonged meditation on suffering. Speaking directly of Job, Ricoeur notes that suffering "is not so much unjust as it is senseless, and it has the result of making every undertaking senseless; in the face of absurdity, everything is equal . . . thus the ethical vision is eaten away right down to the very core of action."[55]

---

54. Habel, *Job*, 235–36.
55. Paul Ricoeur, "A Reaffirmation of the Tragic," in *The Book of Job*, ed. Harold Bloom (New York: Chelsea House, 1988), 11.

"Everything is equal": nothing has meaning, nothing gives direction. Adding to this nondirective meaninglessness, Job is burdened by both the senselessness and arbitrary loss of all he held dear and the unjust nature of his God. Thus for Job—an unusual man, to say the least—in suffering this ethical vision is eaten, as Ricoeur says, "down to the very core of action," a core in which meaning is contingent only on action, on what one does, and every action carries equal meaning. In a crazy-quilt circle, every meaning is equally equal. In Babylonian Wisdom literature out of which the book of Job is born, proposals given as response to suffering include surrender to the inscrutable, modest hedonism, expectation of a miracle, resignation, repentance, death. But Job will accept none of these. He will fight, regardless of consequences:

> What you know I also know;
> I am not inferior to you.
> But I would speak to the Almighty;
> and I desire to argue my case with God.
> . . . .
> See, he will kill me; I have no hope;
> but I will defend my ways to his face.
> (13:2–4, 15)

Since the *ethical* coordinates of the divine had been drawn to such a fine line of sight in Israel, the *crisis* of that vision (as experienced during the Babylonian exile as a people and in Job as an individual) becomes nowhere else so radical.

In the complexity of his speech, Job resolves, even in the face of the absurdity of suffering, to turn a corrupt scheme of justification—the law of retribution—against God. Job knows he is playing with fire, and his intention could drive him over the edge of his already boundless universe; nonetheless he proposes turning a tragic comprehension of God into a potential re-ethicization of God. In doing so he will learn that the moral order in which he dwells, especially that moral order reflected in creation, is not the same as the moral order of the Creator.

In Job's meditation on suffering, he concludes that YHWH

> The terminology of plaintiff and defendant, cases, crimes, deposition, affidavit and subpoena signals what it feels like to be involved in dispute with God. Job has a lifetime behind him of godfearingness (1:1), of calling upon God in reverent prayer and being answered (12:4), of harmonious relation with the divine. In a moment that harmony has been shattered, and he has had to learn a new and more abrasive language to embody the discord in his universe. Now it must be the language of compulsion and division, of contest and defeat . . . what he had known as the language of personal reciprocity [and prayer] has been denatured into a language for isolation and conflict.
>
> David J. A. Clines, "A Brief Explanation of Job 12–14," in *Sitting with Job: Selected Studies on the Book of Job*, ed. Roy B. Zuck (Grand Rapids: Baker Book House, 1992), 262.

destroys nations to no purpose (12:16–25) and that divine destruction is a matter of caprice. As Leo Perdue points out, Job did have options: "Instead of pointing to the weakness of Yahweh and the greater strength of [the god] Marduk (Ps. 115:3; 137:4), or placing blame on the sinfulness of Judah and/or its leaders . . . , or questioning the delay of God in bringing redemption to his people while the wicked prosper in their evil machinations and deeds (Hab. 1:1–4), or choosing to hide in the darkness of enigma, Job places the blame entirely on the caprice of a malevolent God."[56] In the language of Ricoeur, the action of Job is turning an unworkable ethic back on God and, in a sense, daring God to come back with an *ethical* structure that in some way corresponds to the *power* structure of God. Samuel Terrien's Job wondered if God's power or omnipotence had gotten out of hand and acted without the "control of inner standards or the check of outsiders."[57] Edwin M. Good writes that the "distinction [between divine justice and power] has dissolved into darkness, and Job would rather be dead"[58] as God does not respond. And Schreiner suggests, "Good's Job and Calvin's Job stared into the same abyss. Both experienced what Good calls the 'terrorism' of God or

---

56. Perdue, *Wisdom Literature*, 112.
57. Samuel Terrien, *Job: Poet of Existence* (New York: Bobbs-Merrill, 1957), 108–9.
58. Good, *In Turns of Tempest*, 229.

the 'absent and arbitrary force' of the deity. In the midst of darkness, the Job of all these interpreters searched for the face of God."[59]

Using his own integrity, perception, and personal experience, Job searches for God, regardless of his friends' advice. Job's friends tell him to repent. Job has nothing to repent of. Job's God is to be found not in repentance, not in integrity, not in forgiveness, not in creation. Job prays, "No!"

And the struggle is not to be a battle aimed at triumph and victory, winning or losing. It is rather a battle to reframe the possibilities for connection with God. Job looks, and the God he knew is gone, but the impossible prospect of life void of divine communion and relationship is more terrifying even than filling that void with the false God of his friends. So, Job declares, "I will defend my ways to [God's] face" (13:15). But this is precisely the point, poignant and painful but true. The One to whom he would defend his ways is precisely the One to whom this despondent, alienated man prays but cannot find: "Why do you hide your face, and count me as your enemy?" (13:24).

Like Roots to the Scent of Water

In these three complex and dark chapters there are two points at which Job catches a scent of hope. In both cases, hope evaporates as quickly as its scent is momentarily captured. In the first case, Job even uses the word the word *hope*, though not in reference to himself. "There is hope for a tree," he says, for if it is cut down its stump and its roots remain, and "at the scent of water it will bud and put forth branches like a young plant" (14:7a, 9). But this "hope" is only a poetic counterpoint to the fact that for men and women there is no such hope: "But mortals die, and are laid low; humans expire, and where are they?" (14:10). The second instance in these chapters of a scent of hope comes in momentary speculation about the possibility of immortality (14:13–17). But immortality comes at a very steep price—death—and there is no guarantee of what is on the other side; once again this scent of hope in death is no more than a momentary illusion:

59. Schreiner, *Where Shall Wisdom Be Found?* 161.

For there is hope for a tree

. . . .

But mortals die, and are laid low;
    humans expire, and where are they?

. . . .

But the mountain falls and crumbles away,
    and the rock is removed from its place;
the waters wear away the stones;
    the torrents wash away the soil of the earth;
so you destroy the hope of mortals.

                    (Job 14:7a, 10, 18–19)

In both cases, creation is guided by the most ephemeral of senses, a scent ever so faint of water. Job experiences the power of creation and the power of destruction in nature; he knows God's hands touch both. But in which or either is hope?

FURTHER REFLECTIONS
Creation

The Bible is an out-of-doors book. This is true not only in the sense that its meaning is enhanced when it is read, heard, or meditated on out-of-doors. It is especially true in the sense that, from its opening story of creation, to Jesus' parables drawn from the natural world in which he lived and moved and worked, to the book of Revelation that depicts a new heaven and a new earth, it is a book about creation narrated from a point of view that is out-of-doors.

Sapiential literature is particularly adept at using creation and the natural world as a core theological theme. In his excellent book on wisdom theology in the Old Testament, Leo G. Perdue says bluntly that "even a cursory reading of the wisdom texts indicates that they have at their theological core the theme of creation."[60] The book of Job is no exception. Most sages and wisdom writers would assume that God was good, caring, and just and would provide for

---

60. Perdue, *Wisdom Literature*, 3.

creation accordingly. This assumption is easily extrapolated to the moral sphere and in the book of Job is represented by Job's friends. That Job and Qoheleth question this assumption that God could be expected in every case to support and bless the life of God's creation does not alter the fact that creation is used as a theological theme of primary importance. The metaphors and theology of creation engage and destabilize readers just as any metaphors do: they are ambiguous and capable of carrying an excess of meaning. Creation in the narrative of Job is present and fecund from the animals Job owns and the wind that collapses his house and kills his children in chapter 1 to the theophanic appearance of God in a whirlwind in chapters 38–41. The end of the book of Job not only relies on creation to frame the divine theophany (the whirlwind) but chapters 38–41 are themselves a prolonged monologue by God enumerating divine creations and reminding Job in no uncertain terms that God is Creator, Job is created.

Still, before this divine speech, Job himself often uses creation to undermine God's position as Creator. Perdue, for instance, writes:

> The metaphor of the day, signifying birth and the beginning of life, is destabilized in Job 3. Day, symbolizing life, light, and enlightenment, is replaced by an abysmal darkness of approaching death, the shroud of mystery. . . . Job escapes this imprisonment [of nonbeing] only by unmasking the tyranny and lack of compassion of Yahweh, and thus begins the search for a humanism in which meaning is created by reflective sages.[61]

Several trenchant examples of creation theology and how it is used in Job to subvert the tradition (and initiate escape from imprisonment) are used in chapters 12–14. In 12:7–12 Job reflects on the truths of God taught by creation. He even invites the reader:

> But ask the animals, and they will teach you;
> the birds of the the air, and they will tell you;

---

61. Ibid., 11.

> ask the plants of the earth, and they will teach you;
> and the fish of the sea will declare to you.
>
> (Job 12:7–8)

Here Job is reacting to his friends' advice in a sarcastic vein, but in doing so he uses an example of classic wisdom theology: ask the animals, birds, plants, and fish, and they will declare to you the order, justice, and providence of God, the Creator. The sarcasm exists in the friends' wisdom being inferior even to the wisdom of animals, birds, plants, and fish. The larger section of which this is a part, 12:7–25, gives way in form to doxology or praise, but in Job's mouth the doxology *subverts* the wisdom of creation: "Job continues to destabilize sapiential creation theology by using the language of doxology to describe the destructive power of divine providence in directing human history."[62] Job experiences a destructive, destabilizing power in God rather than trust, goodness, or providential guidance. The animals no longer speak of providential care, but instead:

> With God are wisdom and strength;
> he has counsel and understanding.
> If he tears down, no one can rebuild;
> if he shuts someone in, no one can open up.
> If he withholds the waters, they dry up;
> if he sends them out, they overwhelm the land.
>
> (Job 12:13–15)

As noted below, creation is once again, in chapter 14, described in a way that might lead to hope, but we find, along with Job, that such hope is a mirage: unlike the tree cut down, leaving a stump whose roots can reestablish life, mortals die: no stump, no root, no hope.

Scholars disagree widely as to structure, literary forms, and meaning of Job's speech in chapters 12–14. Complexity is intensified in that in these three chapters Job finds himself at a crossroads and in

62. Ibid., 111.

an agonizing struggle over which of two paths to follow: whether to yield to the friends' counsel, submit to God, and repent; or whether to persist in what they all agree, Job included (4:18–19; 7:11–16; 9:2–3; 11:7–9), will ultimately be a futile effort to obtain justice from the Creator of the world. "Against all odds, Job chooses the latter option. He will argue his case with God, even if it means that in doing so he takes his life in his hands (13:14)."[63]

The genre and form of the speech alternate between wisdom (human and creation), hymn, psalmic doxology and psalmic lament, proverbs, and the courtroom language through which Job considers litigation against God. The mood ranges from sarcasm to sincerity, from bold imagination about what might be to mournful despair about what is and can never be. Echoing Job's struggle whether to accede to his friends or to challenge God, the speech can be divided into two parts according to whom it is addressed: the first portion is to the friends, the second to God. Interpreters disagree as to the exact point of division, but, in the speech to the friends, there is at least no question about the issue to which Job is reacting:

> Eliphaz has argued that no human being can be righteous before God (5:17). Bildad has warned Job against even contemplating that God perverts justice (8:3). Zophar has reminded his friend that God's justice is certain, even if it is beyond human comprehension (11:6). Each in his own way offers the same counsel to Job: *if* he will but seek God, by which they clearly mean that he must repent of his sin, *then* God will restore him (5:8–16; 8:4–6; 11:13–14).[64]

Another way to structure this disputation is thematically. David Clines, for instance, recognizes two primary themes that echo the crossroads struggle: (1) in 12:1–13:28, the friends as conversation partners who represent traditional theology; and (2) in 14:1–22, Job's elegy on the human condition, his most extended meditation on the significance of his suffering for what it can say about human life in general.[65]

---

63. Balentine, *Job*, 197.
64. Ibid.
65. David J. A. Clines, "A Brief Explanation of Job 12–14," in *Sitting with Job: Selected Studies on the Book of Job*, ed. Roy B. Zuck (Grand Rapids: Baker Book House, 1992), 262–63.

A second thematic proposal divides the speech into three sections, finding in each a key word that sets tone and marks boundaries. These sections are 12:1–13:5, where the thematic word "wisdom" (*hokmah*) controls the monologue; 13:6–28, in which God's "face" (*panim*) as a kind of theophanic participant in Job's growing demand for a courtroom debate is key; and 14:1–22, because at the close of each of Job's speeches to this point he meditates on the miserable mortal (3:20; 7:20; 10:18; 13:24), asking why (*lama*), and Job does essentially the same at 14:21–22.[66]

A third, helpful thematic ordering notes the continuity between the lament of chapter 3 and Job's speech in chapters 12–14. Key terms link the two speeches, suggesting that Job is continuing his charge that suffering like his must make some claim on God's moral governance of creation. The most revealing of these terms are "trouble" (*rogez*) in 3:17, 26, and 14:1, and "deep darkness" (*tsalmaveth*) in 3:5, 10:21, and 12:22. "Trouble" and "deep darkness" are the lenses through which Job struggles to see God.[67] Marking a transition in Job's thinking and feeling and in his strategy to get at the truth of his suffering in relation to God, Job in these chapters makes a number of critical accusations and decisions. Suffering, disorientation, and confusion still mark his speeches, contributing to the complexity of the chapters. All in all, the image of "aimless wandering"[68] may, in the end, be the most comprehensive, short summation of Job's words and thoughts to this point.

FURTHER REFLECTIONS
Hope

The Joban poet reveals a stark edge of Job's tortured, wandering journey between truth and illusion by introducing a flash-point moment of hope, perhaps even of immortality, brought on by the vision of a tree. This moment of hope is bracketed by a series of

---

66. Habel, *Job*, 215.
67. Balentine, *Job*, 197.
68. Habel, *Job*, 217.

crises: Job is becoming a laughingstock to his friends (12:4), lamenting how God has drawn him into endless wandering on pathless wastes (12:24), refusing to keep silent or relinquish his integrity as arrows of false speech attack him from all sides (13:5–7), daring to suggest that God be brought to trial and made to explain God's ways even though believing that such a trial would most likely end in his death (13:3–19), searching, but finding only the hidden, absent face of God (13:24), perceiving endless troubles and a useless, fleeting life (14:1–6), "feeling only the pain" (14:20–22). Following these, the poet uses a brief moment of hope to heighten the poignancy of the lament; conversely, the litany of abandonment only serves to make hope seem like just another poisonous arrow that pierces Job to the heart:

> For there is hope [*tiqvah*] for a tree,
> if it is cut down, that it will sprout again,
> and that its shoots will not cease.
> Though its root grows old in the earth,
> and its stump dies in the ground,
> yet at the scent of water it will bud
> and put forth branches like a young plant.
> (Job 14:7–9)

Here, in a few short lines in a poem reeking of death and loss and betrayal, the poet gives a beautiful image of a tree, the tree's death, the earth (*adamah*) -compacted roots, a stump that revives the tree, resurrection. The "scent of water" is a particularly striking image: the faintest of the senses, smell, depicted in its most ephemeral form here as a mere "scent," becomes the image for hope. But can hope pick up a mere "scent"? The vision of the tree quickly dissolves, and Job returns with a thump to his present reality, to hopeless suffering and the insight that "mortals die, and are laid low; humans expire, and where are they?" (v. 10). And the Creator, also, is the Destroyer of hope:

> But the mountain falls and crumbles away,
> and the rock is removed from its place;

the waters wear away the stones;
the torrents wash away the soil of the earth;
so you destroy the hope of mortals.

(Job 14:18–19)

The Joban poet is not finished revealing the raw uncertainty, confusion, and wandering coordinates of Job's state of mind as Job meditates in turn on endless troubles and a useless, fleeting life:

O that you would hide me in Sheol [bish'ol],
that you would conceal me until your wrath is past,
that you would appoint me a set time, and remember me!
....
[Then] You would call, and I would answer you;
you would long for the work of your hands.[69]
For then you would not number my steps,
you would not keep watch over my sin [hatta'ti];
my transgression [pesha'] would be sealed up in a bag,
and you would cover over my iniquity ['awon].

(Job 14:13, 15–17)

As he does in all his speeches, Job moves rapidly from hope to despair and back again. Having hoped for new life, then resigned himself to the oblivion of death, Job now takes a detour back to the possibility of the hope of resurrection, perhaps even of immortality. But this too is only a momentary fantasy.

Job ends this particular wandering simply: "You [YHWH] prevail forever against them [humanity], and they pass away; . . . All he feels is his flesh's pain, and his soul [nefesh] laments against him" (14:20a, 22a; Habel). The scent of death is permanent, irredeemable, final; the scent of hope transitory.

---

69. Here Job envisions that YHWH might "long for the work of his hands" (ma'aseh yadeka), 15b, where earlier Job charged that YHWH "despised [his] hand's toil" (yegia' kappeka) in 10:3. The difference in the two passages underscores their difference in hope and tone.

A Structure Built on Tears

The structure, the themes, the literary devices, and the theology of chapters 12–14 work together to form a meditation on suffering in which Job tries to call God to account for injustice, abuse of power, and God's crushing, capricious providence. Lacking hope, Job still chooses integrity; lacking means or experience to justify faith, Job still chooses to resist; lacking guidance, Job chooses to continue to follow the faint scent of a strange, new truth.

At the beginning of this section, we spoke of Job's speeches as imaginative "aimless wandering," of the ironic way in which Job's personal integrity contributes to his suffering, and of Job's meditation on suffering as an intricate dance with no apparent moral boundaries, or at least boundaries and dance steps completely new and heretofore unimagined. Rilke writes of this later aspect of Job in a slightly different way: there are boundaries, but not of clay—as Job's friends would like him to believe. Rilke's boundaries are the blindness, the heavy, the iridescent curve, the brittleness that leaves the sufferer empty. Using Rilke's images, there is no "clay" structure in this Joban poetry, only Job's meditation on suffering that renders Job "empty" but for a few tears by which he "humbly hollows [him]self" in his wandering, righteous search for his God.

Sad Wisdom and an Emerging Self

Job's experience of wisdom is no longer that of his friends; their wisdom (to which he formerly subscribed) is an empty wind: for Job (12:24), God "strips understanding from the leaders of the earth, and makes them wander in a pathless waste" (*tohu*, cf. Gen. 1:2). Job

> Other vessels hold wine, other
>   vessels hold oil
> inside the hollowed-out vault
>   circumscribed by their clay.
> I, as smaller measure, and as
>   the slimmest of all,
> humbly hollow myself so that
>   just a few tears can fill me.
>
> Wine becomes richer, oil
>   becomes clear, in its vessel.
> What happens with tears?—
>   they made me blind in my
>   glass,
> made me heavy and made my
>   curve iridescent,
> made me brittle, and left me
>   empty at last.
>
> Rainer Maria Rilke, "Little Tear-Vase," in *Ahead of All Parting: The Selected Poetry and Prose of Rainer Maria Rilke*, ed. and trans. Stephen Mitchell (New York: Modern Library, 1995), 159.

"grope[s] in the dark without light; he makes them stagger like a drunkard" (12:25). Job's journey is toward wisdom, but at this point in the story the journey is pathless and even pathetic; it is a journey of sadness and tears. But, though he does not yet see it clearly in any concrete sense, Job is beginning to find, in the vortex of his wandering, a new kind of wisdom, not in the friends' platitudes, not in theological or material or social or even spiritual security, but, ironically, in the psychic wandering itself. Perhaps like a "drunkard" this wisdom is to this point remembered only as a numb need for another drink, the need to take another staggered step of forgetting in order to remember a kind of wisdom he has forgotten. Without pushing this simile too hard, Job is "intoxicated" in the sense of an altered consciousness brought on by suffering.

Something new is emerging in Job that he does not yet fully recognize. It is, even for the reader, as yet unsayable: it has something to do with Job's experience of a hidden, silent, and absent God, something to do with the process of disordering and desacralization of creation and the consequent destabilization of a recognizable moral order, something to do with destructuring the correspondence between divine power and divine justice, something to do with a darkness at the heart of God, and something to do with the path of tears and the transformative process that path inflicts. There is also a nostalgia to this emerging self; old patterns are painful to disassemble. And if this tentative groping into new, darker relationship with the sacred requires that Job regress from time to time, it is a healthy regression: he will still choose death, he still feels the shame of the all-seeing celestial

> Mellas raged inwardly . . . But just below the grim tranquility he had learned to display, he cursed with boiling intensity the ambitious men who used him and his troops to further their careers. He cursed the air wing for not trying to get any choppers in through the clouds. He cursed the diplomats arguing about round and square tables. He cursed the South Vietnamese making money off the black market. He cursed the people back home gorging themselves in front of their televisions. Then he cursed God. Then there was no one else to blame and he cursed himself.
>
> Karl Marlantes, *Matterhorn: A Novel of the Vietnam War* (New York: Atlantic Monthly Press, 2010), 212.

eye, he still seeks justice even in the form of a knock-down, drag-out fight to the death with YHWH, whether hand-to-hand battle or in a courtroom, it would matter little: "I am finding a way through this suffering, and I am innocent!"

In Job's lostness, we *can* say that he is beginning to solidify into the wisdom of Rilke's "little tear-vase" that only shapes itself to the tears of the lost or wandering because only the lost can be found: "Rejoice with me, for I have found my sheep that was lost" (Luke 15:6). "Rejoice with me, for I have found the coin that I had lost" (Luke 15:9). "'And get the fatted calf and kill it, and let us eat and celebrate; for this son of mine was dead and is alive again; he was lost and is found!' And they began to celebrate" (Luke 15:23–24).

Job's whys begin to take on the stench of a curse. His curses remind us of the *satan's* taunt and we are left to ask: Is Job cursing God, as the *satan* wagered that he would? Is he cursing himself for thinking God really cares? In the novel *Matterhorn*, the protagonist, Mellas, changes and is changed, something new emerges by the end of the story, but the whys, the curses, never go away. One thing we can say about Job is that he remains in conversation with God; it is one-sided, to be sure, but it is conversation. It is cursing, yet even in that sense it is prayer.[70] He is reaching out for an unseen holy, he is speaking to a Silence in the rage of a prayer.

---

70. Cf. Steven Chase, *The Tree of Life: Models of Christian Prayer* (Grand Rapids: Baker Academic, 2006). Part of what is unconditional about each model is that prayer is a way of life and that regardless of circumstance—blessed or cursed, divine presence or absence—prayer is a practice of the presence of God.

15:1–21:34

Second Poetic Dialogue Cycle

15:1–35

Eliphaz's Second Response to Job:
Job the Irreligious, Job the Unwise

Equating Wisdom and Religion

In the first cycle of speeches between Job and his friends, the friends showed some deference and respect toward Job. Beginning with this second cycle, it is clear that they believe he has crossed some line, a line that calls not for deference or respect, but for reprimand, condemnation, Job's immediate repentance, and a complete reversal in Job's thinking about his relation to God and his place in the created order. Strikingly, the friends move from innuendo to outright accusation. The passion of accusations is so strong that it is clear that Job has touched a nerve, pressing on issues very near and dear to the friends' hearts and transgressing something that they hold sacred.

What is it that is so threatening to Job's friends? Scholars have answered this question in a variety of ways.[1] These include the idea that Job has committed some serious sin made obvious to them by his continued suffering, and in his refusal to acknowledge personal sin Job in effect attacks the justice of God (see Gordis, *BGM*, 85)— Eliphaz especially characterizes Job's speech as so much hot air (15:2–3) and accuses him of subverting religion itself (15:4);[2] the

---

1. Many of these scholars recognize others' suggestions; the examples given are what appears to be the particular scholar's primary reason for the increased emotive and accusative responses of the friends.

2. Cf. J. Gerald Janzen, *Job*, Interpretation (Atlanta: John Knox Press, 1985), 115–16, 118–19.

"windy" and deceitful language of Job itself (Good, 242); the hubris and arrogance toward God in what the friend's see as Job's deception (Habel, 252); or, in speaking of what his eyes have seen and his ears have heard (13:1), Job's claim to know and "understand the sinister secrets of God's design for creation" without consulting the tradition of the "gray-haired and the aged," based on his experience alone, which for the friends is an illegitimate form of wisdom or piety and is not traditional (15:10; Balentine, 233–34).

These reasons for the friends' increased enmity toward Job all point to Job's unyielding insistence that wisdom as he experiences it has to be severed from religion. The very ground of confidence and assurance by which the friends practice religion is based on the wisdom of tradition and of its theology; Job is violating the connection between wisdom and religion in important ways.

Eliphaz in fact *equates* wisdom and religion. In his first speech to Job, Eliphaz "sought to counsel Job as one wise man to another, offering him an assuring 'word' (*dābār*, 4:2, 12) and a constructive 'message/argument' (*millīn*, 4:2, 4)."[3] But Job's response, according to Eliphaz, amounted to no more than wind and hot air (15:2–3). Moreover, because Job is relying on personal experience, he is "doing away with the fear [*yirah*, "fear" or "reverence" toward God] of God, and hindering meditation before God" (v. 4). Traditionally, "fear of God" is the root and foundation of wisdom, while "hindering meditation" is hindrance of communal religion. Job, according to Eliphaz, "limit[s] wisdom to [him]self" (v. 8b), thus making Job not the wise man (*hakam*) he claims to be (12:2–3), but a fool. Those who have "stretched out their hands against God" (v. 25a) practice neither piety nor religion and have a common fate: "they will live in desolate cities" (v. 28a); "they will not be rich, their wealth will not endure" (v. 29a); "emptiness will be their recompense" (v. 31b); "their branch will not be green" (v. 32); "the company of the godless is barren" (v. 34a); and "they will conceive mischief and bring forth evil and their heart prepares deceit" (v. 35). Eliphaz never names Job, but the inference is clear: he is describing what Job has become. In the context of the whole, once again the poetry in chapter 15 is magnificent. And

3. Norman C. Habel, *The Book of Job: A Commentary*, Old Testament Library (Philadelphia: Westminster, 1985), 252.

> All arrogant persons have this characteristic that when they have a right notion, though the thing is little, they wrest it to serve their pride. By the same act from understanding they attempt to raise themselves higher. From swollen pride they fall into the pit of self-exalting and account themselves better instructed than the learned. They exact respect for themselves from their superiors and stand upon it to teach as with authority those who are holier people. Hence it is now said, "I [Eliphaz] will demonstrate; listen to me." (vv. 17–18).
>
> Gregory the Great, *Morals on the Book of Job*, 12.40, in ACCS, 87–88.

once again its brilliant quality only serves to enhance Eliphaz's own deceit as he carelessly rattles off the fate of the unwise in ways that just happen to correspond precisely to the fate that has befallen Job: they correspond but they do not bring wisdom.

Job equates wisdom with personal experience. It would be premature to try to describe what Job's *religion* might be at this point in the narrative; Job's religion is emerging, it is not complete (and may have as one of its attributes that it never will be complete). Yet there are hints about what this religion might include: though he could accuse any number of people for his suffering, he turns only in one direction, as if in prayer. In anger, in despair, lost, without hope, without faith, without friends, he turns only toward the face of YHWH. This may be a part of the prayerful equation that will rekindle—though not in a way the friends might recognize—Job's own wisdom and religion.

The Second Cycle of Speeches

Though the second cycle of speeches does not represent a progression of thought so much as an essentially more passionate restatement of points already expressed, there are some noticeable differences in the way the friends address and respond to Job:

— The range of their concern narrows to focus almost exclusively on one theme: the fate of the wicked, with no parallel treatment of the fate of the righteous.

— Their tone is much sharper, indicating that they are stiffening in their response to Job.

—They offer no word of encouragement to Job, only increased warning, rebuke, and opposition.

—There is considerable repetition in their speeches, an indication that they are increasingly mired in intransigent dogma and theory that will not, and cannot, deal with the substance of Job's charges.[4]

—Eliphaz's speech at chapter 15 introduces the idea that even during the period of his ostensible prosperity the sinner lives in trepidation, never knowing when the blow will fall. His psychological punishment begins long before his physical doom (15:20–22).[5]

15:1–16 *Job's Foolish Claim to Wisdom?*

Eliphaz begins this chapter, and indeed never really stops, with the harshest condemnations of Job's actions and words and thoughts, believing that he and not Job is in sole possession of the wisdom of "the aged." Eliphaz is ruthless in his challenge of Job's perspective on the nature and origin of wisdom, that wisdom can originate from personal experience. Eliphaz accuses Job of things about which he has no proof; but of course for Eliphaz, the proof of Job's corruption and iniquity is Job's suffering. As his true nature emerges, Eliphaz can be brutal because he prefers his religion comfortable, his wisdom straightforward, and any ambiguity detached from his piety.

We have already noted that Eliphaz begins by comparing Job's words and arguments to wind, hot air, unprofitable talk (15:2–3). But he is just warming up. Next he accuses Job of ignoring the essential core of Hebrew wisdom: "you are doing away [*parar*; "sever," Good; "subvert," Habel] with the fear [*yirah*, which means "reverence," another example of scribal reversal—as with bless and curse—due to unwillingness to pass on irreverence] of God" (v. 4). Eliphaz's comments show that Job's words have the "potential to destroy religion as [Eliphaz] knows it *and needs it* to be." This "fear of God" is the essence of piety; it is the "devotion and reverence that

---

4. First four points of difference from Samuel E. Balentine, *Job*, Smyth & Helwys Bible Commentary (Macon, GA: Smyth & Helwys, 2006), 229.
5. Final point of difference from Robert Gordis, *The Book of God and Man: A Study of Job* (Chicago: University of Chicago Press, 1965), 86.

the faithful exhibit when they order their lives in accord with God's design for the world."[6] The "fear of God" passes through all periods of the Christian spiritual tradition as the first stage of wisdom. Toward the same man who (in 1:1, 8; 2:3) does in fact "fear God," Eliphaz could not have begun his attack with a more devastating accusation.

And yet he nearly manages to find an accusation even more devastating: Job is "hindering [*gara'*, "diminish, reduce, subtract"] meditation before God" (v. 4b). This charge, with the word *gara'*, means to be in prayer or meditation or devotion before God! Job's "wisdom" is such that Eliphaz cannot recognize it as devotion or prayer. The irony increases when we recall that in his integrity and scorching truth Job never ceases to place himself before God, whether it be in anger or confession or confusion or even madness. The word translated "meditation," *sihah*, is ambivalent. "It may refer to 'prayer' . . . or to the practice of musing or meditating aloud on God's *torah*. . . . In both cases, it signifies a mode of speaking that conveys the deep inner feelings of a pious person."[7] It may also be used to indicate "complaint." Job's meditation is a kind of complaint meditation (7:11, 13; 9:27; 10:1; 21:4; 23:2), which only enhances the meaning that signifies and conveys "deep inner feelings of a pious person." Job does not "fear" or "meditate" on God in the way Eliphaz is comfortable with. Eliphaz is comforted by the idea that only the blessed commune with God; Job is blazing a trail through a jungle of sorrows. All the while, in a way inexplicable to Eliphaz, Job is fearing, meditating, complaining, communing with God. Job is wise in his way and religious in his practice.

FURTHER REFLECTIONS
Innocence and Guilt in a Piety of Conformity

From Job 1 through chapter 15, one of the most striking developments is the change in tone between Eliphaz's first speech and his second. In the first speech, Eliphaz clearly expresses the doctrine

6. Balentine, *Job*, 232.
7. Ibid., 232.

of retribution and his belief in it. On the basis of the doctrine, he hints and makes a few innuendos gently implicating Job in his own suffering. Eliphaz makes no attempt to specify Job's iniquity, but he does say that Job's suffering will stop if he will only repent of his sin and ask God for forgiveness. He is ham-handed in the way he presents this solution to Job, but we do get a sense that in his awkward way Eliphaz is trying to bring some comfort to Job.

Between that first speech of Eliphaz and the one in chapter 15, Job has had plenty of time and plenty of words to express what he thinks of his friends' advice, what he thinks of a God who would subject him to such suffering, and, in one of his harsher wishes, what he thinks about the night of his conception and the day of his birth bringing him life. As the chapters progress, it is clear that Job does not buy this doctrine of divine retribution. He knows many cases in which the wicked prosper, as do their children: that is not supposed to happen. He is innocent, he suffers; the wicked are guilty, they prosper: the foundations of blessing and curse undergirding the doctrine of retribution have been turned upside down. That is not supposed to happen.

By his second speech Eliphaz is fuming: he sees the innocent and the guilty as exactly opposite from what Job claims. What is so striking, overwhelming really, is how Eliphaz's doctrine has become his religion. As his religion the doctrine is his foundational system of belief, and on it rests his piety; on it rests his relationship, commitment, and intimacy with God. But what does Eliphaz mean by "guilt" and "innocence"?

One way of looking at these emotionally laden terms is to say that *guilt* is the judgment (or condition or feeling) that a person has failed in moral responsibility to somebody else, and in that failure has caused suffering. One may speak of degrees of guilt that correspond to the degree of moral failure and the extent of suffering that results from failure. *Innocence* is the judgment (or condition or feeling) that a person has not failed in moral responsibility to somebody else, and in that moral integrity has not caused suffering.[8]

---

8. John E. Thiel, *God, Evil, and Innocent Suffering: A Theological Reflection* (New York: Crossroad, 2002), 27.

According to this definition, Job sees himself as innocent on the basis of judgment and feeling (his moral integrity has not caused the suffering). Eliphaz finds Job guilty on the basis of judgment and condition, and believes that Job's suffering stems from failed moral responsibility.

Another way of understanding what is going on between Job and Eliphaz (and his other friends) is to see Job as moving toward a crisis of abandonment (his situation leaves him with no other con- clusion than that a hidden God has abandoned him) more grave than the crisis of justice. Job can choose one of two strategies for distancing himself from his growing sense of abandonment: denial or displacement. "In denial, one suppresses the pain entirely, banish- ing it from sight. In displacement, one allows the pain to emerge into consciousness but associates it with a problem that, however troublesome in its own right, can in some manner be acknowl- edged and engaged."[9] Eliphaz is in extreme denial concerning both Job's crises of abandonment and justice: we could even say that his piety is an act of conformity to this denial. Job, on the other hand, chooses the path of displacement, allowing the pain to emerge and engaging it.

Job's anguish can also be looked at using Robert Frost's distinc- tions between griefs and grievances. Borrowing from Frost, J. Gerald Janzen writes that one can argue over a grievance, which is clearly Eliphaz's route, "But one cannot handle grief that way. A grief can only be lamented."[10] Job, then, displaces, allowing pain to emerge and engagement in pain to happen; he allows grievance from time to time, which is natural and human; but mostly he travels the route of grief, which is similar in effect to displacement as a way to face suffering. Frost developed his distinction between griefs and griev- ances in his essay "Introduction to E. A. Robinson's 'King Jasper,'" where he writes:

> Grievances are probably more useful than griefs. . . . Griev-
> ances are certainly a power and are going to be turned on. . . .
> But for me, I don't like grievances. I find I gently let them alone

9. Janzen, *At the Scent of Water: The Ground of Hope in the Book of Job* (Grand Rapids: Eerdmans, 2009), 82.
10. Ibid., 83.

> wherever published. What I like is griefs and I like them Robin-
> sonianly profound [or we could say, Jobanly profound].... He
> asserted the sacred right of poetry to lean its breast to a thorn
> and sing its dolefullest.... A few superficial irritable grievances,
> perhaps, as was only human, but these are forgotten in the
> depth of the grief to which he plunged us. Grievances are a
> form of impatience. Griefs are a form of painful patience.[11]

Job is a man willing to "lean [his] breast to a thorn and sing [his] dolefullest." On the basis of absolutely no evidence, on the basis of the internal logic of the doctrine of retribution only, here are a few of the "sins" that Eliphaz, in his self-defined innocence, finds Job guilty of. Grouping them together in this way shows something of the magnitude of Eliphaz's own anxiety, denial, and religious "grievances":

They [implying also Job] argue in "unprofitable talk"	15:3
"You are doing away with the fear of God"	v. 4a
(discussed above)	
You are "hindering meditation before God"	v. 4b
(discussed above)	
"Your iniquity teaches your mouth"	v. 5a
"You choose the tongue of the crafty"	v. 5b
"You limit wisdom to yourself"	v. 8b
"The consolations of God [are] too small for you"	v. 11a
"You turn your spirit against God"	v. 13a
You are "abominable and corrupt"	v. 16a
You "drink iniquity like water"	v. 16b
You "stretched out [your] hands against God"	v. 25a
You "bid defiance of the Almighty"	v. 25b
You run (as in battle) against God	v. 26a
You "trust in emptiness"	v. 31a

It is true that in a real sense Job does trust emptiness; emptiness is what he finds within himself in the presence of the hidden God.

---

11. Robert Frost, *Collected Poems, Prose, and Plays* (New York: Library of America, 1995), 742–43.

Finally, to show that ideas such as displacement and denial, grievance and grief, guilt and innocence are not only modern lenses, it is
fitting to end with a word from a fifth-century Latin writer, Philip
the Priest: "With these words [Eliphaz] identifies holy Job as a rob-
ber and a pretender who hides his violent actions. He had also spoken so against Job in his first speech, when Eliphaz had compared
him with a lion, a lioness and a cub of lions and tigers. But we must
believe in God, who by praising Job did not call him a deceiver but
declared him to be innocent and simple."[12]

15:17–35 *The Fate of the Wicked*

Continuing to link the doctrine of divine retribution with wisdom,
Eliphaz now concentrates on the fate of the wicked. Applying the
internal logic of the doctrine, he no longer suggests but directly
accuses Job of wickedness, based on Job's fate. Ironically, Eliphaz too
relies on personal experience: where Job had made the claim, "Look,
my eye has seen all this, my ear has heard and understood it" (13:1),
Eliphaz responds in kind, mocking Job, "I will show you; listen to
me; what I have seen I will declare" (15:17).

While the first section of Eliphaz's speech (vv. 1–16) is an indig-
nant rebuke personally addressed to Job, this second section (vv.
17–35) is "an extended portrayal of the wicked man as a type. Here
allusions to Job are ironic and oblique,"[13] but nonetheless intended
as a justification, according to the "sages," for Job's suffering. The fact
that they are types of the punishment portioned out to the wicked
man are further indication that Eliphaz really does not see what is
happening to Job; he again sees only the typological truths of a doctrine. Devoid of empathy, full of inference and innuendo, complete
with self-righteousness, inferring a connection between Job and the
wicked, Eliphaz says of the wicked

— They "writhe in pain all their days" (v. 20).
— "Terrifying sounds are in their ears" (v. 21).

---

12. Philip the Priest, *Commentary on the Book of Job* 15 in ACCS, 89.
13. Habel, *Job*, 248.

—"They despair of returning from darkness" (v. 22a).

—"They wander abroad for bread, saying, 'where is it?'" (v. 23a).

—"Distress and anguish terrify them" (v. 24a).

—"They will live in desolate cities" (v. 28a).

—Their "houses [are] destined to become heaps of ruins" (v. 28c).

—"They will not be rich, and their wealth will not endure" (v. 29a).

Obviously, he is describing Job, the wicked.

Eliphaz describes but does not see; he understands the wisdom of the "gray-haired" generations but he does not know his friend. In his unyielding need for a certain kind of "religion" he frames Job safely within a litany of iniquity rather than release him into the creative freedom of innocence. Edwin M. Good captures the self-serving perspective of Eliphaz nicely when he says that "Eliphaz proves to be consistent: when he claims to have seen, he is not to be trusted."[14]

Doctrinally, as chapter 15 concludes, we are left with two contrasting positions with regard to evil, with regard to distributive justice, with regard to the very nature of what it means to be a human being, and with regard to the place of the human in creation and in relation to God. Eliphaz is by now certain that commitment to God requires that conventional wisdom take precedence over personal

> [The dialogues] present the two visions in counterpoint. The true revelations of the persecuted alternate with the untruthful sacralized speeches of the persecutors. . . . Sometimes we do not even need this counterpoint. In some of the arguments I have quoted—those of Eliphaz for example . . . the scapegoating is so evident that we have no need to compare the two types of speech. . . . The difference in perspective on the same act of collective violence [Job's suffering] is the true subject of the Dialogues. The sacred lie of the friends is contrasted with the true realism of Job.
>
> René Girard, *Job: The Victim of His People* (Stanford, CA: Stanford University Press, 1987), 32.

---

14. Edwin M. Good, *In Turns of Tempest: A Reading of Job with a Translation* (Stanford, CA: Stanford University Press, 1990), 244.

experience and that, according to that conventional wisdom, Job has no commitment to God and Job is wicked. Unlike in his earlier speech, Eliphaz no longer even bothers to encourage Job to repent and change his ways: Job is a sinner and Eliphaz is not afraid to tell this to Job's face.

Job, on the other hand, is admittedly awash in despair and hopelessness and suffering, and there is no doubt that this affects much of what he says and how he says it. But Job is emerging, slowly, even in the trauma of his loss, into a new religion, a new way of being committed to God. Conventional wisdom does not inform Job's predicament; Job is finding that personal integrity transforms suffering into the ephemeral, "the scent of water." And that ephemeral "scent" is also Job's new and growing dream of God that is becoming radically separate from Eliphaz's certain reality. As we cringe at the insensitivity of Eliphaz, we begin to experience Job's integrity and commitment as a surprising, perhaps personal and potentially creative, "scent of water."

16:1–17:16

Job's Second Response to Eliphaz:
Prayers of Despair

If the poet intends that Job's jangled nerves, crushed heart, and frayed mind be reflected in the style, images, and language of the poem, this soul-wrenching speech by Job serves the poet well. Many, if not most, of Job's images and claims of lament from his earlier speeches are compressed into these two short chapters. Job's words tumble quickly out of his mouth as he seems to grasp one idea, then another, then another in a desperate attempt to find some coherence, internal logic, or justification for his pain. The effect of this compression and mental trembling is to portray in Job a man struggling desperately to maintain a semblance of communication with the outside world while his inside world is being stripped of meaning. The effect is of a man trying to remember himself well enough to assemble a personal identity strong enough to make it through yet another day of horror and betrayal. If this is the poet's intent, he is exceedingly successful in this speech in using Job's language and words to give us clues that Job may be collapsing under the strain.

The disjointedness of this speech alone indicates Job's fragile condition. In no particular order or sequence Job returns to earlier ideas, as if the moment they pop into his mind they are fresh, yet singularly all he has to hold on to. He cannot pin down these thoughts, so foreign to his former way of thinking, and they come out as from the lips of a man losing a battle with sanity. As in earlier poems he berates his friends; he realizes that whether he speaks or not makes no difference: his pain remains; he returns for a few lines to his ongoing fantasy of meeting God in a court of law, a fantasy that begins to sound like the character Gollum in the *Lord of the Rings*, whose only hope is also a fantasy, the ring, "my precious"; he describes in gruesome detail the battle God is waging against him; he claims again that his prayer is pure, that his hands are clean, and that he himself is not a man of iniquity; as he had in chapter 9 and will again in chapter 19, Job imagines the possibility of an advocate, a mediator in heaven who would adjudicate his complaint; then he realizes that as a mortal he will anyway be gone, out of sight, never to return again; he speaks again of being ready for the grave and the grave ready for him; he is mocked, a byword of the people, spit upon; his body no longer casts a shadow: it *is* a shadow; he has a momentary insight on the meaning and intention of the righteous, then abandons it; once again day is night and night is day; he lingers with death as a possible hope for relief from suffering, then realizes hope is no more than a temporary narcotic and death is no more than dust.

Job has expressed most of these views before. Some are new. But the almost desperate, quick succession by which they are brought together reaches our ears and hearts more like talismans than like answers. As Bishop Bossuet put it in the seventeenth century in a sermon on death, Job is so small and insignificant as to be slowly trapped outside time while descending into a mad concoction of nothingness: "If I look backward, what an infinite expanse of time in which I do not exist! And if I looked forward, what a dreadful continuation in which I no longer exist! And that I shall occupy so small

In the second cycle [and particularly this speech], the speakers do not allude to each other as much as they did in the first cycle. . . . These references and allusions [to the friends] are fewer in number and less subtle and powerful than were the earlier ones. Perhaps Job and the friends increasingly talk not to each other but past each other. . . . The other noticeable factor in this speech is the paucity of Job's remarks to the god. In earlier speeches, except for chap. 3, he always speaks directly to the deity. . . . From this speech on, except for a brief address to the god almost exactly in the middle of his last speech (30:20–23), and the two responses to YHWH's speeches in 40:4–5 and 42:2–6, Job addresses the god very seldom and only in quick snatches, sometimes no more than a single line.

Gordis, *Book of God and Man*, 86.

a space in this immense abysm of time! I am nothing—an interval so small is not capable of distinguishing me from nothingness."[15]

Still, in his smallness, in his descent into nothingness, Job prays, and through his prayer we glean new insights into theology as a way of life.

16:1–6 *The Pastoral Art of Soul Sympathy*

The content as well as the style of this speech indicate that Job's state of mind, body, and soul are deteriorating. Readers of these chapters have noticed other differences between these two chapters and Job's earlier speeches. One commentator writes, "Communication between Job and his friends has now all but disappeared. Their concept of God is meaningless for him."[16]

And Job has had it with his friends. They have long since ceased being comforters. Not only has he heard over and over their conventional, dull doctrine, he knows that were he in their place, "I also could talk as you do" (16:4a). But presumably Job, having suffered, would act differently: "Job knows how to nod his head (v. 4b: *nw'*; cf. 2:11) as a gesture of sympathy. He knows how to string together encouraging words,

---

15. Cited in Thomas McFarland, *Coleridge and the Pantheist Tradition* (Oxford: Clarendon, 1969), 125.
16. Gordis, *Book of God and Man*, 86.

and he knows how to maintain sympathetic silence when the occasion calls for it (vv. 4–5)."[17] But the friends' words are anything but encouraging; they only increase his sorrow, his misery (*'amal*; cf. 3:10, 4:8), and his guilt; they are "worthless physicians" (13:4). They are not good counselors; they are not good spiritual directors.

In fact Job's disparaging words about the pastoral ability of his friends are much stronger than "worthless physicians" and are missed in most English translations. Job's friends fail not simply because they are poor listeners or speakers, not simply because they attempt to inflict Job with doctrine that does not address his condition, and not simply because they are "poor counselors." More importantly, they fail to find an empathetic mode in which they can share their "soul" (*nefesh*) with Job's "soul's place" in any sympathetic way. A literal translation of the Hebrew is "if your soul were in my soul's place" (v. 4b: *lu yesh nefshekem tahat nafshi*).

A rare translation that does catch this important nuance is the King James Bible: "I also could speak as ye do: if your soul were in my soul's stead, I could heap up words against you, and shake mine head at you" (v. 4).

To put "your soul in [another] soul's place" is not only a source of comfort, it is a phrase that describes the art of spiritual direction, as the spiritual director accompanies another on the journey of the soul into God; it is truly to see and be with another.

Not only do the friends fail to see Job in the way of a true friend, more importantly they refuse to see Job's soul, his essence, his place

> Thou must join in with the beginnings of life and be exercised with the day of small things, before thou meet the great things, wherein is the clearness and satisfaction of the soul. The rest is at noonday; but the travels begin at the breakings of day, wherein are but glimmerings or little light, wherein the discovery of good and evil are not manifest and certain; yet there must the traveler begin.
>
> Isaac Penington, "Letter to Bridget Atley," 1665, in *Quaker Spirituality: Selected Writings*, ed. Douglas V. Steere (New York: Paulist Press, 1984), 144.

17. Balentine, *Job*, 250. Job is also turning Eliphaz's description in 15:35a of the wicked as "conceiving mischief" (*'amal*) back on Eliphaz, castigating his friends as "miserable [*'amal*] comforters." Cf. Good, *In Turns of Tempest*, 245.

of God's abiding; they, unlike Job, are unable to exchange places, to experience that place where every traveler must begin. They have neither soul-identity nor soul-words.

FURTHER REFLECTIONS
Windy Words

Dialogue between the friends and Job is of course a dialogue of words and silences; they are speeches meant to be heard, to persuade, and to change behavior. In this sense the words of the dialogue are not unlike the tradition of Hebrew wisdom itself, in which wisdom is not only a body of knowledge, but also a process that forms character and virtue, and right action in relation to God, creation, and others. In verse 3 Job characterizes Eliphaz's words as "windy" (*ruach*), echoing Eliphaz's gibe that no wise person would articulate knowledge that was mere "windy knowledge" (15:2, *da'at ruach*). Ironically, Elihu (a fourth friend) later makes a fool of himself by claiming to be filled with a "wind" (or "gas", 32:18) that would answer all their questions (cf. Habel, 271). Both the friends and Job are now accusing one another of useless "windy words" (16:3, *dibrei ruach*; in 8:2 Bildad asks Job how long "the words of your mouth [will continue to] be a great wind") that have no meaning or persuasive power. Both partners in the dialogue consider the other's speech empty of content. This is all the more troubling, since at the beginning of the book, the sign that Job has not cursed God is that he does "not sin with his lips" (2:10). As can be seen in the progression below, over the course of the book words and speech (the stuff of wisdom and conversation in Job) go from a sign and seal of integrity and righteousness to the torments of wind that mock and break a man in pieces:

2:10   Job does not "sin with his lips."
  3:1   Job "opened his mouth" (after a week of silence).
  4:2   Eliphaz: "If one ventures a word with you, will you be offended?"

8:2   Bildad:"Words of your mouth [are] a great wind."

10:1   Job:"I will give free utterance to my complaint."

11:2   Zophar:"Should a multitude of words go unanswered?"

13:6   Job:"Hear now my reasoning; listen to the pleadings of my lips."

13:17   Job:"Listen carefully to my words; let my declaration be in your ears."

15:2   Eliphaz:"Should the wise answer with windy knowledge?"

16:3   Job:"Have windy words no limit?"

18:2   Bildad:"How long will you hunt for words?"

19:2   Job:"How long will you torment me, and break me in pieces with words?"

The words continue to fly, and many, though cutting, will continue to be complex and beautiful. But ultimately, as is presaged here, Job's most intimate connection with YHWH will not come through ear, but rather through eye. Job will understand partially through what he has heard, but will understand most fully according to what he sees: within the wind (*ruach*), the whirlwind, he sees the face of God (cf. 40:5; 42:5).

16:7–17 *"Like a Warrior" God Attacks*

Having found words to be of little help in convincing his friends, bringing him comfort, or persuading God to ease his suffering or at least show God's face, Job gives a short description of what God has done to him: "And he has shriveled me up, which is a witness against me; my leanness has risen up against me, and it testifies to my face" (16:8). Here for a moment he falls into his friends' logic as his body provides the witness and testimony of his sin. As Job describes God as a warrior attacking him, Job looks at his body and wonders if this body indeed "testifies" against him: perhaps he has sinned. Job's integrity shines through at this point: true integrity passes through trials, yet here Job maintains integrity by admitting the possibility of that to which his body testifies. Job witnesses to truth both in body and in spirit. His integrity helps him read the signs

In accusing God of assailing him Job uses the Hebrew word *śāṭam*, 'hate actively'... which is similar in sound to, if not directly related to, Heb. *śāṭān*.... Unable to fathom God's role in his affliction, Job fears that God has become his enemy.... He identifies God as his enemy rather than as his advocate. At this crucial point he is tested to the ultimate.

Hartley, *Job*, 260.

his body shows while the integrity of his spirit remains certain of his righteousness.

In 15:25–26, Eliphaz accuses Job of attacking God as if Job himself were the warrior. Now, "in his wrath" (*appo*, "anger," 16:9a), God "tears" (*taraf*, v. 9a) Job apart, God is Job's "adversary" (*tsari*, v. 9c), God is the attacking warrior: God "rushes at me like a warrior" (*gibbor*, v. 14). God not only attacks the weakened Job, "God gives me up to the ungodly" (*avil*, v. 11a; Habel translates: "El delivers me over to the evil").

The attack on Job continues to be ruthless, described in graphic detail: God's attack tears him apart like a pack of wild animals (16:9–10). God gives Job over to the wicked, perhaps to evil itself (v. 11). God breaks Job in two, seizes his neck and dashes him to pieces, sets Job up as a target for archers, slashes open his kidneys, pours out his gall/bile on the ground, bursts upon him again, then again, then again. Job's face becomes red with weeping and once again, "deep darkness is on my eyelids" (vv. 12–16). In language hard and unsettling, Job experiences all this as *God's* doing, as *God's* attack, which, as the reader knows from chapters 1 and 2, it in fact is. Job is accurate in accusing God: Job's friends are not responsible; Job's wife is not responsible; Job's community is not responsible; Job is not responsible; God is responsible. God attacks Job. This is hard; it is hard to assimilate; it is difficult to stand or live in the midst of this reality, that suffering has not always a human or even random cause, but is divinely caused. The poet Anne Sexton comments on her poem, "The Dead Heart": "After I wrote this, a friend scrawled on this page, 'Yes.' And I said, merely to myself, 'I wish it could be for a different seizure—as with Molly Bloom [a character speaking at the end of James Joyce's novel *Ulysses*] with her "and yes I said yes I will Yes."'" But Sexton's poem reads in part:

> It is a dead heart.
> It is inside of me.
> It is a stranger . . . [18]

"It is a dead heart." Job, describing his suffering as attacks from God, is describing his "dead heart." Job did not create the dead heart; indeed, it's a wonder this heart still beats. What Job is doing is anything but irreverent; he is refusing to deny who he is and what is happening to him. Job's friends will not admit that innocent suffering has a place in creation; for them there is no room for "a dead heart." But here in Scripture, in the book of Job, whether we like it or not, in Job there is just such a "dead heart."

But perhaps most important of all, the entirety of this lament is prayer. Job ends this section having "sewed sackcloth upon my skin, and . . . laid my strength in the dust" (v. 15). He is moving into the prayer of detachment, of letting go, of self-surrender. But of two things Job is certain: even in the midst of this frontal attack by God, Job himself has done no violence and "my prayer is pure" (v. 17).

16:18–17:2 *Wisdom of the Heart*

The Latin patristic writer Jerome, who also translated the complete Bible into Latin (*Biblia Sacra Vulgata*), once described the book of Job as a slippery eel around which one squeezes one's two hands, and the harder one squeezes the more it slips away.

The book of Job is, in this way, just such a slippery eel. It is like a bag of groceries slightly too large for the arms that slowly, no matter how hard we try to balance it against the heart, begins to slip and fall to the ground. The suffering is something we want to fix. With the groceries we can try to stack them in a better load, but we will fail. We have means to better stacking by which we can grasp and comprehend things in different ways: with our hands, with our minds, and with our hearts. But as Jerome pointed out long ago, we cannot comprehend or grasp Job wholly with any of these; the eel is too slippery. We have seen that Job is not fully comprehensible to our minds

---

18. Anne Sexton, *The Complete Poems* (New York: Houghton Mifflin, 1981), 439.

alone: the book is about relationship and wisdom as much as it is about understanding, and it is filled with paradox, ambiguity, and misdirection. With Job we must also try to "stack them in a better load" with the heart, with the imagination, with creative intuition.

How can we understand the merciless attack on Job by God, this attack on a man who is already "shriveled" and "lean" (16:8)? Unlike a doctor treating a broken arm, a parent with a crying child, or a plumber with a broken pipe, we cannot "fix" or comprehend in the sense of "grasp" or "seize" or "stack a better load." It is what the *heart* is able to comprehend—a comprehension no doubt beyond all the "windy words"—that is the way, the tool, the only organ that will be of use in "fixing" in the sense of understanding Job.

After the attack and the momentary dream of the heart's comprehension, Job is exhausted, hardly more than a ghost: "My spirit is broken, my days are extinct, the grave is ready for me" (17:1). This is a very difficult section; some of the best commentators simply admit the truth is not ascertainable at all in this section. But, hope abides: the truth is at least approachable within the wisdom of the heart. It is only with the heart that Job can maintain righteousness as passionately as he protests against power, aggression, violence, and capriciousness. Perhaps he is at prayer.

17:3–10 *Job at Prayer*

My spirit is broken, my days are extinct,
    the grave is ready for me.

(Job 17:1)

Between the brutal attack by God, wisdom which only the heart can see, and the friends, Job finds himself utterly lost, alone, once more abandoned: God will not answer him. As he says, his spirit (*ruach*, "breath," "wind") along with his days—future and past—are extinct; he is already dead inside and prepared for burial; his grave is open and awaiting him. He is a broken man physically, psychologically, and spiritually; he can barely draw a breath, his limbs are withered, he has become a laughingstock, his shadow appears at times more real than his emaciated body. Yet he continues to pray;

prayer is all that remains of Job this side of death: he *is* prayer. All of Scripture, indeed, is prayer.[19] Job simply shows us a part of our lives we would normally think inappropriate or not worthy of turning to God as prayer. Yes, Job prays for his children in chapter 1 and the prayer is good. He prays for his friends at the end in chapter 42, and God accepts the prayer. In between these acceptable prayers to God, Job learns a new, equally acceptable, vocabulary of prayer. It *is* hard to say just what Job has become in terms of prayer. Elie Wiesel has his character, Berish, "pray" in a similar way in his play, *The Trial of God* (cf. Berish's prayer of truth quoted, pp. 71, 72).

Examples like Berish and Job help us build a composite impression of another human as living prayer. In the Psalms creation itself is constantly at prayer (see Pss. 145; 148). Thomas Merton said, "A tree gives glory to God by being a tree."[20] A tree is prayer. Brother Lawrence, a seventeenth-century Carmelite monk, forms himself into the likeness of Christ through what he calls "the practice of the presence of God." Job, his God seemingly absent and abusive, nonetheless practices the presence of God; in doing so he is prayer.

17:11–16 *Death and Despair in Dust*

The reality and confusion of his own suffering floods over Job once again, and the metaphors of hope and death enter a deadly combat, as if Leviathan and Behemoth of the latter chapters of Job turned on each other in ferocious anger. Job's thoughts take on a frustrated and obscure quality as, abject and wearied, in his fantasy he languishes as if he *were* in Sheol, finding there a ghastly home and family, a deep-dark comfort. Job now expects death and Sheol; in ironic references to lost hope compared to his lost family, he can even draw his own family into the hallucinatory images of his deathly despair. He says of "the Pit" [v. 17:14a: *shachath*[21]], "You are my father," and

---

19. On the notion of all Scripture being prayer, whether as fruit for *lectio divina*, as word and story for meditation, or as inspiration for prayer when our prayer is dry and the Spirit intercedes for us, see Steven Chase, *Tree of Life: Models of Christian Prayer* (Grand Rapids: Baker Academic, 2005).

20. Thomas Merton, *New Seeds of Contemplation* (New York: New Directions, 1961), 29.

21. The "pit" (*shahath*) refers to the underworld as the domain of corruption, filth, and the fallen. The "worm" (*rimmah*) is likewise a symbol of death, the mark of one decimated by decay.

of the Pit's maggots and "worms" Job says [17:14b: *rimmah*],"My mother," or "My sister" (v. 14c). The pit of Sheol is his father, maggots and worms are his mother and sister. "Where then is my hope? Who will see my hope?" (v. 15). This is hopelessness beyond the precious, minute hope we last saw expressed as the root of a tree responding tentatively to "the scent of water" (14:9). This is a sickness unto death, total identification with loss, abandonment, and grief. Job, a man who, finding hope only in death, clings to shadows thinking they are light and in a final grief-surrender is so accustomed to complete loss that he identifies the horrors of death with the closest members of his family.

FURTHER REFLECTIONS
Frantic Hopelessness

Austrian composer Hugo Wolf paints a painful situation—similar to Job's contrast between hope and death—in which the external world of light, warmth, and creation that is visible but unreachable contrasts to Wolf's inner world of darkness and aridity that is far too attainable and real:

> To describe … I would most like to hang myself on the nearest branch of the cherry trees standing now in full bloom. This wonderful spring with its secret life and movement troubles me unspeakably. These eternal blue skies, lasting for weeks, this continuous sprouting and budding in nature, these coaxing breezes impregnated with spring sunlight and fragrance of flowers … make me frantic. Everywhere this bewildering urge for life, fruitfulness, creation—only I, although like the humblest grass of the fields one of God's creations, may not take part in this festival of resurrection, at any rate not except as a spectator with grief and envy.[22]

Like Wolf's vision of fecund spring that is alive and beautiful but beyond his reach, the hope of the tree's root tracking the scent of water is not Job's to grasp. Though no less than "the humblest grass

---

22. F. Walker, *Hugo Wolf: A Biography* (London: J. M. Dent & Sons, 1968), 322.

of the fields [that is] one of God's creations," Roethke, Wolf, and Job
are each resigned, and realistically so, to finding only "Sheol as my
house" (17:13a), where they will dwell with the "muck," their father,
and the "worms" and "maggots," their mother and sister. In 14:19
Job accused God of providing hope for the tree but destroying his
hope by sending him to the grave. Wolf's hope dissolves into "grief
and envy." The "purity of pure despair" is Roethke's hope. And Job's?
Job's hope is now no more than a question:

> Where then is my hope?
> Who will see my hope?
> Will it go down to the bars of Sheol?
> Shall we descend together into the dust?
> (Job 17:15–16)

18:1–21

Bildad's Second Response to Job:
"The light of the wicked is put out"

Expressing frustration with Job even in his first speech, Bildad opens
his second with the same two words as his first: "How long?" (18:2;
8:2). But between his speech in chapter 8 and his words in chapter
18, Bildad has had a radical change of perspective. He still assumed
Job to be righteous in the first speech, but now he gives up any pre-
tense of comfort or pastoral compassion. Bildad is interested only in
instructing Job about the life and fate of what he has come to believe
Job to be: wicked. Given Job's predicament and behavior, there is
really only one conclusion Bildad feels he can make, that Job has cast
his lot with the wicked. What is new is Bildad's additional willing-
ness to let Job know something of the terrifying fate of the wicked:
horrendous suffering in this life, and complete annihilation (complete consumption)—eating flesh and skin and limbs—by the king
of all terrors, Death (vv. 13–14). He paints a picture devoid of hope.

The structure of the speech is simple: a complaint against Job (vv.
2–4) and a graphic enumeration of the terrifying consequences and
fate of the wicked (vv. 5–21). The latter is developed through images

Bildad's request for respect seems innocuous enough. Sometimes, however, insistence on civility can be a means of control by those who do not want a discussion to disturb the foundations of things in which their security and their very identities are invested. A comparable rhetorical strategy is evident in Bildad's characterization of Job as one who "tears" himself "in his anger" (v. 4a). Bildad recasts Job's serious attack on the foundations as mere self-destructive behavior. His own words have subtle overtones of animality ("tear," *taraph*, is used of animals attacking prey) and of madness, since only if he were insane would Job mutilate himself in his anger. By these means he belittles Job's words and patronizes him.

Carol Newsom, "Job," in *NIB* (Nashville: Abingdon, 1996), 4:467.

of extinguished light (vv. 5–6), loss of movement (v. 7), entrapment like a hunted animal (vv. 8–10), predation by the forces of destruction (vv. 11–13), seizure by death's servants (v. 14), annihilation of all traces of existence, including place, home, progeny, memorial or memory (vv. 15–19). The speech concludes with a universal reaction of horror at the fate of the wicked (v. 20), and Bildad's summary (v. 21). In this speech Bildad has arrived at three conclusions: (1) based on the doctrine of retribution and his refusal to repent, Job is a wicked person; (2) on the basis of the wisdom tradition of the time, Job is not wise; and (3) Job has abandoned verbal, traditional, and historical foundations upon which a legitimate, moral discourse might be engaged.

18:2–4 *The Complaint against Job*

Each friend, and Job as well, has by now accused the other of this third point of preventing legitimate, moral dialogue. In Bildad's case, such a conversation can take place only within a framework of shared presuppositions and in an atmosphere of respect. Bildad thinks Job has insulted the friends, asking of Job, "Why are we counted as cattle? Why are we stupid in your sight?" (v. 3). Bildad would also like Job to stop talking long enough to "recognize" the certain things that are essential to civil conversation of respect (*bin*, v. 2b; "consider," NRSV; "be sensible," NIV).

Images in verse 4 such as "the earth" and "the rock" emphasize this need to secure foundations in order to ensure legitimate discussion and a structure of respect. But it is too late to lay ground rules for civil discussion. Between Job and the friends, language has already broken down; civil interchange and mutual understanding, from this point onward, are no longer possible.

18:5–21 *The Life and Fate of the Wicked*

Introducing his extended monologue on the fate of the wicked, Bildad, the traditionalist, suggests images or motifs that together make it difficult to imagine a more hopeless picture of human desolation. The images, primarily of disintegration, starting from verse 5 include light turning to darkness, the strong animal trapped, the strong man enfeebled by sickness and marched to death, descendants killed, the memory of the person dissolved, and the removal of the wicked from the land of the living.[23] The primary motifs of the annihilation of the wicked are removing the wicked from the land of the living and destroying their dwelling place, their habitation, their community, which is loss not only of identity but of the protection of the community, which at the time of the writing of Job would have been essential for survival.

If Job cannot or will not accept that these are the conditions and fate of the wicked, Bildad has no further grounds for conversation. Again, Bildad is the traditionalist who insists on a formula of religious practice that flows from a just moral order. That is, there will always be a religious practice provided for the righteous sufferer that will, according to Bildad's vision, eventually return balance to the moral order and relieve suffering in this life. The practice is simply to repent and to pray to a compassionate God for forgiveness. In his first speech, this is what Bildad urges Job to do. Unfortunately there is no comparable practice for those wicked who, like Job, do pray but exchange lament for repentance. Lament, according to Bildad, will not reverse the suffering of the wicked. Bildad sees Job's lament as

---

23. Good, *In Turns of Tempest*, 253–54.

the ravings of an evil madman, which, with regard to relieving suffering, are less than useless to Job.[24]

Verses 5–6 begin Bildad's description of disintegration by using a classic symbolic association in Wisdom literature, light/life and dark/death. This symbolism is common in Job (3:20; 10:21–22; 15:22; 17:13). To affirm that the doctrine of divine retribution is operative, Bildad quotes a proverb (Prov. 13:9, "the lamp of the wicked goes out"; see also Prov. 20:20; 24:20) that implies that the fate of the unrepentant wicked is not to be overturned: "The light of the wicked is put out" (Job 18:5). Bildad's fondness for these familiar images and phrases has, in Bildad's mind, the effect of making his own words a conduit of that authoritative tradition of the ancients. None of the verbs in this section carries an active agent. Neither Bildad, Job, nor God, nor even a wind, extinguishes the light. Rather the light simply "goes out" (*da'ak*) and "grows dark" (*hashak*); the flame "does not shine" (*lo'-yiggah*), the lamp "goes out" (*da'ak*).[25] In the passive voice or simple present, the implication is that in Bildad's well-ordered moral universe the wicked can expect one thing: one way or another, their light will go out and they will be encased in darkness, regardless of how active or passive one is.

Even the strong are eventually ensnared (passive voice) and "their own schemes throw them down" (v. 7). In verses 8–10, Bildad describes the fate of the wicked in terms of entrapment and in doing so provides fascinating clues, nowhere else available in Hebrew literature, to ancient hunting methods. Bildad is a knowledgeable hunter. In illustrating the idea that wicked people are sure to be ensnared in their own schemes, Bildad uses six different words for trapping devices, some of which we know little about and are referenced nowhere else in any ancient language. Devices used to trap birds and animals are used as symbols for traps that ensnare the wicked: a "net" (*resheth*) spread over a pit to tangle the feet of birds and small animals (v. 8a); a "webbing" (*sebakah*; "pitfall," NRSV), a large mesh of branches spread over a pit (v. 8b); a "snare" (*pah*;

---

24. See Carol Newsom, "The Book of Job: Introduction, Commentary, and Reflections," in *NIB* (Nashville: Abingdon, 1996), 4:468, on wisdom and relief from suffering.
25. Ibid.

"trap," NRSV), an unknown type of trap that grasps the victim's heel (v. 9a); a "snare" (*tsammim*), a little-known word, perhaps another trap that closes on its prey (v. 9b); a "noose" (*hebel*; "rope," NRSV) set to ensnare and raise the animal from the ground (v. 10a); a "trap" (*malkodeth*), a general term for a snaring device.[26] The tradition of wisdom also incorporates crafts-manship and other technical skills; using the wisdom of hunting, Bildad insinuates not only that the

> **Bildad says these things using the metaphor of the birds or the animals that are captured in the hunt. In fact, as they can no longer escape after falling into snares and nets, so the impious are caught by inevitable calamities that overwhelm them.**
>
> Olympiodorus, *Commentary on Job* 18:7–9 in *Commentary on Job*, ed. Ursula Hagedorn, PTS 24 (New York: de Gruyter, 1984), 59, in ACCS.

wicked are caught in their own scheme, but that the agent setting the trap is also varied: perhaps it is the wicked people themselves who set their own snares, in the passive voice Bildad implies that some traps must be laid by God, and some traps are simply hidden, a natural part of the landscape over which the wicked must walk and are thus taken down.

Holding back nothing, Bildad next throws plagues, terrors, deso-lation, and death at Job; he is ready for the kill. As for the wicked themselves, realizing the true nature of the path they must walk and the hidden snares that will surely entrap them, they will be seized by "terrors" (*ballahoth*, v. 11), all the while knowing that they will be consumed by Death itself. The imagery has shifted from traps to aggressive, predatory horror leading to calamity, disaster, and finally to death. Verse 11 describes the chase, verse 12 the cornering of the prey, and verse 13 devouring by Death. Terrors does not primarily refer to subjective psychological reactions but to the servants of per-sonified Death.[27] What are the servants of Death to which Bildad refers? Certainly calamity and disaster are two. Textual problems and grammatical ambiguities in verses 11–14 permit varied translations

---

26. John E. Hartley, *The Book of Job* (Grand Rapids: Eerdmans, 1988), 276.
27. Nicholas J. Tromp, *Primitive Conceptions of Death and the Nether World in the Old Testament* (Rome: Pontifical Biblical Institute, 1969), 74.

that actually accentuate the graphic nature of the "terrors" awaiting Job. One viable and respected translation[28] suggests that the servants of Death, the terrors Job will have to confront, include:

> Death's terrors frighten him all around
> And tangle him up in his feet.
> The Hungry One will be his strength,
> Calamity ready as his escort.
> He consumes his skin with both hands;
> Firstborn Death consumes with both hands.
> He is snatched from his secure tent
> And marched off to the King of Terrors.
>
>   (18:11–14)

What vision are Job's "miserable comforters" trying to convey to the man with the diseased skin and limbs, being told he will be consumed by the Firstborn of Death, a ravenous glutton consuming the captured, evil unfortunates with both hands? The oldest, Eliphaz, the more subtle theologian, gives a portrait of the terrors of suffering and death in which he stresses the psychological fear the wicked can expect. Bildad, the theologian of tradition, the hunter at home in the physical world, presents the same horrors as realities of the underworld, servants of King Death itself, attendants of the king of terrors who consumes earth and sky and all things wicked in between.

Job has traveled a long path since chapters 1 and 2. His friends seem to have traveled even farther; they have become something very like the traps and snares Bildad describes; they are long past thoughts of comforting Job and well into their own needs to verbalize the values of their own moral universe, justifying themselves on the basis of a simple doctrine that is itself a grotesque minefield.

As a final jibe at his victim, Bildad ends by referring back to his sarcastic insult to Job in verse 4, "shall the earth be forsaken because of you, or the rock be removed out of its place?" That is, even given Job's endless lamenting and suffering, will even the smallest rock be moved out of its "place" for Job's convenience? This is linked to the

---

28. Habel, *Job*, 280.

final verse of the chapter, in which Bildad, still referencing Job, says that the underworld of the dead is "the place of those who do not know God" (v. 21). The irony is that Job knows God only too well.

FURTHER REFLECTIONS
Wisdom

Wisdom is not just what we might think of as the characteristic of a "sage" person. Wisdom in the ancient Hebrew tradition has many components. It is a body of knowledge set forth for understanding God, creation, human nature, and human society; it is a discipline structured to shape behavior and formation of character to actualize virtue in discourse and action; it is a body of knowledge concerning how to maintain moral discourse and behavior in society through adherence to beauty, order, justice, truth, and abundant life; it could manifest itself in the areas of court wisdom dealing with education, service in the bureaucracy, reading, writing, copying, debating, and maintaining traditions of society; it includes the wisdom of artisans skilled at producing both artistically pleasing and pragmatically needed products and services (such as Bildad's hunting wisdom).

It is easy to see how righteousness would be linked to wisdom and how wickedness or evil would be linked to the undermining of wisdom. However, these links also became intertwined with the doctrine of retribution, so that not only were the punished obvious perpetuators of corruption and sin, but also those who suffered punishment undermined the moral balance of wisdom. Those who, like Job, suffered rather than prospered were not wise, they were fools; indeed they were evil fools. It is easy to understand (though even easier to disagree with) Bildad's devastating remark at the end of his speech that what he has described as Job's fate "is the place of those who do not know God" (v. 21). Wisdom and knowing God in the sense of having fellowship with God would have been the most coveted form of righteousness. Job is angry at God beyond measure, but to be told that he does not know God is an affront, devastating and demoralizing.

As is often reiterated in Hebrew Scriptures, the fear of God is the first stage of wisdom (Prov. 1:7; Ps. 111:10; cf. Prov. 3:7; Isa. 11:2; Mic. 6:9). This "fear" is fear not only of the transcendent power and justice of God, but fear also in a more immanent sense, the *mysterium tremendum*, wherein knowing God means to have fellowship with God, even fellowship with the numinous mystery that is God. This fear is traditionally also terrifying, but in this case it is terror that is the stuff of prayers, the vision of saints. The sight of Job's emaciated body fires Bildad's rhetoric, while he shows no compassion that would encourage Job to seek God. This all happens when Job is the *only one* of these men who is maintaining relationship and fellowship with God, as God will make clear at the end of the book.

In a culture grounded in fear in the sense that Bildad uses it to terrorize Job, or in our own culture of fear today, there are many manifestations of what some would call the fate of the wicked and sinful life that are present for all to see, most of which are named or alluded to in this chapter through Bildad's accusation of Job. These include an arrogant attitude toward God or, perhaps worse, a complete lack of knowledge of God (of which Bildad accuses Job, v. 21). The wicked have no habitation, no "place," be it tent or dwelling or house, to serve as a grounded point that is the locus of meaning, order, or community. There are also "a number of obvious polarities operative within Bildad's portrayals of the wicked. The imagery and language associated with these oppositions include veiled allusions to the speeches of Job which provide evidence for Bildad that Job is indeed one of the wicked."[29] These include polarities of light/darkness (already a strong image in chapter 3) that have their correspondences to life/death and wicked/righteous. Another is that of trap/trapped and hunter/hunted. Job had accused God of attacking him, of shooting arrows at him, of being a hunter who pursued Job as if Job were prey, and scheming as the Creator to make Job his sacrificial victim (6:4; 10:13–16; 13:27). Bildad sees these as traps Job can expect and deserves.

As strongly as Bildad and the other friends, Job believes that there are correspondences between human actions and predicaments

---

29. Ibid., 284.

and divine agency and will. The difference is that the friends and Job have parted ways regarding the contingencies, connections, and balance between human action and providence. Job is practicing a devotional discipline that disallows guilt and shame, even in the context of suffering. The friends continue to seek balance in a moral configuration that hinges on guilt and shame and punishment. Both approaches are difficult to abandon. But by the end of the book of Job the friends' primary categories are cast in moral exigencies of cursing and wickedness which are condemned by God, while Job's categories, though still tender and in need of nurturing, emerge into what is for him the recently lost world of blessing, and are affirmed by God.

The wisdom of the friends is faulty both from the perspective of the reader (at least most readers) and from the divine perspective of YHWH, who says to Eliphaz at the end of the book, "My wrath is kindled against you and against your two friends; for you have not spoken of me what is right, as my servant Job has" (42:7). Nonetheless, the dramatic poetry of the three speeches on the fate of the wicked (chaps. 15, 18, 20) are among the most compelling in the book of Job. They also model a provocative way of imagining evil and people who embody evil, even today. The moral imagination of the poetry may seem strange at first, but one may recognize in Job some familiar and disturbing modes of thinking present in modern culture.

The understanding of good and evil as active forces affecting both life and death is an ancient as well as contemporary model that envisions the world as a holistic environment in which what is good is nurtured and what is evil is isolated and expelled. Nevertheless, this way of imagining evil and the world's response to it can be deeply disturbing. The fact that "elements of this perception are present in modern culture is evident from the common reactions of fear, disgust, and even hatred that people sometimes experience when confronted by a person whose body is deformed or disfigured by illness and suffering. These reactions are residual elements of a subconscious, subrational chain of association: a horribly suffering body, which death is so visibly claiming, is seen as a body rejected by life and all goodness associated with life. It is seen as a body cursed, and therefore, a presence of evil."[30] In a very real sense Job has changed from a man who "did not sin with his lips" (2:9) to a man in whose deformed, diseased, dying body his friends see the curses of evil and, not unlike the Nazis' depiction of the Jews, they seek to eliminate evil by eliminating Job.

19:1–29

Job's Second Response to Bildad:
Vindication and Redemption

In this, the briefest but also one of the most celebrated of Job's speeches, Job covers more emotional and psychological territory than in any of his previous dialogues. Unjustly accused, he moves from near-suicidal despair over the varied attacks of his God and the breakup of his community, to a brief pinnacle of ecstatic, nearly christological hope, only to fall once again into the fear of the sword of judgment (see v. 29).

This chapter of emotional upheaval has received enormous exegetical attention. The focus of attention is on verses 25–27, which can hardly be heard or spoken without the majesty of Handel's *Messiah* coming immediately to mind: "For I know that my Redeemer lives, . . . then in my flesh I shall see God" (vv. 25a, 26b). This familiarity is a problem in interpreting the speech as a whole: the familiarity covers Job's true intention with layers of meaning that even this NRSV translation struggles to remove. The lines also remain heavily invested with theological associations mostly having to do with resurrection, redemption, and immortality focused on the Redeemer as Christ, which of course is not a theological issue of Job's. Adding to the problem of understanding is that these verses and those surrounding them are notoriously corrupt, the text remains very unclear, and, as we shall see, emendations abound.

The speech can be divided into thematic focuses: an opening rebuke to the friends (vv. 1–5); a traditional lament form that places guilt not on Job himself but on God (vv. 6–22); God's violent attacks

---

30. Newsom, "Book of Job," 471.

on Job (vv. 6–12); alienation from Job's community caused by God (vv. 13–19); concluding description of further deterioration of his body (v. 20); and a return to the issue of Job's captivity by friends and by God in which closeness becomes as unbearable as alienation. Traditional laments end with a plea to God for restoration and aid against enemies; ironically Job turns to a pitiful plea to his friends instead[31] (vv. 21–22), presumably because God is Job's enemy. Job then turns not to prayer, but to a wish that his words could be permanently preserved (vv. 23–24). Finally Job envisions a redeemer or avenger that he hopes will erase all unjust accusations and return him to his former state of blessing, in the course of which his connection with God would be redeemed (vv. 25–27). Job ends the speech, for the first time not with a meditation on death, but with a rebuke and warning to the friends (vv. 28–29).

From Innocent Suffering to Unjust Accusation

A part of the genius of the book of Job is that over the course of its story, the character of Job undergoes slow, subtle, yet discernible growth and transformation, a transformation in which none of the initial spirit or personality of Job is lost, but in which the spirit and personality are rather integrated, transformed, and enhanced. The transformation is as much theological as it is psychological; chapter 19 is in all these, a crucial transitional point in Job's transformation.

Job's emotional state has risen and fallen many times to this point; yet his shift in moods in chapter 19 is the most striking in the book. In chapter 3, for instance, the focus is on innocent suffering, and Job wishes for nothing less than oblivion and death as a means to end that suffering. Job's capacity for irony and parody give him some energy (chaps. 7, 9, 12), but he continues to end his speeches with meditations on death (chaps. 10, 14, 17). Slowly, however, Job begins to find some hope in the idea of a trial in which he can argue his case before God and reverse both the divine and his community's unjust accusations. Though he continues to struggle with despair and self-doubt, his response slowly begins to become more aggressive and his attacks on God and on his friends likewise become more violent.

31. Ibid., 474.

In the paradigmatic story of the unjustly accused, there comes a time when the accused must make a crucial decision: whether to give up and even participate in the conspiracy of lies, or to fight back. To fight back is a gamble: it is usually a fight of the powerless against the powerful, and even if the inequality of power is overcome, justice does not always win out. Tormented and broken as he is (19:2), Job decides to take the gamble.

19:1–5 Rebuke of Friends: "You have become my superiors!"

Once again Job laments his friends' reactions, reaching a new intensity with his familiar complaint. It is familiar in that Job claims once again that it is the friends' very "words" that torment and break him (v. 2; cf. "if you would only keep silent," 13:5; "windy words," 16:3). It is familiar as well in that the friends remain "miserable comforters" (16:2), creating more pain than they come to relieve. But with that familiarity comes a new intensity: the "words" now "torment" and "break" (v. 2) Job; the "comforters" only "cast reproach" and "wrong" (v. 3) him. The verb for "torment" (*yagah*) is used elsewhere only of God, who in anger inflicts cruel suffering on God's own people (Lam. 1:5, 12), while the verb for "break" (*dak'*; also to "crush" or "oppress") recalls Job's earlier lament that God would "crush" him

---

My mistress was, as I have said, a kind and tender-hearted woman; and in the simplicity of her soul she commenced . . . to treat me as she supposed one human being ought to treat another . . . [but] Slavery proved as injurious to her as it did to me. When I went there, she was a pious, warm, and tender-hearted woman. There was no sorrow or suffering for which she had not a tear. She had bread for the hungry, clothes for the naked, and comfort for every mourner that came within her reach. Slavery soon proved its ability to divest her of these heavenly qualities. Under its influence, the tender heart became stone, and the lamb-like disposition gave way to one of tiger-like fierceness. The first step downward was in her ceasing to instruct me [to read] . . . nothing seemed to make her more angry than to see me with a newspaper. . . . I have had her rush at me with a face made all up of fury.

Frederick Douglass, *Narrative of the Life of Frederick Douglass, An American Slave* (New York: Barnes & Noble Classics, 2003), 43–44.

to death as a means of alleviating his pain (6:9).[32] Thus the friends' "words" and "comfort" actually "cast reproach" (*kalam*; "humilitate," Habel; "insult," Good) and "wrong" (*hakar*; "abuse," Habel).

The poet organizes much of the rest of Job's short speech around paired but opposite images of distance and closeness and of travel and staying at home. For example, as Good translates v. 4:

> Have I truly strayed?
> My straying stays at home with me.

Job's theological and spiritual journey is an itinerary both straying and staying in place. "Strayed" (*shagah*; "erred," NRSV) and "my straying" (*meshugah*; "error," NRSV) have more the sense of aimless wandering than of moral "error." "Stays" (*lin*; "remains," NRSV) is better translated as "lodges," lending another nuance to "home." Job says, in effect, his friends are taking up permanent residence in Job's journey of suffering and injustice.

19:6–12 *God Attacks Job*

Job once again wants his friends to know that it is God who has "put me in the wrong" (v. 6). The Hebrew translated "wrong," *'iwwet*, means literally "bend" or "make crooked," and in using it Job not only implies that he has been wronged unjustly, but refutes Bildad's major premise that God does not pervert (*'iwwet*) justice (8:3). From Job's perspective, God does in fact pervert justice, God has "closed his net around me."[33]

> **Job cannot forego either his own truth or God.**
>
> Martin Buber, quoted in Harold Bloom, ed., introduction to *The Book of Job* (New York: Chelsea House, 1988), 2.

With the description of the "net" we are also reminded of Bildad's elaborate vocabulary for traps in 18:8–10, a vocabulary Bildad had intended to use as metaphors of human agency as the provocateurs of sin: humans trap themselves. For Job it is God who traps.

32. Habel, *Job*, 299.
33. Cf. Hartley, *Job*, 284.

In verses 7–12 Job describes God in an attack mode, while verses 13–20 describe the dissolution of his community. The former—depicting God in attack mode—uses a series of travel images to describe polarities between travel and stability. The images of travel or journey and home are core themes in Hebrew theology and spirituality. There is wisdom to be gained in the freedom and change brought about by a spiritual journey; there is wisdom to be acquired also in stability, in tradition, in routine. But in the verses having to do with journey and travel, Job is attacked and his way is blocked by God. God has put a net around Job's path (v. 6); God has "walled up my way so that I cannot pass" (v. 8a); God "has set darkness upon my paths" (v. 8b). God's own "troops" (*gedud* can mean "gangs" or "raiding parties")[34] come together and build "siegeworks against me" (v. 12). These ways, these paths, blocked, even the place of former stability can become traps for attack. The prey of these elaborate attacks is, as Job points out, his simple "tent" (v. 12). "Tent" is a Hebrew image for family. Thus Job's journey is blocked on every side and the stability of home, Job's flimsy "tent," by now provides nothing at all like the securities and rest of a home.

Thus God has "subverted" (v. 6a, *avath*; Habel) Job's way; the images of that subversion suggest a directed military attack on Job's person and community:

> 19:6 He throws up siegeworks *against me* (*'alay*; Habel)
>
> 7 I cry out, "Violence!"
>
> 8 He has walled up my way and sets darkness *against* (*'al*) my path
>
> 9 He has stripped my glory *from me* (*me'alay*) and taken the crown from me
>
> 10 He breaks me down *on every side* (*sabib*)
>
> 11 He has kindled his wrath *against me* (*'alay*)
>
> 12 They have thrown up siegeworks *against me* (*'alay*) and encamp around my tent.

---

34. Good, *In Turns of Tempest*, 255; 422 n. 40 makes a case for "gangs" at 19:12 and "troops" (*rabbim*) only at 16:13, but Habel, Gordis, Hartley, and NRSV maintain "troops," thus emphasizing the military metaphor as well as the journey/home metaphor, and thereby greatly enriching the depth of Job's laments.

The language reflects a siege mentality. Six times the poet uses the preposition *'al* ("against") to express the intensity of the divine opposition, and twice the preposition *sabib*, ("on every side").

In the midst of this complaint comes an ironic allusion to an earlier statement on hope made by Job. The allusion is clear, unavoidable, powerful, and pitiable. In verse 10b Job says, "He [El] has uprooted my hope like a tree." We are reminded again of chapter 14, where Job expressed at least the possibility for hope: "For there is hope for a tree, if it is cut down, that it will sprout again, and that its shoots will not cease" (v. 7). Now there is not even a hope for hope: God uproots Job's hope like a tree.

But Job's lament is only getting started.

19:13–22 *"Those whom I loved have turned against me"*

The one against whom Job screams "Violence!" (v. 7) attacks from the outside, but Job now turns from a lament in which all his ways are blocked to a lament in which he is alienated and betrayed by his community from within.

Job's complaint against God is in part for alienation from family and community. Verses 13–19 use "some twelve different terms for social and kinship categories. Unfortunately, the precise meaning of many of them is unknown or disputed. Even without such knowledge, however, one has the impression that Job is giving a detailed map of the relational world from which he is now excluded."[35] The implication throughout is that

> Is not God wicked? Is it not the possibility that the believer evokes when he prays: "Lead us not into temptation"? . . . The theme of the wrath of God, the ultimate motive of the tragic consciousness, is invincible to the arguments of the philosopher as well as of the theologian. For there is no rational vindication of the innocence of God; every explanation of the Stoic or Leibnizian type is wrecked, like the naïve arguments of Job's friends . . . as soon as meaninglessness appears to swoop down intentional on man, the schema of the wrath of God looms up and the tragic consciousness is restored.
>
> Paul Ricoeur, "The Reaffirmation of the Tragic," in *The Book of Job*, ed. Harold Bloom (New York: Chelsea House, 1988), 19–20.

35. Newsom, "Book of Job," 476.

Job experiences these rejections because God has caused them. The verbs move from passive rejection (distancing, estrangement, failing, and forgetting, vv. 13–15a) to an upheaval in social relations (vv. 15b–16), followed by a description of repulsion and loathing and active despising (vv. 17–18), leading finally to the turning away from Job by those whom Job loved (v. 19). The social relations Job names move in a progression from distant to intimate: kin, extended family, acquaintances, relatives, close friends, servants (which break the progression but serve as poignant irony, as explained below), houseguests, his wife, intimate friends, and those whom he loves, all of whom have turned away from him because, as Job sees it, of God's whim.

Perhaps the most cruel indignity is shown in Job's relations with his servant (v. 16). He "calls" (*qara*; "summons," Habel) but gets no "answer" (*anah*) and must therefore degrade himself by meekly "pleading" (*hanan*). As Habel has commented, "Because God would not 'answer' as a normal adversary at law, Job would be obliged to 'entreat' his accuser for mercy. Job is a man without an answer, be it from God, from heaven, from his friends, or from his own kin. Even his 'servant' does not answer! He stands alone, alienated from all in heaven and earth."[36]

Job's community reads the signs and responds to the divine curse placed on Job. Thus even his "intimate friends" (*math-sod*; literally "intimate men" or "intimate counsel," v. 19a) and "loved ones" (*aheb*, v. 19b) who have given a lifetime of love and concern have read and interpreted the signs and deserted and distanced themselves from him. These images of distancing and alienation are then suddenly replaced by images of claustrophobic closeness: his skin and flesh "cling" (*dabaq*) to his bones (v. 20); God's hand "touches" (*naga*, v. 21); both the friends and God "pursue" Job (*radaf*, v. 22).[37] The nightmare of divine attack, social ostracism, unbending application of the painful piety of divine retribution, and palpably pathological reaction to closeness combine pitifully: "Have pity on me, have pity on me, O you my friends" (v. 21).

36. Habel, *Job*, 301–2.
37. Cf. Good, *In Turns of Tempest*, 256.

19:23–24 *"O that my words were . . . engraved on a rock forever"*

In this preliminary vision Job moves from images of change, psychological and spiritual distance of the human community, a lament over interior and exterior closeness, to a shift to images of permanence: he envisions immortality etched not in change, but in stone:

> Would that my words were written,
> Would that they were engraved in an inscription,
> With an iron stylus and lead
> Forever in rock they were incised.
>
> (19:23–24, Good)

Writing lasts longer than speech, and imagining writing "incised" in rock with letters filled with lead lasts even longer; ironically, even in rock with lead the words remain ambiguous. As Good writes, "Incise them, engrave them, fill the hollow spaces of the letters with lead and the meaning of the marks will go on eluding everyone who reads them."[38] And so this vision, solid as it appears, is hollow. We must remember again also that Job's emotions, intellect, and soul are in such a state that they are anything but rock; they are more like water, floating, sinking, struck down, caught up, once more sinking, moving from despair to hope to despair. It is in this state that Job has his second, most famous vision, his closest flirtation with new hope and perhaps even immortality.

> Writing is not necessarily permanent, but it persists longer than speech. . . . And this writing is to be "forever" "incised" in rock with an iron tool, with the incised letters filled with lead. . . . The irony is, of course, that Job's words *are* written, nothing but written. The thought of reclaiming an "original," spoken Job is impossible. But the second irony of writing is that, however permanent the words may be, they remain as ambiguous as ever. Incise them, engrave them, fill the hollow spaces of the letters with lead and the meaning of the marks will go on eluding everyone who reads them.
>
> Good, *In Turns of Tempest*, 257.

38. Ibid., 257.

19:23–29 *"I know that my Redeemer lives"*

Chapter 19 is probably the most famous in Job. We come now to a passage containing a set of verses about which one commentator has written, "The literature on vv. 25–27, perhaps the most famous and difficult passage in the book, is enormous,"[39] while another acknowledges, "Verse 25 is probably the most celebrated in the book of Job, and the riddle of its meaning continues to exercise the ingenuity of scholars."[40] One writes of Job's "mystic vision . . . aggravated by grave problems in the text,"[41] while yet another writes of verses 28–29, "These lines are a jumble of verbiage and possibly the text is damaged or misplaced."[42] Of verses 25–27, still another: "This passage gives everyone fits, both of furious activity and of blank despair. In 35 years of trying to perceive sense in these verses, I have found it only in the first line." This commentator then proceeds with an otherwise illuminating translation, simply omitting verses 25b–27 from it.[43] Famous and notoriously difficult, these verses are a formula for an avalanche of opinion and paucity of agreement. But that is also a part of the reason that they draw readers and commentators back to this passage again and again. The NRSV renders verses 25–26:

> For I know that my Redeemer lives,
>   and that at the last he will stand upon the earth;
> and after my skin has been thus destroyed,
>   then in my flesh I shall see God.

In addition to the echoes of Handel's *Messiah*, it is easy to see in this passage how generations of Christian exegetes could find explicit christological meanings in the word "Redeemer" and more than hints of the doctrines of immortality and bodily resurrection in the phrase "then in my flesh I shall see God." Such allegorical or tropological readings see the Redeemer as Jesus and the later phrase as

---

39. Gordis, *Job*, 528.
40. Habel, *Job*, 303.
41. Gordis, *Book of God and Man*, 89.
42. Marvin Pope, *Job* (Garden City, NY: Doubleday, 1965), 147.
43. Good, *In Turns of Tempest*, 100–101.

a literal allegory of what is yet to come. But even without the Handel melody and christological allegories, commentators are unanimous about only one thing concerning the passage: it is difficult.

What does *Job* mean when he says, according to the NRSV, "I know that my Redeemer lives . . . then, in my flesh I shall see God?" He has just given voice to his predicament by lamenting God's ruthless attacks and how his community, from child to wife to prince to servant, has turned against him. He has pictured an impossible dream of his words carved in stone. Now he speaks what is in essence a mystical vision engraved in his decrepit flesh. He begins with a strong "I know," which reaches beyond the wish formula, "O that" or "O if only," of the previous verses (23–24) and announces a strong, though fleeting, new conviction.

FURTHER REFLECTIONS
My Redeemer Lives

Chapter 19 is not the first time Job has found a short-lived hope that a deliverer of some kind will bring relief from his suffering and from divine injustice. Including chapter 19 these are

9:33	*mokkiah*	arbiter, adjudicator, "umpire" (NRSV)
16:19	*'edh*	witness
19:25	*go'el*	redeemer, avenger, kinsman, rescuer

Were Job given any of these "mediators," each would be progressively more active in a court of law on behalf of Job as defendant against YHWH as prosecutor and judge.

Why does Job hope for a *go'el*? It is possible that Job chooses a *go'el* because of its strong associations with the role of blood avenger. Earlier Job had appealed to the earth not to cover his blood because the violence he has experienced at God's hands is equivalent to murder (16:18). Job gives a similar declaration of "Violence!" as a complaint against God in 19:7. A full appreciation of the role of *go'el* must also take into account the context of this speech and previous relevant speeches. It is clear that God is the enemy who has attacked Job violently and left him a physical and spiritual wreck (16:9–14). It is also apparent that Job considers God his accuser and adversary at law.

As Job, enraptured, swings from lament to ecstatic vision, who or what is the *go'el* he foresees? The literature on this question is overwhelming, but two major interpretive answers predominate: the *go'el* is either God or a third party who acts as Job's defender/advocate in his legal suit against God. Those who argue for the former are in the minority. Theologically based reasons for this view include (1) the God that Job expects to "see" (v. 26) is the same as the *go'el* Job expects "at the last" who will "stand upon the earth" (v. 25b), thus lending an eschatological dimension to the "Redeemer," a dimension that neatly incorporates all history into the redemptive work of God; and (2) the claim that the uncompromising monotheism of the book of Job militates against a third party playing the role of the redeemer.

Those who argue for the *go'el* as a third party are, by far, in the majority. Reasons for this interpretation include (1) there is no logical textual reason why Job should expect the *go'el* to be God; the expectation is purely that of a defender figure for Job *against* God; (2) the allusions to God as Redeemer in the Psalms are not pertinent: the need for Job is deliverance from God, not by God; (3) the appeal to an uncompromising monotheistic theology is misleading; the hope for a third party is not inconsistent with the theology or cosmology of Job; (4) viewing God as the *go'el* would mean a complete reversal in the pattern of Job's experience of God as the adversary, a pattern continued throughout much of the rest of the book.

Norman C. Habel's "obvious solution" to the problem of the identity of the *go'el* "is to identify the *gō'ēl* with a figure like the celestial witness (*'ēd,* 16:19) and arbiter (*mōkīaḥ,* 9:33) of previous hope speeches. Both these figures are clearly distinguished from God and viewed as vehicles for bringing Job's case before an impartial court."[44]

An answer to when Job may expect the *go'el* to rise and testify on his behalf is also split into two camps: the first that the *go'el* will

44. Habel, *Job,* 306.

rise in court before Job dies, and the second that the *go'el* will rise in court on Job's behalf sometime after he dies. Theologically this question has immense resonance if the *go'el* is allegorically interpreted as Jesus. The question of ante- or postmortem vision of the *go'el* could be answered "both/and" for certain forms of millennialism, "antemortem" by a number of Christian mystics, and "postmortem" by most Christian denominations and rites confessing resurrection of the body.

Albert Barnes brings together a helpful compendium of arguments on one final hotly debated question arising from this text: does the passage refer to the Messiah, and to the future resurrection of the dead? (Barnes does not separate the issue of the Messiah from that of resurrection.) He concludes:

> The opinion [against the *go'el* as the Messiah] which has now been expressed, it is not necessary to say, has been held by a large number of the most distinguished critics. Grotius says that the Jews never applied it to the Messiah and the resurrection. . . . Calvin seems to be doubtful—sometimes giving it an interpretation similar to that suggested above [against], and then pursuing his remarks as if it referred to the Messiah. Most of the fathers, and a large portion of modern critics, it is to be admitted, suppose that it refers to the Messiah, and to the future resurrection.[45]

Whatever Job's vision of the "Redeemer" that Job hopes to see "in his flesh," it is a vision grounded in Job's experience of injustice and suffering. Job's sense of a moral and just universe is now maintained in ephemeral hopes of these fleeting visions.

19:26b–27 *"In my flesh I shall see God"*

Even given the textual difficulties, it is clear that Job believes that he will see God. Just how shall he see? Job's flesh is as corrupted as the text. The phrase *umibbe-sari* is more properly rendered, literally, as "from or out of my flesh" or even "without my flesh."[46] Whatever

45. Albert Barnes, "Job 19:25–29," in *Sitting with Job*, ed. Roy B. Zuck (Grand Rapids: Baker Book House, 1992), 283–97.
46. Ibid., 288.

the phrase means, it does not mean "in." Dhorme thinks it means "behind my skin . . . as behind a curtain,"[47] and the curtain may be death. Once again the question of immortality and the afterlife is raised, but once again it is ambiguous: for instance, the skin may need to be peeled off before Job sees God (i.e., in death); or it may mean a robust and renewed vision "from out of my flesh" in this life.

Another question concerns just what kind of seeing is meant. Suggestions have ranged from physical vision to mystical, imaginary, visionary, or disembodied experiences. To these we could add more spiritual senses, such as seeing with the eyes of the heart, the eyes of the mind, or, given Job's now long process of purgation, the eyes of contemplation.

However we choose to answer these questions, the importance for the narrative is that Job is ravaged by God, abandoned by friends, almost hallucinating airy words—though he wants them preserved in lead and stone, and groping for a way to express a hopeful memory of divine presence.

FURTHER REFLECTIONS
"From my flesh I perceive":
Premodern Readings of 19:25–29

Is there an afterlife? Will and how will we see God? How does Jesus cast an enlivening shadow over the Hebrew Bible? These are the kinds of questions asked by premodern commentators when they turned to these problematic verses in Job. As a rule, they were more likely than modern or postmodern readers to interpret verses 25–29 in eschatological terms. For some the afterlife, as a form of future reward, is also an obvious inference of verses 25–26. For Christian interpreters, the verses most often represent an allegorical allusion to Jesus as redeemer, especially in the sense of an intermediary figure between God and innocent (or sinful) sufferers. "The interpretation of these verses as a doxological pronouncement of faith in the

---

47. Édouard Dhorme, *A Commentary on the Book of Job* (Nashville: Thomas Nelson, 1984), 248.

resurrection of the dead and in redemption through Christ was to become a dominant theme in medieval literary and artistic representations of Job."[48]

Numerous Jewish commentaries on Job also survive from the medieval period. One such Jewish commentator was Saadiah Gaon (882–942), who also provided one of the first translations of the Hebrew Bible into Arabic. His commentary on Job is a combination of close linguistic analysis and philosophical interpretation. Saadiah provides two reasons for the suffering of the righteous: (1) they are punished for sins they have committed, or (2) God is testing them, in which case there are two reasons for such trials: they allow the righteous to demonstrate their devotion to God and thereby earn reward in this life and the next, or righteous individuals are actually blessed by God through such suffering, providing inspiration and hope for others. Leaning toward an eschatological perspective, Saadiah believes that Job is undergoing a test that, if passed, will lead to future reward, and that Job will "see God" in the afterlife.

Like Saadiah, Christian exegetes as early as the patristic period saw the solution to the challenge presented by Job's innocent suffering in the notion of the afterlife and resurrection. Ambrose, Cassiodorus, and Gregory the Great held this position. The same understanding was upheld in the medieval period by Thomas Aquinas, who also interprets God's rebuke of Job's friends as grounded not in a rejection of belief in providence (which, with Job, they upheld), but because they rejected belief in the afterlife (cf. Schreiner, 73–77). However, other Christian thinkers who also believed in the afterlife were reluctant to place such insight into this doctrine in the mouth of Job. Wanting to accentuate Job's patience in the face of trial, these Christian readers felt that patience would be compromised if Job were aware of some future reward. This, for example, was the position of John Chrysostom.[49] Saadiah differs from Chrysostom only in seeing Job's suffering having an afterlife as it will be passed on to future generations so that the righteous of the future will be better equipped to suffer the arbitrary afflictions

---

48. Lawrence L. Besserman, *The Legend of Job in the Middle Ages* (Cambridge, MA: Harvard University Press, 1979), 29.
49. See Besserman, *Legend of Job*, 27–30; 160 n. 28.

with fortitude. Thus while some Christians envision a personal reward and afterlife, Saadiah suggests that Job's trials are ultimately for the community: Job's suffering has its afterlife in the life of the Jewish community.[50]

Thomas Aquinas also suggests this intriguing conclusion that Job's suffering has an afterlife, even an eschatological trajectory, not individually, but through and for the sake of the community. Aquinas writes: "Just as gold does not become true gold but its real nature is manifested to men as a result of the fire, so Job has been tested through adversity not so that his virtue might appear before God, but so that it might be manifested to men."[51]

Thomas Aquinas also illustrates the most common premodern Christian interpretation of verses 25–26: that the *go'el* or redeemer (*redemptor* in Latin Vulgate) is Christ:

> Therefore, he says expressly *For I know*, namely, through the certitude of faith. Now this hope is in the glory of future resurrection, concerning which he first assigns a reason when he says *my redeemer lives*. And here one should consider that man, who had been constituted immortal by God, incurred death through sin, according to the text of Romans 5:12: "Through one man sin entered into this world, and through sin, death," and from this sin, of course, the human race had to be redeemed through Christ, a redemption which Job foresaw through the spirit of faith.[52]

John Calvin, while using a Thomistic framework to explain the meaning of immortality as a key to understanding the meaning of Job's story, also uncovers a surprising form of mysticism in the fact of divine hiddenness. As Susan E. Schreiner writes, in the doctrine of the afterlife proclaimed explicitly in these verses, according to Calvin, "we are led to the heart of the tension between visibility and concealment that runs throughout Calvin's *Sermons on Job*. This tension finds expression in ... his use of the doctrine of immortality to set up ... a perceptual opposition between Job and his friends."[53]

---

50. Comments on Saadiah Goan based on Robert Eisen, *The Book of Job in Medieval Jewish Philosophy* (Oxford: Oxford University Press, 2004), 17–41.
51. Aquinas, 23:8–13, 302–3.
52. Aquinas, 19:21–25, 269.
53. Schreiner, *Where Shall Wisdom Be Found?* 122.

But Calvin's fine sense of the mystery or hiddenness of God is also awakened by the great depth of Job's faith and of his hope and is measured not in terms of what he can see, but rather in terms of what he cannot see. Calvin writes: "Here is a man who surmounts things present, he does not show then the faith and the hope that he has in God, because he can see and comprehend by his natural senses, but he passes beyond the world; as it is said, we ought to hope beyond hope, and hope is of things hidden."[54] Thus when Job says "in my flesh I shall see God," Calvin can write,

> when Job declares that he will have his attention fixed on God, and no other, indeed, although he may be entirely consumed (v. 26a); it is as if he said that the hope that he has in God he will not measure according to what he can see; but that when nothing appears, yet he will not cease to look at God.[55]

Possibly because of the content as well as the difficulty of this passage, it draws passionate interest and questions from Christians: Is there an afterlife? Will and how will we see God? How does Jesus cast an enlivening shadow over the Hebrew Bible? A short comment from Ephrem the Syrian (ca. 306–373) sums up these questions, as alive today as they were in premodern times: "'For I know that my Redeemer lives and that at last he will be revealed upon the earth.' Here the blessed Job predicts the future manifestation of Emmanuel in the flesh at the end of time."[56]

Job 19:28–29 *Job's Fire: Both Smoke and Flame*

Job once again shifts emotional tone from the height of his theophanic vision back to the labor of condemning his friends and assuring himself that he will be vindicated. While God is not mentioned in these verses, it is clear that Job draws some parallel between the friends' continual pursuit and the celestial Hunter himself. Once again the text is unclear, with verse 29b alone being rendered variously as "for wrath brings the punishment of the sword" (NRSV);

---

54. Calvin, Sermon 9, 123.
55. Ibid., 122.
56. Ephrem the Syrian, *Commentary on the Book of Job*, 19.25, ACCS, 105.

> In the melancholic . . . the spirits were somber and dim; they cast their shadows over the images of things and formed a kind of dark tide; in the maniac, on the contrary, the spirits seethed in a perpetual ferment; they were carried by an irregular movement, constantly repeated; a movement that eroded and consumed, and even without fever, sent out its heat. Between mania and melancholia, the affinity is evident: not the affinity of symptoms linked in experience, but the affinity—more powerful and so much more evident in the landscapes of imagination— that unites in the same fire both smoke and flame.
>
> Michel Foucault, *Madness and Civilization: A History of Insanity in the Age of Reason* (New York: Vantage Books, 1965), 132.

"the sword that sweeps away all iniquity" (NEB); "for yours are crimes deserving of the sword" (Gordis); "for these are sins worthy of the sword" (Habel). What is clear and new is that "just where one expects a despairing meditation on death, Job instead speaks boldly of judgment against his accusers. After chap. 19, Job does not again speak of death, either in longing or in despair."[57]

It is equally clear that in chapter 19 Job's suffering has brought him once again near to a psychological breaking point. His moods and words, his swings of emotion from exalted excitement to deep despair are, in their extremity, symptomatic of what today we would term bipolar or manic-depressive disorder. Michel Foucault gives a dynamic account of the manic-depressive sufferer that, while it does not capture the theological content of Job's suffering, exemplifies the psychological and spiritual content of that suffering as both "smoke and flame."

20:1–29

Zophar's Second Response to Job: Fate and the Wicked

Seemingly unable to contain himself, Zophar, the youngest, the most brash, the most dogmatic and assured in his theological

57. Newsom, "Book of Job," 479.

perspective, turns on Job as if he has been attacked: "Pay attention! My thoughts urge me to answer, because of the agitation within me. I hear a censure that insults me, and a spirit beyond my understanding answers me" (vv. 2–3, NRSV). Zophar takes what Job says as a personal humiliation and insult. His own emotional state seems out of control: he leaps at Job in a state of "agitation" (*hush*; "in the sense of hurry") yet at the same time with what he calls a "discerning spirit" (*ruach binah*; "spirit of understanding," Habel). A traditionalist with what he understands to be an impeccable story of balance between the fate of the wicked and that of the righteous, Zophar "sees" Job, yet never lets the facts of what he sees get in the way of his precious theory. Job has just suffered a full-frontal attack from God; Zophar reconfigures the attack to fit his theology so that he manages to rebuke Job for humiliating *him*. At the same time Job somehow hopes the friends will offer some solace or at least relent in their accusations. Job begs: "Have pity on me, have pity on me, O you my friends, for the hand of God has touched me!" (19:21). Pity, unfortunately, is not a characteristic Zophar is familiar with; his "discerning spirit" hears and sees only suffering—and that can mean only one thing. In a parody of sympathy, Zophar tells the barely human mass of flesh and skin and bone sitting on a dung-heap outside the city pleading for pity to "Pay attention!" (v. 2a)

Like a thoughtless child torturing a bug by directing the sun's rays through a magnifying glass until the bug slowly shrivels, crisps, and burns, Zophar only magnifies Job's own suffering. If Job has a fleeting moment of encouragement in his vision of the *go'el*, avenger, or redeemer (19:25–26), Zophar is determined to quash even this short, ecstatic breath of hope. After his initial rebuke, the rest of Zophar's speech is devoted to a single topic using multiple images: the certain and desolate pains of the wicked. After a short synopsis of the negative side of this doctrine of retribution (v. 5), Zophar describes the fate of the wicked, first using images of their invisibility in God's eyes, followed by images of food and eating in relation to the wicked in which the governing metaphor is evil as food or committing evil as eating (vv. 12–28): what the evil eat turns to poison, they know no quiet in their bellies, they fill their belly to the full.

20:4–11 *Those Who Saw Him Say, "Where Is He?"*

From the narrative core of his moral universe, Zophar sums up what he believes to be the true story of the fate of the wicked, and directs this directly at Job:

> Do you not know this from of old,
>   ever since mortals were placed on earth,
> that the exulting of the wicked is short,
>   and the joy of the godless is but for a moment?
>   (Job 20:4)

In the verses to follow, "the wicked" are spoken of in the third person, but it is clear that the object of Zophar's agitation is Job. Following Bildad (8:8) and Eliphaz (15:18–19), as the source of his teaching, Zophar appeals to tradition. And as light is the most primordial of created things ("God said, 'Let there be light'; and there was light" [Gen. 1:3]), to be counted among the "wicked" or the "godless" is to be deprived of light, in effect again to be unseen. Zophar also uses a series of images to highlight the notion that since the wicked are without light, since they are unseen, they are outside the created order. Like the poor and dispossessed, like the homeless and the wanderers, they are unseen. In this sense, to be unseen is to be unclean, cast out from social structures, lacking identity, denied even the dignity of a place to lay one's head. Even though the wicked "mount up high as the heavens" (v. 6a) they will "perish forever" and "those who have seen them will say, 'Where are they?'" (v. 7); they will "fly away like a dream" (v. 8a) and will be "chased away like a vision of the night" (v. 8b); the "eye that saw them will see them no more, nor will their place behold them any longer" (v. 9). Job has repeatedly lamented the all-seeing eye of God that will give him no rest, but at the same time has warned his friends that they too will return to dust and be seen no more. As Norman C. Habel writes, "Perhaps Zophar's sharpest jibe is found in his allusion to the recurring surveillance motif of Job. The 'Seeing Eye' (ʿēn rōʾī, 7:8) of God which 'spied' (šwr) on Job is transformed into 'the seeing ones' (v. 7b) who say 'Where is he?' and 'the Eye' which 'spies' on the wicked

(v. 9a). Zophar seems to imply that Job, as one of the wicked, is paranoid about the 'seeing ones' and the 'eye' of God watching for his sins (cf. 7:8, 19–20; 10:4–7, 13–14; 13:37)."[58]

20:12–29 *Sweet Food Made Bitter*

In these verses Zophar centers on images of eating and food to highlight the fate of the wicked. Food and eating in companionship ought not only to be a pleasure, they are life sustaining. But for the wicked, according to Zophar, food becomes a poison, causing signs and symptoms that correspond to a slow death. To make his point, Zophar first relates a story of misery related to food and eating: wickedness itself becomes "sweet in [the wicked's] mouth" and loathing to let it go (v. 13) they begin to "hide it under their tongues" (v. 12); yet all the while any food they eat "is turned in their stomachs"

> The world was void,
>
> . . . .
>
> A lump of death—a chaos of hard clay.
> The rivers, lakes and ocean all stood still,
> And nothing stirr'd within their silent depths;
> Ships sailorless lay rotting on the sea,
> And their masts fell down piecemeal: as they dropp'd
> They slept on the abyss without a surge—
> The waves were dead; the tides were in their grave,
> The moon, their mistress, had expir'd before;
> The winds were wither'd in the stagnant air,
> And the clouds perish'd;
> Darkness had no need
> Of aid from them—She was the Universe.

George Gordon, Lord Byron, "Darkness," in *The Last Man*, Mary Shelley, vol. 1 (London: 1826), lines 29, 72-82, http://www.rc.umd.edu/editions/mws/lastman/bydark.htm.

and becomes like "the venom of asps within them" (v. 14); they swallow riches "then vomit them up again" (v. 15a), as "El forces it up [*yarash*, Good; AV: "vomits"] from their stomachs" (v. 15b, Habel). They "suckle [*yanaq*] the poison of asps" (v. 16a, Good) and the "tongue of a viper will kill them" (v. 16b); the wicked will "never admire the streams of honey and milk" (v. 17, Habel); the wicked will receive no enjoyment from their "toil," indeed, again reversing the images of food and eating, they "will not swallow it down" (v.

---

58. Habel, *Job*, 316–17.

18). Though he is not done with his story of misery and food, at this point Zophar makes it clear that he is not as interested in the demise of the wicked as he is in the moral principles that they abuse. Thus in a lightly veiled accusation against Job, Zophar says of the wicked:

> For they have crushed and abandoned the poor,
>   they have seized a house they did not build.
> They knew no quiet in their bellies;
>   in their greed they let nothing escape.
>
> (vv. 19–20)

Having introduced what he considers to be an inescapable moral principle, Zophar now begins to associate food and eating with material wealth—the righteous enjoy and keep the wealth of their toil; the wicked cannot enjoy and in fact lose the riches once sought, once so sweet: the wicked "know no quiet in their bellies, in their greed they cannot escape" (v. 20); there is "nothing left after they have eaten . . . their prosperity will not endure" (v. 21); "In full sufficiency they will be in distress" (v. 22). In a move not unfamiliar in contemporary religion, Zophar links material wealth to moral rectitude: do the righteous, those for whom wisdom has brought not only understanding but the joy of ownership, "crush and abandon the poor"? In chapter 22 Eliphaz will, based on Job's words and Job's predicament, accuse Job directly of a particular sin; here in chapter 20 Zophar implies that Job has done something as radically immoral as to "crush and abandon the poor."

Job's condition, his loss, his grief, his need to lament are all a result of a wager between God and the *satan* regarding the issue of disinterested piety. As the reader knows, Job's only sin is in the eyes of his friends. Yet the relentless attack on Job's character and moral wisdom begins to wear down even the reader. One begins to wonder. Zophar calls down cosmic forces that readers may have experienced themselves: "To fill their belly to the full God will send his fierce anger into them, and rain it upon them as their food" (v. 23); the wicked are subject to "utter darkness" and "a fire fanned by no one will devour them" (v. 26); a flood will wash away their household (v. 28a); "the heavens will reveal their iniquity" (v. 27a). One begins to wonder; do the heavens not reveal our iniquity as well? What is happening here? Is the poet, through Zophar, intending that these metaphors that describe the fate of the wicked also mirror the experience and fate of the reader?

> They will flee from an iron weapon;
>> a bronze arrow will strike them through.
> It is drawn forth and comes out of their body,
>> and the glittering point comes out of their gall;
> terrors come upon them.
>
> (vv. 24–25)

FURTHER REFLECTIONS
The Moral Order Reordered

Is there some truth to what the friends say? Are there links between the way we live in moral context and the blessings (or lack of them) that mark our lives? Knowing as we do the details of Job's predicament, as readers we identify with Job. Nonetheless, the arguments begin to mount up and the evidence for a retributive perspective on justice begins to accumulate. And regardless of its distastefulness, retributive justice is impossible to disprove. Though we identify with Job, the cumulative pressure on Job of three friends impresses upon us at least the *possibility* that there may be something of truth in what they say, that suffering does in fact indicate sin. With their repeated arguments of the dark fate of the wicked, the friends are admittedly extremely poor comforters. But does that mean they are also poor theologians?

Recent commentators on Job have begun to call into question the outright dismissal of the doctrine of retributive justice as expressed by Job's friends. Carol Newsom writes, "For myself, I do not know whether I believe the story told by the friends about the fate of the wicked is true. I do, however, think that it is one of the most complex, difficult, and provocative claims made in the book,"[59] and she adds that in her experience the claim has yet to be adequately refuted.

---

59. Newsom, *Job*, 118.

As a literary critic as well as a theologian, Newsom notes that these poems on the fate of the wicked have several common rhetorical features: their tight focus, the nature of the warrants that introduce them, the way that they represent tradition in the form of ancestral knowledge, as Zophar says, "from of old" (20:4), and the nature of the rhetoric by which they are developed. The poems are intensely imagistic and create a dramatic tableaux of the wicked meeting a violent and desolate end. Rhetoricians commonly observe that topics may be argued or developed in two ways: by arguments or by tropes. Job includes both.

Though much of Joban biblical poetry is highly imagistic, much can be found that proceeds and develops its points by argument. However, the arguments are only from Job's side; in the speeches of the friends no arguments appear, only descriptive images and metaphors. Moreover, although the imagery of each poem has a distinctive profile, all of the images in the poems are repetitive variations on a single figure, the insubstantiality of the wicked.

It would be a mistake to equate the truth claims regarding the righteous and the wicked as claims similar to those in, say, physics. But the surface rhetoric of the friends' claims sometimes appears to be similar kinds of truth claims. "Yet," as Newsom wryly notes, "if such statements were intended as universal, exceptionless claims, only a deluded fool could believe them, and whatever the friends may be, they are not fools."[60] Instead, to understand the truth claims of the poems it is necessary to consider their distinctive rhetoric.

Tropes (i.e., images and metaphors, pictures and vignettes) also carry the rhetorical power of these poems. From the friends' side, the fate of the wicked is assumed, and the distinctive quality of a particular fate is evoked in image and metaphor rather than argument. Along with the friends, Job too attempts to portray the nature of the moral order in which they find themselves through distinctive images, but Job also adds rational arguments. The poems that deal with the fate of the wicked are not intended as empirical description but as the evocation in poetic form of the life of the world. In other words, Job and the friends are not out to prove the veracity or even the legitimacy of the doctrine of retribution; they are, rather,

---

60. Ibid., 119.

in poetic form attempting to depict their place in the organic life of the moral order of the world as they see or believe it to be.

Of infinitely more help than veracity or legitimacy (both components of power and punishment) are the images and how they are utilized. In chapter 18, for instance, Bildad uses the image of extinguished light to describe the wicked: the statement could be taken literally as light going out, but also with its traditional metaphorical resonances as "life," "vitality," "presence," and so forth also being extinguished. Later, using an array of traps, Bildad forms a cluster of images around arrested movement and death. Common among all the friends is the image of predators. Here in chapter 20, Zophar makes this metaphor a centerpiece of his own imagery wherein the wicked are both consumers of bitter fruit and are themselves consumed: the wicked are trapped, consumer and consumed.

The stories of the friends concerning the moral order are "iconic narratives": they encode fundamental commitments, social roles, and profiles of virtue so that "these narratives ring true because they define the horizon of meaningful action within an already given social and moral world."[61]

This is all very well, except that the friends fail to understand that these "iconic narratives" change and transform and that Job is a prime example of that transformation. Instead the friends continue to hand Job images of cultural mechanisms that have in the past served to regulate social, economic, and spiritual structures with almost mechanical ferocity. Even so, it is possible to give at least a partially sympathetic reading of the friends who at least give voice to a moral order that has been of value in the past.

But Job is caught up in a new ethical equation that transcends even what the friends have previously experienced, a redistribution of power and justice that renders the traditional moral code obsolete. In this new cosmic setting, with this perhaps new God, the link between innocence and nonsuffering is severed. Rhetorically, this cannot be argued "right" or "wrong"; it can only be expressed poetically in image and likeness.[62]

---

61. Ibid., 123.
62. See Newsom, *Job*, 115–25, on relation between the moral imagination and Job's battle with the doctrine of retribution.

In a moral world governed by generations of faith and witness to the Deuteronomic Code, the relation between thoughts, behavior, and action and their consequences had been clear. The code was also serviceable in reverse, so that even the unknowable thoughts or hidden actions of another were knowable and open through outward signs. We can ask ourselves how and to what degree we, the readers of Job, share something of this perspective of connection between ethics and reward or punishment. It is easy to dismiss Job's friends, but they are in fact the "religious" of their day, and though they show little sympathy, they are anything but stupid. How many times today do we walk by a disheveled, disoriented, and destitute person and entertain the fleeting thought that he or she "deserves" it? What are your own moral prejudices in the relation between the blessed and the wicked . . . and those who dwell somewhere in between?

For Job's part, he has yet much to endure, but he is also headed toward the wonder, the astonishment, the surprise of his life.

21:1–34
Job's Second Response to Zophar: Job at Prayer

In a direct attack on his friends' uncaring theodicy, Job concludes the second dialogue of speeches by turning from a focus on his own suffering and his legal complaint against God to a refutation of the friends' assertion of just retribution for the wicked. To this point Job has emphasized his distrust in this doctrine by focusing on the suffering of the righteous, his own condition. Now Job focuses on another implication of the doctrine, arguing that in fact the wicked are not punished but "live on, reach old age, and grow mighty in power. Their children are established in their presence" (vv. 7–8a). Eliphaz (15:17–35), Bildad (18:5–21), and Zophar (20:6–29) each in their turn have focused on the fate of the wicked as it stands within the moral order of the universe, given the doctrine of just retribution. Job, urging the friends to listen (v. 2), also appeals to their own perceptual acuity: "*Look* at me, and be appalled" (v. 5a). But once again Job speaks to what we know to be a prejudiced audience.

Job begins (v. 2) and ends (v. 34) this speech by attacking the friends' misguided efforts to offer him "consolation" or "comfort" (the same root, *naham*, occurs in both places). They have failed him not only because their theology is wrong, but because they will not (or dare not) listen to or look at the man sitting before them. In between Job raises a series of questions that reference, then challenge, the friends' previous, precious assertions.

21:1–6 *"Shuddering seizes my flesh"*

Previously we asked whether the friends' assertions concerning the fate of the wicked might be at least partially correct: perhaps there is some truth to the idea of a connection between evil and just punishment. In this speech Job dedicates himself not to demolishing a connection between blessing and justice, as he has in the past, but to reversing the connection espoused by his friends—that punishment is the result of a sinful life—with the assertion that the evil are not punished but in fact prosper. In doing this, as we have seen, Job rejects the vast majority of Old Testament wisdom.

In moving toward his new assertion, Job experiences a kind of existential dread at the terrifying injustices he sees and describes: "Look at me, and be appalled" (*shamma*; also "desolated, horrified"; v. 5a). "When I think of it [that the wicked live on in old age, wealth, and power] I am dismayed [*bahal*; "disturbed, terrified"], and shuddering seizes my flesh" (v. 6). As usual God is not mentioned, but Job is "appalled" and horrified both at the bumbling "consolation" of his friends and at the seemingly random injustice that he sees and experiences as the divinely ordained moral order. It makes his flesh creep.

> There is silent and long-suffering sorrow to be met.... It withdraws into itself and is still. But there is a grief that breaks out, and from that minute it bursts into tears and finds vent in wailing. ... But it is no lighter a grief than the silent. Lamentations comfort only by lacerating the heart still more. Such grief does not desire consolation. It feeds on the sense of its hopelessness. Lamentations spring only from the constant craving to re-open the wound.
>
> Fyodor Dostoevsky, *The Brothers Karamazov*, trans. Constance Garnett (New York: Barnes & Noble Classics, 2004), 53.

The friends' diatribes have momentarily silenced Job's sorrow and brought it to the surface as anger. As Dostoevsky points out, there is a need both for silence and for lamentation. The friends give Job ample need for both. God will give time for both as well, and as God does it is good to note that both silence and anger can be prayer. Job prays *to* God and *for* God in silence and in lament. Scholars have generally taken the question at verse 4, "Is my complaint for *adam* ["people"; NRSV "mortals"]?" to be a rhetorical question that assumes a negative answer: "No, it is not for mortals, but for God." But there is also a sense in which Job calls out in prayer *for* mortals as well *to* God even as he urges his friends to "be appalled," and a shudder takes hold of Job's flesh (v. 6).

21:7–34 *Job's Plight as Prayer*

The friends have sought to comfort Job and, failing that, to convince him—on the basis of tradition, piety, and even visions—that he suffers for a reason. The friends have begun to describe the behavior of the wicked in ways that parallel Job's predicament, slowly implicating him with sin. By the time of Zophar's speech in chapter 20, his description of the wicked is very much a description of Job. Explicit sins Job is supposed to have participated in are named. It is an incomprehensible move—nothing in the text would implicate Job in iniquity in the way his friends begin to describe—but the accusations continue, and the assertions of particular wickedness become more and more outrageous.

Imagine friends coming to your "tent" to grieve, say, the loss of a spouse, children, or a job. They do look at you and hear you to a degree, because after a time of silence they go through a process in which they, first, do describe exactly how you are feeling. But a change begins to take place: an anxiety develops within them as they begin to hear from you what they would expect to hear only from one who has sinned. You feel as though you have sucked "the poison of asps," as if "the tongue of a viper" is killing you, you know "no quiet" in your belly, as if "a bronze arrow" has pierced you and come out your back, with its "glittering point" dripping gore and gall and blood, as though "terrors" have come upon you and what is left in your tent has been "consumed" (cf. 20:16, 20, 24–25, 26). This *is* how you feel. But a poison works within the words themselves. The friends begin to declare impossible impieties, yet you, like Job, refuse to share their connections:

> Look at me, and be appalled,
>> and lay your hand upon your mouth.
> When I think of it I am dismayed,
>> and shuddering seizes my flesh
>
> $$(21:5–6)$$

Job knows the bitter reality of his suffering and though a shuddering seizes his flesh, he stands his ground, speaking once again out of the bitterness and suffering that now define him, but also out of truth and reality. Job has descended into a kind of hell, but this hell transforms; in heaven or in hell, truth and reality given to God— absent or present—are always prayer.

FURTHER REFLECTIONS
Job's Complaint as Prayer

Some commentators claim that Job's "complaint" (*siyah*) of verse 4 is "the legal complaint he had lodged against God."[63] But the nature and complexity of Job's complaint goes much deeper; it is a component of his ongoing communication with YHWH, a component of his ongoing prayer of lament and grief. Job asks in verse 4, "Is my complaint for *adam*?" Many of the Psalms witness to the idea that complaints are prayer. Some people may feel uncomfortable with the idea that complaint of Job's intensity is prayerful, but a closer look at the meaning and implications of the word *complaint* will show that it is indeed a way of prayer, finding precedence not only elsewhere in Job, but throughout the Old Testament.

In Old Testament usage, *siyah* does have the connotation of "complaint," but usually of a complaint in the context of prayer

---

63. Habel, *Job*, 326.

addressed to God. Usages of *siyah* in the Hebrew Bible include connotations of meditation, musing, prayer, contemplation, talking, and
communication: all forms of prayer. Uses of the word outside Job
in the Old Testament help put Job's use of the word in a meditative, prayerful perspective. At the beginning of 1 Samuel, Hannah,
childless, presents herself before the Lord, as she has done yearly. Eli
the priest, standing nearby in the temple of the Lord, hears her. "She
was deeply distressed and prayed to the LORD, and wept bitterly" (1
Sam. 1:10). "Hannah was praying silently; only her lips moved, but
her voice was not heard," and Eli mistakenly assumes she is drunk.
Accused of drunkenness, Hannah says, "Do not regard your servant
as a worthless woman, for I have been speaking out of my great anxiety [*siyah*] and vexation all this time" (v. 16). Eli, corrected, says simply, "Go in peace; the God of Israel grant the petition you have made
to him" (v. 17). Like Job, Hannah prays while she is "deeply distressed"
and weeping "bitterly"; she prays out of her distress and she prays
about her distress. Her prayer comes from deep vexation and, like
Job, she does not hide but rather boldly prays her great complaint.

The Psalms are especially rich in explicit complaint as prayer.
Psalm 55 begins in prayer: "Give ear to my prayer, O God; do not
hide yourself from my supplication" (v. 1). It is clear that the prayer is
from one distraught and confused: "Attend to me, and answer me; I
am troubled in my complaint [*siyah*]" (v. 2). Psalm 64 likewise comes
right to the point, incorporating complaint as prayer in the first
verse: "Hear my voice, O God, in my complaint [*siyah*]; preserve my
life from the dread enemy." The AV is perhaps the clearest English
translation linking prayer to complaint, as in the superscription of
Psalm 102: "A prayer of the afflicted, when he is overwhelmed, and
poureth out his complaint [*siyah*] before the LORD." Elsewhere the
psalmist is not afraid to meditate on complaint: "May my meditation [*siyah*] be pleasing to him, for I rejoice in the LORD" (104:34), and
"With my voice I cry to the LORD; with my voice I make supplication
to the LORD. I pour out my complaint [*siyah*] before him; I tell my trouble before him" (142:1–2).

From these examples it is clear that Job is in good company as
he pours out his complaint as prayer before the Lord. He has prayed
his complaint before the example from Job 21:4 (cf. 9:27; 10:1), and
he will do so again (cf. 23:2). One of the great lessons of Job is that

throughout his innocent suffering, the uncaring, windy comfort of his friends, and the seeming absence of God, Job continues to communicate through prayer to his God. It is not comfortable, it is agitated, and it is complaint, but it is persistent prayer.

How the Wicked Prosper

Because of his friends' attacks and God's apparent abandonment, Job is appalled, dismayed, agitated, and horrified, yet he stands his ground. As he ends this second cycle of speeches he barely mentions his own righteous suffering, turning instead to confute his friends' position on the prospering of the wicked. Job's words are also an indictment of God and a prayerful complaint, but Job builds a case diametrically opposite that of his friends. He does this by first listing a long series of counterexamples to the friends' general position, then raising a series of issues that are direct quotes or paraphrases of the friends' previous assertions about the wicked, then challenging those assertions with concrete examples.[64] Robert Gordis writes, "As against the comfortable doctrine that the wicked are ultimately destroyed, Job paints a more realistic picture of the malefactors enjoying happiness and security during their lifetimes and dying quickly without pain."[65] The most helpful way to follow Job's speech as "a more realistic picture of the malefactors" is to note his counterexamples that illustrate the prosperity of the wicked and then to address the more specific issues raised by the friends as Job insists that some who are wicked encounter no calamity at all. Some of Job's comments are sarcastic, some ironic, some direct; all are intended to demolish the friends' comfortable positions.

21:7–16 Job's General Observations on the Prosperity of the Wicked

Job is very clear about his claim about the prosperity of the wicked. The wicked, he says, reach old age and grow in power (v. 7, *hayil*, meaning "physical health" as well as "material wealth" or "economic

---

64. Robert Gordis was among the first to point out this structure, and most commentators since have followed him. Cf. Gordis, *Job*, 223–26; Gordis, *Book of God and Man*, 90–92; and Balentine, *Job*, 322–37.
65. Gordis, *Book of God and Man*, 90.

prosperity"); their children flourish (v. 8) and lead idyllic lives, play with the lambs, dance, sing, rejoice (vv. 11–12); the houses of the wicked are safe from fear (v. 9); they live in "prosperity" (*tob*; "good, happiness, pleasantry, well-being") and "in peace [*shalom*] they go down to Sheol" (v. 13); they are secure in their own self-sufficiency; they say to God, "Leave us alone! We do not desire to know your ways"; they ask why "serve Shaddai," what is the "profit" in praying to the Almighty? (vv. 13–16).

21:17–34 Job's More Direct Response:
Do the Wicked Suffer Calamity?

Using a slightly different perspective, Job also responds to the question of whether the wicked suffer calamity. Bildad had claimed that the light of the wicked grows dark and that their lamp fails (18:5–6). Job asks ironically how often this really happens. Zophar predicts the end of the wicked in gruesome detail and claims that the allotted portion (*heleq*) of the wicked is calamity (*'ed*, 20:20–29). Job ridicules these ideas. He claims instead that the light of the wicked does not fail and that the allotted destinies espoused by the friends are pure fabrication in light of human experience and historical reality.[66] Moreover the "anger" (*'ap*) of God is not visited on the wicked, there is no alleged "day of anger" as Zophar had described (21:17c); indeed it is Job, not the wicked, who has become straw and chaff blowing in the wind of divine anger (v. 18).

Job responds to another assertion of the friends that once again lacks forgiveness, saying that they declare, "The sinner is being saved for the day of calamity; on the day of wrath, he will be led to his doom"

> At bottom, to dismiss sin as negative is to demonstrate a failure of imagination.
> As the writer Garret Keizer asserts in *Help: The Original Human Dilemma*: "Everyone believes in sin, the people who charge their peers with political incorrectness and the people who regard political correctness as the bogey of a little mind." He adds, "What everyone does not believe in, as nearly as I can tell, is forgiveness."
>
> Kathleen Norris, *Acedia & Me: A Marriage, Monks, and A Writer's Life* (New York: Riverhead Books, 2008), 117.

66. Cf. Habel, *Job*, 328.

(v. 30, Gordis). But, says Job, if this is true it is not just, especially in this life: the sinner ought to be denounced to his face; God has not established any authority on earth powerful enough to repay such an evildoer *for what he has done.* As a result evildoers are given a dignified burial even though they have lived as they pleased. With great pomp they are "carried to the grave," even "a watch is kept over their tomb" (v. 32), thus continuing the honor into death and the memory into life. Zophar has said that for those who do evil, "wickedness is sweet in their mouth" (20:12a). In a final thrust of sarcastic irony toward those wicked untouched by fate, Job alludes to Zophar's claim. In reality, says Job, even in the midst of a lavish burial, there is more indignity to the righteous in the out-and-out flourishing of the wicked. Even in death, as the wicked are buried, "The clods of the valley are sweet to them; everyone will follow after" (v. 33).

After this prolonged prayer of complaint that also outlines the prosperity of the immoral, Job saves a final verse to let his friends know what he thinks about their advice and comfort to date:

> How then will you comfort [*naham*] me with empty
>   nothings [*havel*]?
> There is nothing left of your answers but falsehood
>   [*maal*].
>
> (v. 34)

With seven occurrences, the theology of comfort, *naham*, has a fascinating trajectory within the book of Job. It first appears in 2:11, where its usage is straightforward and honest: Job's friends "meet together to go and console and comfort [*nacham*] him." By chapter 7 the friend's "comfort [*nacham*]" is only so in an ironic sense, in that the "comfort" serves rather to "scare me with dreams and terrify me with visions" (7:14). By chapter 16 Job refers to his friends as "miserable comforters (*nacham*)" (v. 2) and comments that if what he has heard so far is to be the tone of his friends' comfort, he would rather they were silent. "Comfort" occurs three more times in the book, twice in the final chapter. A certain nuance develops over these last three uses but never reaches the level of how we would normally think of comfort, as some form of consolation.

"Empty nothings" (*havel*) from the NRSV has the connotation of mere "vapor" or "breath," and in the figurative sense, "vanity." Job uses the word as a key term in an earlier meditation on death and, significantly, in the context of begging his friends to leave him alone, to cease their efforts at "comforting": "I loathe my life; I would not live forever. Let me alone, for my days are a breath [*havel*]" (7:16; cf. 9:29). But the usage of *havel* that most captures how Job is characterizing the friends comes from the mouth of Qoheleth: it is the word translated "vanity," with no fewer than thirty occurrences in Ecclesiastes. One verse illustrates this usage and is illuminating as we recall that the same word is used by Job to characterize his friends' advice: "Vanity [*havel*] of vanities [*havel*], says the Teacher, vanity [*havel*] of vanities [*havel*]! All is vanity [*havel*]" (Eccl. 1:2). The friends' "comfort" is *havel*: "vanity," a "vapour," a mere "breath," "empty nothings."

Worse perhaps than vanities and empty nothings, the friends utter "falsehood" and "lies" (*maal*). This word also has connotations of a treacherous or unfaithful act against God, hence impiety. Thus Job accuses the friends of not only lying to him, but worse, of unfaithfulness to God. Robert Gordis notes that

> the connotations of the root *maal* are noteworthy. It is a priestly term occurring in the Priestly Code, . . . in the meaning of "violation of a sacred object" and, by extension, treachery . . . by Israel against God (Deut. 32:51; Ezra 10:2, etc.). Here, Job declares the friends' answers to be an act of faithlessness against the truth and by that a token against God.[67]

The words of Job in verse 34 offer a fitting closure to his speech and to the second cycle of dialogues. The friends are wretched comforters who offer lies rather than concern for Job's struggle. They prefer the neat packaging of the doctrine of retribution, a doctrine that frees them from guilt and convinces them of their own righteousness and distance from the paths of the wicked. But Job not only condemns them for their bumbling efforts at consolation and their untenable theology, he hints that their intransigent positions

---

67. Gordis, *Job*, 236.

represent an unfaithful orientation toward God. We begin to sense that the friends are growing as distant and merciless and unjust and cruel toward Job as we perceive God to have been toward Job from the beginning. They lack the power of God to initiate Job's suffering (as the *satan* also lacked the power). But short of that lack, we can picture the friends' self-perception as comfortably ensconced within the circle of the "heavenly beings" (1:6; 2:1), judging Job guilty, reporting to the same God, and congratulating themselves for the cleverness by which they are able to see Job's suffering for what it really is: a sign of sin and a good bet that Job will, in the end, curse God!

22:1–27:23

Third Poetic Dialogue Cycle

22:1–30
Eliphaz's Third Response to Job:
"There is no end to your iniquities"

The third cycle is one of the most subtle pieces of writing in the book of Job, while its structure, intentionally confused and confusing on the surface, remains a vivid transition piece between the well-worn arguments of the friends and the new arguments, wisdom, and shocking appearance of God that are to come.

Most commentators concentrate on the repetition and shopworn character of the ideas and arguments of this third cycle in Job. But in fact this cycle introduces new arguments, suggests deeper insight into ideas introduced in previous chapters, and wraps the whole in new poetic imagery that is not only fresh in itself but also adds resonance and character to earlier images in Job. Many of these new images refer back to other books of Scripture as well, especially— since Job is at its core Wisdom literature and therefore focused on creation and the Creator—to the creation stories in Genesis.

Among the new arguments or fresh perspectives in this third cycle are accusations by Eliphaz of very specific sins committed by Job; Job himself speaking more confidently and with a certain hope based, ironically, on the very qualities of his character that attracted attention in the first place, his integrity and righteousness; Job remaining a desperate and abused man yet showing hints of an evolving understanding of the meaning of an absent God; Job begin-ning to consider divine omnipotence in new ways, not the least of which is this very absence of God, now expressed as a divine darkness or divine emptiness that itself represents potential paths to discernment; Job, who had tried to separate himself from others who suffer (as a way of manifesting his righteousness), now beginning to identify himself with the innocent sufferers of the world; the idea introduced by Eliphaz of the doctrine of "horizontal responsibility" whereby Job's repentance will not only free Job from the consequences of sin (vertical responsibility) but will also have positive effect in his community (horizontal responsibility); and finally, an argument by both Job and the friends that "chaos" is also a characteristic of the wicked, thus foreshadowing some of the content and intentions of the divine speech from the whirlwind.

Though the third cycle introduces new arguments and imagery and moves the narrative forward, the speeches seem to be disintegrating and the friends and Job, more than ever, are speaking at cross-purposes. The arrangement of the text as we have it today contains only an extremely short speech by Bildad (25:1–6), an unusually long speech by Job (chaps. 26–27), and no comment by Zophar at all. Some "try to restore the symmetry of the dialogues, hence the order of the drama by rearranging the text to what is assumed to be its original form. Bildad's speech may be lengthened by subtracting 26:5–14 from Job's words and adding them to Bildad's. Zophar's speech may be reconstructed from parts of Job's speech in 27:13–24."[1] Balentine suggests that a wiser course is to allow the text to remain as it is and in doing so to serve as an interpretive guide.[2]

The textual integrity of the third set of dialogues is also questionable. Good, for example, essentially throws up his hands when he writes, "Chapter 24 is complex in its images, ambiguous in its syntax, full of verbs with unspecified subjects and of pronouns with uncertain antecedents and referents."[3]

Gracefully and with humor, Habel suggests that like the friends in the older Babylonian Theodicy we can at least agree that "the gods give perverse speech to the human race."[4]

---

1. Samuel E. Balentine, *Job*, Smyth & Helwys Bible Commentary (Macon, GA: Smyth & Helwys, 2006), 339.
2. Ibid.
3. Edwin M. Good, *In Turns of Tempest: A Reading of Job with a Translation* (Stanford, CA: Stanford University Press, 1990), 279.
4. Norman C. Habel, *The Book of Job: A Commentary*, Old Testament Library (Philadelphia: Westminster, 1985), 355.

> Virgil is stunned: "Who has forbidden me the halls of sorrow?" . . . But the City of Dis [the lower rungs of Dante's hell] is not a prison to keep the most sinful souls in; it is a fortress built to keep God out.
>
> Hubert Dreyfus and Sean Dorance Kelly, *All Things Shining: Reading the Western Classics to Find Meaning in a Secular Age* (New York: Free Press, 2011), 125.

In the third cycle of dialogue in the book of Job, the gods may indeed be giving "perverse speech to the human race," but in the hands of the poet of the book it is a perversity that is chilling in its bright, chaotic audacity and acuity.

Guilty! And What Job Ought to Do about It

Samuel Terrien has written that as the dialogues limp to an end, the friends *lose* and Job *gains* focus. The friends become more and more impatient, disconcerted, and angry. Job becomes more and more determined, stable, and resolute.[5] This may be true, but it is not the case in chapter 22, where Eliphaz, though his logic and perceptions are fundamentally flawed, sarcastic, and self-righteous, focuses his indignity on Job with laser sharpness intended to sear Job's heart and move him to contrition and repentance. This third speech of Eliphaz is made up of three sections. In the first (22:1–11) Eliphaz charges Job with specific sins based on his moral failures. Verses 1–5 ask rhetorical questions concerning the relationship between humanity and God, verse 5 claiming that, with no evidence other than Job's current suffering, "there is no end to [Job's] iniquities." He gives the particulars of Job's sins in verses 6–9 and the consequences he can expect as a result of those sins in verses 10–11. In the second section (vv. 12–20) Eliphaz makes a case for Job's sin and guilt based on his theological failures (siding with the wicked) and on a transcendent God who in his mercy fills the houses of the righteous and the innocent with good things. The third and final section (vv. 21–30) is a summons for Job to repent, in effect to agree with the friends' theological perception of the reasons for Job's suffering.

---

5. Samuel Terrien, "The Book of Job," *Interpreter's Bible*, ed. G. A. Buttrick (New York: Abingdon, 1954), 3:1072.

FURTHER REFLECTIONS
Original Sin

Though original sin is not named in the book of Job, the tradition of Joban interpretation has linked Job's innocent suffering to the doctrine of original sin.

There are two primary reasons that the church, in the past, has chosen to deny innocent suffering, as Job's friends do in their argument with Job. One reason is theological: the doctrine of original sin maintains what some have called the "divine omnies"; that is, that God is omnibenevolent (all good), omnipotent (all powerful), omniscient (all knowing), and omnipresent (all present). Thus the *denial* of innocent suffering has the theological advantage of *affirming* the innocence and omnipotent perfection of God; or put another way, the guilt rests not with this God of perfection but with imperfect humanity and creation. If God were to allow innocent suffering, God would be complicit in either the creation or continued existence of evil in the world.

A second, psychological advantage to denying innocent suffering satisfies an emotional need: denying innocent suffering allows us, at least, to address feelings of *guilt* (that is, given original sin, the emphasis is on the inevitability of sin; human evil cannot be avoided), whereas accepting innocent suffering leads to a general sense of *helplessness* (that is, in accepting innocent suffering the emphasis shifts to the inevitability of suffering; we remain innocent, helpless victims of suffering). The inevitability of sin that is a result of denying innocent suffering is at least, though burdened with feelings of guilt, something we can attempt to address, we are not helpless: we can pray, ask forgiveness, confess, seek reparation, reconciliation, redemption, and so forth. The friends are a perfect example of those who deny innocent suffering, who focus on sin and guilt but at the same time deny that Job is helpless and in varying ways insist that he reject his helplessness and "work" to return to a "right relation" with God and with Job's community. Job, of course, accepts innocent suffering: he knows that he is innocent. Job's emphasis is thus naturally shaded toward his suffering and given his innocence, he is focused on his helpless inability to understand suffering and his inability to "fix" or redeem his suffering while at the same time remaining true to himself and to the justice he demands. Thus, Job's friends attempt to accuse Job and get him to accept his guilt; Job himself does not accept the guilt but lives in a deteriorating state of helplessness.

In the Christian tradition, the development of a doctrine of original sin allows us to deny innocent suffering. The result has been a general substitution of helplessness with guilt. The results are visible even today: we live (whether we like to admit it or not) in a culture of guilt that has constructed a radical denial of helplessness. Many struggle to rid themselves of guilt, but to do so is a difficult journey. The acceptance of helplessness is a form of mindfulness, of spiritual dispassion or letting go, a practice of deep humility. These are also difficult journeys, but closer to the spiritual journey Job finds himself walking.

In the prologue chapters to the book of Job, there is no question that Job is innocent: even God declares this in no uncertain terms (1:8; 2:3). The prologue also sets a scene in which Job as a man of integrity suffers mercilessly at the hands of God in seemingly arbitrary ways. Thus from the beginning we have to affirm both Job's innocence and his suffering. In this sense, though the book of Job does not deal directly with the doctrine of original sin, it affirms innocent suffering as a counterexample to most of the rest of Scripture as well as much of Christian theology.

A modern strategy to address the issue of suffering and its relationship to innocence and guilt is based on confidence in human reason and its ability to construct a reasonable defense of God's goodness and power even in the face of evil: this has come to be known as a *theodicy*. (See "Further Reflections: Theodicy." For a brief description of modern and postmodern approaches to the fluidity of divine attributes making the project of theodicy irrelevant, see William Placher's commentary on Mark from this series.[6] As we will see, the theme of divine transformation is nowhere better illustrated than in the book of Job.)

6. William C. Placher, *Mark*, Belief (Louisville, KY: Westminster John Knox, 2010), 11–12. Cf. also Ronald Goetz, "The Suffering of God: The Rise of a New Orthodoxy," *The Christian Century* 103, no. 13 (April 16, 1986): 385–89.

To this point Job and his friends have discussed the righteous and the wicked in relatively general terms. As the dialogue has proceeded, accusations of Job's sinfulness have progressed from explicit implications to implicit irony and sarcasm pointed ever more clearly at Job's wickedness and sinfulness. Yet no one has, to this point, directly and unambiguously accused another of a particular sin. Now in chapter 22 implication moves to direct accusation: not only does Eliphaz accuse Job of enormous crimes and depravity beyond bounds (v. 5), Eliphaz proceeds to enumerate Job's sins, both moral and theological, in explicit, unambiguous, specific terms. It is as if Eliphaz is accusing Job of not only guilt, but, in order to enumerate specific sins, declaring him guilty of "original sin."

At this point we need to remind ourselves that neither Job nor any of the Hebrew Bible is burdened with the traditional Christian notion of original sin. Working from the assumption of divine, retributive justice, the participants in the Joban story assume that some individuals are righteous, blessed, and without sin (Job being the primary example of this), while others are wicked. Since the results of sin, in this narrative, are obvious and observable, sin is not assumed as a human birthright but is rather implied in outward and visible signs.

But the doctrine of original sin used to deny innocent suffering requires the assumption that humanity is born into a state of sin and so stands helpless and guilty before God at birth. That is, no suffering is innocent, since from birth sin is a part of humanity's DNA. Conversely, truly innocent suffering would undermine the doctrine of original sin. The serpentine twists and turns of original sin were initially developed to maintain and preserve divine attributes such as power, goodness, and wisdom. But given what we know of Job, we can ask: is there a way to conceive of the pervasiveness of sin as a part of the human condition, yet continue to affirm innocent suffering?

In his treatment of sin and innocent suffering, John Thiel develops an understanding of original sin that is compatible with the claim that innocent suffering exists. He writes that "the doctrine of original sin can be articulated in a way that yet acknowledges the reality of innocent suffering [and] . . . explains how God's goodness

remains credible before the moral fact of such suffering."[7] In order
to do this Thiel first presents what he calls "A Short History of Sin."

The doctrine of original sin does not appear among the beliefs
of the earliest Christians. No mention of it is made in the New
Testament or the Hebrew Bible. Paul's writings on sin (especially
in Rom. 5) were an important precedent to what the doctrine was
to become, but nowhere does Paul claim that human sin is inherited
at birth, though he does say that sin is inescapable. Paul's primary
contribution to the doctrine was the early Christian assumption
that the first sin of Adam and Eve brought God's retribution in
death, which subverted humanity's created immortality. Augustine
then, also using death as divine retribution for sin, incorporates this
idea into later writings as he engages in theological battle with the
Pelagians in the early fifth century on the subject of grace. Augustine's earlier writings, such as *On the Choice of the Free Will*, are quite
removed from a doctrine of original sin. In fact, the early Augustine
has such confidence in human moral capacity that he describes
human reason as naturally oriented to divine, natural law and says
that it is a guide, with the aid of grace, to every virtuous act. Thus
for the early Augustine, grace rather than sin is "original." But by the
time of the *Confessions,* hints of a doctrine of original sin begin to
emerge. Only slightly later, as he enters into a full-fledged battle
with the Pelagian teaching of heroic asceticism as the model of
Christian discipleship, does Augustine's emphasis on grace find its
necessary correlate in original sin. Augustine's panegyric writings
on grace during this period are more often remembered than the
writing's implications for sin, especially original sin. But grace and sin
need each other like bread and wine: if an argument against Pela-
gius required Augustine to insist on absolute, free, and unimpeded
grace, the other side of this doctrinal equation required original
sin. With original sin all humanity is condemned, making salvation
possible only in Christ through this absolute, free, and unimpeded
grace.

Over the centuries different Christian traditions maintained the
doctrine of original sin, though with many differences regarding

---

7. John E. Thiel, *God, Evil, and Innocent Suffering: A Theological Reflection* (New York: Crossroad,
2002), 125. Discussion of innocent suffering in Christian tradition is based on Thiel, 1–31,
102–42.

the relation between sin and grace. Augustine intertwined the doctrines, as did Luther, Zwingli, and Calvin. The Roman Catholic Council of Trent (1545–63) condemned several of the Reformers' teachings on sin and grace, qualifying their strong emphasis on human corruption by rejecting any understanding of original sin that made humanity utterly powerless before God's grace.

The "functionalist" view of human sin suggests what it calls "precedent sin," a power of sin that precedes human sin but that is precedent not in the human sexual act or in the consequent child resulting from procreation, but in evil itself. This raises questions of predestination. But it has an advantage over original sin in that while it does precede any individual or group act, it does not subvert real acts of virtue arising from the free choice of the human will. Contemporary theology gives several illustrations of how precedent sin might affect evil in the world: for Gustavo Gutiérrez, the misuse of economic and political power are examples of precedent sin; for feminist and African American theologians, the power of prejudice is precedent sin; and for René Girard, the precedent is victimizing sin in the practice of scapegoating.

In the first two chapters of Job, we have God's word that Job is righteous, a man without sin. In the final chapter God proclaims, "You [Eliphaz and the friends] have not spoken of me what is right, as my servant Job has" (42:7). Eliphaz and the friends take the routes of divine retribution, they deny innocent suffering, and their reasoning implies the doctrine of original sin. Job did not come into the world contaminated in mind, body, and spirit by sin—neither by the sins of the first parents, of his ancestors, or of his father or his mother. By divine decree he is a righteous man. But he is up against such comforters as Eliphaz who see suffering, think guilt, move to sin, and end concluding that Job's "wickedness" is immense (22:5a), and that there "is no end to your iniquities" (v. 5b). In doing so, the friends deny innocent suffering and unknowingly support an early doctrine of original sin.

22:1–11　*Guilty: Job's Moral Failures*

Eliphaz begins with a series of sarcastic, cruel questions intended not only to justify his depiction of Job as steeped in sin, but also to protect his God from any hint of weakness or flaw. The questions Eliphaz asks about the fate of the righteous and wise are rhetorical, but obviously directed at Job. Through his questions Eliphaz makes an emphatic point that God is sufficient unto God's self and hardly needs Job's righteousness or sin to aid God's active justice and power. Eliphaz asks, can the "hero" (v. 2a, *gaver*, Habel; "mortal," NRSV) "be of use to" (v. 2a, *sakan*; "endanger") God? Can the "wisest" (v. 2b, *sakal*; "a sage") be of service to God? "Is it any pleasure to the Almighty if you are righteous?" (v. 3a, *tsaddiq*). Is God's own power or justice enhanced in any way simply because Job's "way" (v. 3b, *derek*) is "blameless" (v. 3b, *tamam*; "perfect") or because Job's "piety" (v. 4, *yirah*; "reverence") is beyond reproach? For Eliphaz, the implied answer to all these questions is no!

The book of Job is both endlessly intriguing and tirelessly frustrating in part because every conceivable combination of perspectives on the relationship between humanity and God in the context of divine power and justice and human righteousness and sin are explored. In addition, one character in the story will voice one point of view only to contradict it later, more often than not in the interest of fitting the facts to a truth if the truth does not fit the facts. Complexifying these aspects of the story is that there is at least a kernel of truth in anything the participants say that does in fact conform, at least in part, to the truth of the narrative as it unfolds. Often this is recognizable only later, but it has the overall effect of adding density, depth, and insight to the story.

As one example in chapter 22, Eliphaz asks, "Can a mortal be of use to God?" Can even the "wisest," "righteous," "blameless," or pious be of use to God? (vv. 2–4). Of course for Eliphaz, God has no need even for the best of these; yet there *are* righteous people whom YHWH does notice and respond to (and Job is one of them, in chaps. 1 and 2 and 40–42). Though Eliphaz intends these cynical and acerbic rhetorical questions to humiliate Job and to set the stage for a description of his wickedness, Job *is* one of those righteous, wise, pious mortals who are "of use to God" (v. 2a). In fact, the bits of truth are planted even deeper: Eliphaz is so wrong about divine action in the world that not only does the divinity "care" about the righteous, this same divinity "cares" also about the unrighteous and, in yet another loop in the slippery eel of a narrative, Eliphaz *himself* is among the *unrighteous* "mortals . . . of use to God."

Nonetheless, Eliphaz does not bother to hide behind the ironic sarcasm of rhetorical questions, nor does he bother with evidence. He now makes straightforward accusations (vv. 6–11) that are breathtaking in their audacity and arbitrariness, enumerating Job's moral crimes and theological short-comings (vv. 12–20), which seem to merge easily into his moral faults. As astonishing as his lack of evidence for his accusations is Eliphaz's complete certainty of Job's guilt.

> It was woe on woe and within the lowest deep a lower deep.
>
> James Clarence Mangan, *Autobiography* (Dublin: Dolman Press, 1968), 26.

Unable to imagine a moral behavior or theological world that corresponds to his own understanding of the good and the true and the pious, Eliphaz constructs one, one that just happens to correspond exactly to Job's moral world filtered through Eliphaz's eyes. While imagining his moral accusations against Job, Eliphaz, ironically, completely misrepresents the morality or action of Job but does describe exactly Job's current physical, emotional, and psychological reality. Put another way, Eliphaz's accusations falsely depict Job's active behavior but truthfully represent Job's passive reception of suffering:

"You have exacted pledges from your family for no reason."	v. 6a
You have "stripped the naked of their clothing."	v. 6b
"You have given no water to the weary to drink."	v. 7a
"You have withheld bread from the hungry."	v. 7b
"You have sent widows away empty-handed."	v. 9a
You have "crushed" "the arms of the orphans."	v. 9b
Therefore "snares are around you."	v. 10a
"Sudden terror overwhelms you."	v. 10b
There is "darkness so that you cannot see."	v. 11a
"A flood of water covers you."	v. 11b

Obviously, some of Eliphaz's necessary fantasy echoes earlier words of Job; the rest stems only from Eliphaz's need to implicate Job's suffering in Eliphaz's own Deuteronomic system of justice. Samuel Balentine sharpens this focus well when he writes that there is, "one important difference between what has already been said and what Eliphaz now solemnly declares. The judgment Eliphaz decrees is no longer an abstract fate only generally applicable to the wicked at large. It is now a concrete reality that is prepared specifically for a wicked person named Job."[8]

22:12–20 *Guilty*

Having accused Job of an outrageous list of sins that are real only in Eliphaz's own imaginings, Eliphaz moves on to Job's supposed theological faults. Given what we know of Job and what he has said, Eliphaz does little better in representing the theological Job than he does the moral Job. He "quotes" Job using words Job has not spoken. Eliphaz thus imagines and falsely claims deeds Job has not done and words Job has not spoken. Eliphaz claims,

> Therefore you say, "What does God know?
> Can he judge through the deep darkness?
> Thick clouds enwrap him, so that he does not see,
> and he walks on the dome of heaven."
>
> (vv. 13–14)

Eliphaz misrepresents Job in these verses not only by misquoting him, but also by misrepresenting Job's theology in at least two ways: (1) Job has complained over and over that God sees all too well and all too constantly; adding to Job's many losses on earth, Job complains that God is "all seeing," "all knowing," "judging," the "one who sees" beyond the farthest star and judges and even controls the thoughts and deeds of all mortals. Eliphaz cannot seriously believe that Job thinks clouds hinder divine activity. But he nonetheless puts these wildly exaggerated words in Job's mouth. (2) Eliphaz

8. Balentine, *Job*, 346.

misrepresents Job's understanding and words concerning the doctrine of transcendence itself, implying that Job views God as self-sufficient, unconcerned or unoccupied with the affairs of humanity on earth. In a universe in which all the characters we have encountered to this point in Job assume a doctrine of retributive justice, Eliphaz's claim that Job's theology is that God is unconcerned about the ways of the wicked or of the righteous is absurd. The absurdity can be clarified by looking at the doctrine of transcendence itself.

In accusing Job of walking the "old way" of wickedness and predicting that his continued theological "heresy" will lead to chaos and disorder in his life, Eliphaz makes another allusion to the "high" God of transcendent ambivalence. Job neither watches nor guards (*shamar*) the "ancient" paths. As Edwin Good writes, "Eliphaz is asking not merely whether Job sees that dishonorable path but whether he can be responsible for it."[9] The implied answer is definitely negative. In his roundabout and disingenuous reasoning, Eliphaz is implying once again that God is responsible for the fates of the evil, the worthless, the god-despisers on that path (v. 15), but that Job has sunk so low that he is incapable of seeing clearly the fate of even the worthless; that is, according to Eliphaz, Job himself.

> As Human beings, not only do we seek resolution, but we also feel that we deserve resolution. However, not only do we not deserve resolution, we suffer from resolution.
>
> Pema Chödrön, *When Things Fall Apart: Heart Advice for Difficult Times* (Boston: Shambhala, 2000), 54.

22:21–30 *Guilty: Repent and Then Rejoice!*

It is difficult to read verses 21–30 after reading the first twenty verses of this chapter. We are suddenly greeted with a solution and a possible happy outcome, and it is so simple: just rejoice, Job, all will be well! Eliphaz moves from curses to seemingly warm concern. The radical reversal is no doubt harder on Job than the accusations. But coming on the heels of the gross exaggerations with which Eliphaz

---

9. Good, *In Turns of Tempest*, 275.

has been taunting Job, Eliphaz's words betray his own emotional system wound to the breaking point, an intellect out of touch with reality, and a spiritual sensitivity numbed by self-interest. Having dared to point a finger at Job, accusing him of "unrighteousness" (v. 23, 'awla), the primary evil Job explicitly repudiates (6:24–30; 27:4), and declaring, "Is not your wickedness great? There is no end to your iniquities" (v. 5), having blithely enumerated Job's sins, none of which is based on a single shard of evidence, having topped these off by accusing Job with grossly misguided theological positions, Eliphaz the counselor of chapters 4–5 reappears. Here in chapter 22 he comes across only as a person of duplicity and betrayal. Verses 21–30 ought most appropriately to be placed in the mouth of Job speaking to Eliphaz. Instead, in his speech in verses 21–30 Eliphaz condemns a man drowning in innocence, afire with grief, driven mad by a sense of abandonment, and dying both physically and spiritually.

Eliphaz dares to recommend to Job that Job take "instruction" (v. 22, torah, perhaps hinting at law or regulation) from God. Of course the "instruction" actually comes from the now godlike Eliphaz who, after establishing that God ought to be Job's one and only treasure, allows his own "righteousness" and "wisdom" to instruct Job on the path back to harmony with God. Neither pastoral nor particularly self-aware, Eliphaz offers Job a series of pietistic, penitential verbs and nouns that will supposedly restore Job to God. Eliphaz the instructor of wisdom says, "lift" (nasah, v. 26b) your face to God; "pray" (athar, v. 27a) to God, who will listen; "pay" (shalam) what you "vow" (neder, v. 27b); "decide" (gazar; "decree," v. 28a); and "light will shine [nagah] on your ways" (derek, v. 28b).

Many of Eliphaz's recommendations for restoring Job to God's favor also hearken back to a Joban complaint and could only serve to further enrage him: "The unusual assurance that Job, if penitent, would be 'rebuilt' [v. 23, banah], would hardly be heard with good grace in view of Job's contention that nothing El tears down can be 'rebuilt' (12:14). The promise that 'light' would illuminate Job's 'way' or 'destiny' recalls Job's opening cry that those who suffer under divine oppression come to the 'light' at birth but find their way hidden (3:20, 23). . . . This unusual term for gold [ophar, v. 24] seems to be chosen to associate with the word beṣaʻ, 'gain,' in v. 3. Job's 'gain' is not in his own perfection, but is the 'gold' of Shaddai. Thus Eliphaz's closing assurances are couched in language that recalls his opening indictments,"[10] and even though they sound hopeful enough on the surface, they constitute yet another serious spear thrust at an already completely compromised and debilitated Job.

> Agree with God, and be at peace;
> in this way good will come to you.
>
> (v. 21)

With cruel condescension Eliphaz promises a day in which Job will again reside among the perfect and regain God's favor. Job must be choking with disbelief. A part of the uncompromising design of this speech is that Eliphaz is predicting the process of his own redemption by the man he is now accusing (42:7–10).

We have reached a place in the poem of Job where every word, every simile, every metaphor, every image, every description, every reasoned explanation is fraught with previous and potential

---

Father Zossima, near death, speaking some last words to some of his fellow monks, including the young Alyosha Karamozov:

"When he [a monk] realizes that he is not only worse than others, but that he is responsible to all men for all and everything, for all human sins, national and individual, only then the aim of our seclusion is attained. For know, dear ones, that every one of us is undoubtedly responsible for all men and everything on earth, not merely through the general sinfulness of creation, but each one personally for all mankind and every individual man. This knowledge is the crown of life for the monk and for every man. For monks are not special sorts of men, but only what all men ought to be. Only through that knowledge, our heart grows soft with infinite, universal, inexhaustible love. Then every one of you will have the power to win over the whole world by love and to wash away the sins of the world with your tears."

Fyodor Dostoevsky, *The Brothers Karamazov*, trans. Constance Garnett (New York: Barnes & Noble Classics, 2004), 155–56.

---

10. Habel, *Job*, 337.

meaning. One image conjures another; a single metaphor takes on opposite meaning; a freighted word can become fraught with projected meanings of both shadow and light; the reader brings his or her own meaning to the lushness of meaning on the page; meaning becomes difficult to assimilate when what we hear and see are masks that cover the faces only of emptiness; a shadow is one person's retribution, another's justice. God looks on, seeing all, saying nothing.

23:1–24:25

Job's Third Response to Eliphaz:
"There are those who rebel against the light"

As Job progresses in his journey of suffering, we find in these chapters new meaning in old rhetoric and the germinating seeds of a new theological vision. Theologically, Job bores deeper into the perennial problem of divine justice, and he refuses to let go of the inscrutable tension between a hoped-for divine presence and a felt divine absence or incomprehensibility. Following his own path, he walks a way that is entirely congruent with the way of God. At the same time he dares to demand a face-to-face encounter with God, terrifying as such an encounter may be.

Once again we enter complex textual distortions that have presented scholars with difficulty at the most basic levels of translation. The texts as we have received them are corrupt in many places; the grammar is often maddeningly scrambled, resulting in uncertainty even at the most basic levels of who is speaking and to whom. These textual and grammatical confusions, which are an unfortunate fact of the text's historical transmission, are heightened by intended ambiguity on the part of the poet. The poet is a master at propagating multiple meanings within seemingly simple phrases and verses. Apart from translation difficulties, most scholars assume that they will find a consistent, rational (in Western terms) closure to any doctrine or theological issue. But the author of Job builds a theology of suffering from the ground up that does not explain the ways of God to man (theodicy) but which rather, in staying true to the nature of evil and suffering in the world, dares to ask new and difficult questions that not only have no easy answer but, like suffering itself, evoke not an answer as much as a continuing question of existence.

Chapter 23 is relatively easy to outline. It opens with a complaint from Job (v. 2), moves to a statement of desire to find and enter into God's dwelling or presence (v. 3), returns to Job's ongoing call to face God and argue his case before God in order to redeem justice (vv. 4–7). As often happens with Job, he then turns immediately abject, recalling that no matter where he turns, God is absent (vv. 8–9). He finds this divine absence hard to understand, in that God not only knows Job's path but Job himself has followed God's own path and precepts (vv. 10–12). On the other hand, he recognizes that God is omnipotent and what God desires God will do (vv. 13–14). The chapter ends with yet another shift in Job's thoughts as he realizes that, though he has called out to meet God face to face, were God to show God's face the encounter would crush Job with dread, fear, and gloom (vv. 15–17) regardless of his innocence or guilt.

Chapter 24 is much more difficult to outline. First, it is difficult to determine who or what class of people is speaking and whom they are speaking to. Opinions as to possible outlines and suggestions about who is speaking to whom are given below. A second difficulty, having to do with the nature of suffering itself, is again one of the underlying reasons for the greatness of the poem. The poet pursues the demon of suffering, not as an abstract entity (that we might outline) but as an unsettling evil neither qualifiable nor answerable. This leaves the meaning of evil and suffering open-ended but realistically depicted, even if the result is intentional lack of orderly narrative as a rhetorical approach. Even at the expense of clarity the poet intends to remain true to the nature of suffering itself.

> **The honest rage of Job represents a giant step forward from the insensitivity or dishonesty of the friends, the credulity of those who themselves are fortunate, "the wisdom of the well." . . . Given that one is bitter, perhaps blasphemy is therapeutic, and even heroic; but is it desirable to be bitter?**
>
> John T. Wilcox, *The Bitterness of Job: A Philosophical Reading* (Ann Arbor: University of Michigan Press, 1994), 100–101, 102.

23:1–17 *Seeking God Face To Face*

Job once again opens with a complaint, directed here not so much at the friends but at his God. His complaint now is "bitter" (*mar*, v. 2a) or "defiant," while "God's hand" (elsewhere symbolizing God's unwarranted affliction and endless torment; cf. 1:11; 10:7; 13:21; 19:21) serves mainly to hide God (v. 9). But Job is now intent on pursuing God, which he expresses emphatically in his wishes that he "might find God" (v. 3a) and come into God's presence or "dwelling" (*tekunah*, v. 3b).

The immediate purpose of finding and coming into the presence of God is still to argue his "lawsuit" (*mishpat*, "case", vv. 4a, 7b) before God. But an important theological change focused on divine hiddenness occurs in Job that has tremendous implications for the poem. The changes are not, unfortunately, immediately apparent in the NRSV translation. For example, at verse 4a the NRSV reads, "I would lay my case before him." Earlier, Job had summoned the courage to formulate bold claims about what he would "say" to God (9:27; 10:2). Later he would agonize over the difficulties of presenting his suit "in God's presence" (chap. 13).[11] God's "face" (*panim*) was a key motif in that speech, and now at verse 4a Job actually uses the same word, so that the verse is more properly translated as "I would press my suit to his *face*." In chapter 13 Job was afraid God would "hide his face." Now he is prepared to approach God face to face regardless of the consequences. While in verses 3–7 he still expresses some, no doubt legitimate, misgivings, Job is at the very least confident that he is genuinely "upright" (*yashar*, v. 7a) and that God will hear his case and present God's "face":

> Would he prosecute me by an attorney?
> No, he himself would attend to me.
>
> (v. 6, Good)

Job has considered bringing his case to God before, but always with an intermediary: an "arbiter" (9:33), a "witness" (16:19), and an "avenger" or "redeemer" (19:25). In other words, Job is no longer

11. Ibid., 349.

asking for an intermediary of any sort: he is seeking to enter the divine presence and to confront God face to face.

What is Job asking for? God said to Moses, "you cannot see my face; for no one shall see me and live" (Exod. 33:20), and so God hid Moses in a cleft in the rocks and covered him with his hand. And still, as Moses descended from the rocks the skin of his face shone so that he had to veil it before the people (Exod. 34:33, 35). In 1 John we read, "Beloved, we are God's children now; what we will be has not yet been revealed. What we do know is this: when he is revealed, we will be like him, for we will see him as he is. And all who have this hope in him purify themselves, just as [God] is pure" (1 John 3:2–3). From an Old Testament point of view, Job is asking for a thing pointedly not possible or, if possible, deadly. From a New Testament point of view, Job is asking to see God now, as God is, so Job may be like God. Christian mystics have long described an unmediated presence of God, some in terms of unity or simplicity, some in terms of love, some in terms of beauty, others through an unmediated vision of Christ or an intuitive vision of the Trinity. But in asking for (demanding!) such an encounter, Job questions the theology that is the catalyst and the *shalom* that helps his community cohere. With the exception of Moses, a face-to-face, unmediated encounter with YHWH would destroy not only the individual but also the balance between the community and the sacred. Even Moses, his face covered, returned from the mountain with laws and precepts that were to have profound effect on the community. One of the effects of Moses' encounter was the eventual development of the priestly class whose function was to mediate the divinity through strict and highly formal ceremonies and rites.

Job is taking the chance that not only his face but his very being will be annihilated in such an unmediated encounter. Why? He continues to insist that there is meaning to suffering that he has as yet not been privileged to know, and he is now willing risk all to understand God's causal relationship to his suffering. He demands to know how heavily God's hand rests on evil. We tend to think of the story of Job as the story of individual, innocent suffering. The book of Job speaks to community evil just as strongly: communities that inflict evil and communities that endure evil.

And then in a twinkling Job's fears come to the fore once again. As before, Job feels boxed in by absence. East, west, north, south:[12] to all points of the compass, no matter where he turns, God is "not there" (v. 8a), Job "cannot perceive him" (v. 8b), God "hides" (v. 9a), and again, Job "cannot see/behold" God's face (v. 9). These verses continue the quest Job is undertaking, but now in a pessimistic sense. There is a secret wisdom to God's hidden ways that Job does not possess. This hidden, inscrutable, incomprehensible God is at the heart of Job's search for a place and time of dwelling in divine presence. As in any spiritual journey, there is a period of purgation or purification in which the soul or the people or the body or the person is "tested" like metal in a fire, in this case like the most precious metal, gold (v. 10b). Job will welcome this ultimate testing (in fact he is undergoing it even as he speaks) as long as it will bring him face to face with God. He describes this test, again, in the form of a journey, a path, the "way" (v. 10a, *derek*), which is rich in connotation and carries several meanings as Job uses it. For Job the "way" includes the "way" of God, which Job has kept so unfailingly that

---

"But he knows the way that I take." This is as if he [Job] said in plain terms, "I for my own part search myself strictly and am not able to know myself thoroughly; yet he, whom I have no power to see, sees most minutely all the things that I do." The holy man [Job] compared himself with the one who is being tested through fire as gold. This is not said out of pride. . . . As he was being delivered over to suffer tribulation, he believed that he was being purified, although he had nothing in him to be purified . . . "my foot has held fast to his steps." . . . Every day the righteous are concerned that they test their actions by the ways of truth. So they propose these as a rule to themselves, that they should not turn aside from the track of their right course. Thus, day by day, they strive to move ahead, a step above their present position in proportion as they are being lifted up toward the summit of virtues.

Gregory the Great, *Commentary on the Book of Job*, in A Library of the Fathers of the Holy Catholic Church, trans. Members of the English Church, 44 vols. (Oxford: John Henry Parker, 1881), 21:247–48, 250–53.

---

12. The four points of the compass are determined by the Israelite facing east. Thus east is also "before"; west is "behind" (Isa. 9:11); north is "to the left" (Gen. 14:15); and south is "to the right" (1 Sam. 23:19). The NRSV chooses the less precise spatial metaphors "before," "behind," "left," "right."

his feet follow in the footsteps of God: "My foot has held fast to his steps" (v. 11a). The "way" is also the righteous way of life, a path from which Job does not deviate in his integrity (cf. 31:4–7). But the way also recalls Job's complaint that God confines mortals and prevents them from finding their way (3:23; cf. 12:24).

Taken together, Job's ambivalence and ambiguity are typical of the spiritual journey: one is caught between compulsion to find God and the fear that one may just do so.

FURTHER REFLECTIONS
The Hiddenness of God

Job's question in 3:23 is translated by Good, "[Why is there light] for a man whose way is hidden, whom Eloah has hedged around?" The verse introduces the mystery or hiddenness of God and God's ways that will be at the core of Job's existential despair and inability to move forward beyond suffering. Divine hiddenness is lamented in two ways in this verse.

Lamentation, first, is grounded in the fact that the way (*derek*) of life for man is hidden. In Wisdom literature *derek*, "way," is a symbol of the conduct of life, personal destiny, and the underlying principle of order. For Job, this way of life has been hidden since the onset of the suffering when his "way" was lost. Not unlike Job, Dante Alighieri begins his *Divine Comedy* in a similar place in which the "way" is lost. Notice in these verses the similarities to Job's lament:

> Midway upon the journey of our life
> > I found myself within a forest dark,
> > For the straightforward pathway had been lost.
> Ah me! how hard a thing it is to say
> > What was this forest savage, dark and dense,
> > Which in the very thought renews the fear.
>
> So bitter is it, death is little more;
> > But of the good to treat, which there I found,
> > Speak will I of the other things I saw there.

> I cannot well repeat how there I entered,
>   So full was I of slumber at the moment
>   In which I had abandoned the true way.[13]

The second way divine hiddenness is lamented in Job is more ambiguous: God is absent from the narrative and dialogue, but is Job hiding from God or is God hiding from Job, or both, or neither? In chapter 3 we saw the play on the way in which the deity has put a "hedge" or "fence" (NRSV) around Job. On the one hand, God hides the way through an image of blocking or constriction. But a hedge or fence can also protect people as they travel on their "way." This "hedge" is an obvious allusion to Job 1:10, where the *satan* used the same verb to characterize God's protection of Job. Thus at 3:23 "hedged around" (*yasek ba'do*) indicates God has hidden Job's "way"; at 1:10 "hedged around" (*sakta ba'do*) indicates God has protected Job.

Chapter 24 of Job is interpreted and translated in many different, often contradictory, ways. One illustration from the translation by Edwin M. Good is an example of this diversity and serves as a transition from chapter 23 to chapter 24. In highlighting Good's approach I am not suggesting it is more true to the book of Job than any of the other perspectives mentioned below in the commentary on chapter 24. Good does, however, present an interpretation that finds continuity between the two chapters.

Good begins by saying of chapters 23 and 24 that "the focus of his [Job's] discourse this time, however, is the god's absence."[14] The complaint finished, in fact, Good notes that Job "jumps immediately into the theme of the god's absence (23.3)." Job moves rapidly in these chapters, as noted, between compulsive seeking and deep dread of finding this same elusive God. Thus after some optimism, discouragement returns in force as Job boxes the compass in search of the god in 23:8–9. The search in all directions is unsuccessful. The God is "not there," cannot be discerned (or "understood," *bin*, v. 8b). In any direction Job looks, God is hidden, unseen, secretive. God is

---

13. Dante Alighieri, *The Inferno*, 1.1–9, trans. Henry W. Longfellow.
14. Good, *In Turns of Tempest*, 276.

simply not "placed." God may seem to be avoiding justice as assidu-ously as God is veiled from Job's sight. But Job thinks he knows why: "Because [*ki*] he knows the way I'm on" (v. 10a). As Job describes his unbending adherence to these "ways," each "way" also presents the possibility of becoming lost, even further removing him from the hidden God.

Job has unerringly kept close to the lifestyle prescribed by God: in that prescription, his "way" is true. At one point Job had said, "I am perfect" (9:21, *tam'ani;* NRSV "I am blameless"). This is said by Job less to, once again, remind reader, friends, and God that he is innocent than to emphasize that throughout his innocent suffering there remains this palpable divine absence. God's absence is also illustrated by God's absence of justice and the deity's arbitrariness. Job's terror and dread in chapter 23 are simply the "other side" of a "divine opponent [who] exerts absent and arbitrary force."[15]

Divine absence as the key theme is carried over into chapter 24 starting with verse 1:

> "Why are times not kept by the Almighty,
> And why do those who know him never see his days?"

Since God fails to treasure the "times," humans are bereft of God's guidance and can go wrong. God's seeming aloofness and disregard for the proper "time" or places suggests the victory of chaos over God: moral chaos, cosmic chaos, nature chaos, and soci-ety chaos are mentioned.

Good's own conclusion about divine absence as described by Job is that additional discussion by Job about *Deus absconditus* would not have been helpful. In fact, Good would just as soon end the book at chapter 24: "Delving deep into the ground of human corruption," Good writes, "Job finds there the actions or the absence of the god. Now we know why in chap. 23 he feared the outcome of the trial: a deity who is the source of human corruption is unlikely to acquit an uncorrupted human being."[16] The theme of the divine

15. Ibid., 278.
16. Ibid., 281.

absence is modified by images of an arbitrary, whimsical, and, on the friends' part, unjust presence. But Job returns decisively to absence and challenges both the friends and his absent God to prove, in the friends' case with reasonable words, in God's case with simple presence, that he is wrong about righteousness, goodness, and truth:

> If it is not so, who will prove me a liar,
> and show that there is nothing in what I say?
>
> (v. 25)

Job's grief swirls around an absent, unknown God. Job will surrender to comfort only as this transcendent, unknowable God reveals—in God's final whirlwind speeches—God's immanent knowable presence through and in creation. Sorrow, grief, loss, hiddenness, lamentation are all a part of Job's journey, a journey toward what I consider to be a barely bearable consolation.

24:1–25 *"God pays no attention to their prayer"*

Despite the textual problems of chapter 24, this lovely poem continues refining theological issues that surfaced in chapter 23: the sovereignty of God; the apparent decision of God that Job should suffer; a suggestion of delayed retribution of the wicked, which is different

---

According to his speeches in the central section, his true sorrow in all his sorrows, and therefore the primary subject of his complaints, consists in the conjunction of his profound knowledge that in what has happened and what has come on him he has to do with God, and his no less profound ignorance how far he has to do with God. . . . We see this knowledge and ignorance of God in headlong collision and unbearable tension. This is the depth and essence of the suffering of the suffering Job. . . . Job's particular difficulty is that this knowledge is in tension and conflict with his no less concrete ignorance, which neither he, nor, as the poet plainly thinks, anyone else can overcome without intervention of God Himself. . . . He [Job] does not doubt for a moment that he has to do with this God. But it almost drives him mad that he encounters Him in the form in which He is absolutely alien.

Karl Barth, *Church Dogmatics* IV/3.1, ed. G. W. Bromiley and T. F. Torrance (Edinburgh: T & T Clark, 1961), 401, 402.

from chapter 21, in which the primary theme was how the wicked prosper; and Job's assertion that God seems not to care about the suffering in the world, that God is indifferent to the plight of the oppressed described in chapter 24.

On a journey to God, steep and deep, passing through light and through dark, seeking but not finding, Job searches for comfort and is discomforted.

Chapter 24 is one of the most controversial in Job. Even those affirming coherent unity and lyrical beauty in the poem disagree radically about its meaning. Grammatically, most of the disagreement is focused on who is speaking in the poem and to whom. A variety of proposals purport to reattribute speeches in all of the difficult third cycle to their proper speakers

> No worst, there is none.
>   Pitched past pitch of grief,
> More pangs will, schooled at
>   forepangs, wilder wring.
> Comforter, where, where is
>   your comforting?
>   . . . .
> Here! creep,
> Wretch, under a comfort
>   serves in a whirlwind: all
> Life death does end and each
>   day dies with sleep.
>
> Gerard Manley Hopkins, "No Worst, There Is None," in *The Poetical Works of Gerard Manley Hopkins*, ed. Norman H. Mackenzie (Oxford: Oxford University Press, 1990), 182.

and rearrange verses to fit more clearly with theology expressed by each character. Some of the major (but by no means agreed-upon) proposed changes to chapter 24 to "make the text conform to the speaker" can be summarized as follows:

> (a) the entire speech is to be attributed to Job, with Job either expecting or soliciting the punishment of the wicked (in vs. 18–25); (b) the speech belongs to Job but certain portions (vv. 18–20, RSV; 18–24, Gordis) are a quotation of the friends' position; (c) vs. 18–24 are assigned to Bildad (NAB) or Zophar (Dhorme, Pope); (d) the speech is an independent poem of the author (Fohrer; Snaith; Habel); and (e) certain verses are a pious gloss added to make Job appear more orthodox (Peake).[17]

---

17. Habel, *Job*, 357. See Habel also on the details of each proposed position.

More recently a sixth proposal has been made by David Wolfers, who demonstrates convincingly a coherence for the complete third cycle as it stands, including chapter 24. He writes, with a certain caustic tone, of how these chapters hold together and "how apparent contradictions which the text suggests may properly be resolved without recourse to surgery."[18] The approach is convincing, most importantly for the reason that it allows even more nuance in Job's theology as he wrestles with his predicament and with his God, in the process allowing the poetry free rein to show in ever more subtle ways the complexity of the divine-human relationship in the context of evil. This interpretation makes for a coherent, lyrically beautiful, and closely argued poem that comes solely from the lips of Job, describing the plight of the poor, which Job attributes to the apathy of God. "Job's purpose in this chapter is to demonstrate that God has missed His aim, and is visiting the punishment supposedly reserved for 'the wicked' on harmless men who have simply not had the opportunities which are required for piety and ritual observance— *to know the ways of the Light*."[19]

25:1–26:14

Bildad and Job Respond:
"How small a whisper"

The Third Cycle Breaks Down; The Dialogue Deepens
Where previously the friends make their cases in particular, unchanging order, with Job responding in turn, in chapters 25–27 Bildad's speech is exceedingly short, Zophar does not enter the discussion, and much of what Job says, at least on the surface, sounds very unlike his previous positions. Many claim that the text has been altered, speeches have been moved, and that it is at the very least a challenge to link correct speakers with the proper speeches. Gordis says the third cycle "has suffered great damage" and hence "cannot

18. David Wolfers, *Deep Things Out of Darkness: The Book of Job, Essays and a New English Translation* (Grand Rapids: Eerdmans, 1995), 37.
19. Ibid., 228. Wolfers's emphasis.

be meaningfully interpreted in its present form,"[20] while Perdue finds that only after chapters 21–27 have been "correctly edited to indicate who is speaking" can we fully understand "the increasing crescendo of the three opponents' accusations brought against Job."[21] A variety of approaches for restoring and rearranging the chapters to their original order have been proposed.

FURTHER REFLECTIONS
Masoretic Text and Canon

Ancient scribes and contemporary scholars emend, rearrange, and "improve" Job to an extent rarely appreciated by nonscholars. Concerning the text of Job, the canonical scholar Brevard Childs has written, "The Masoretic text is not identical with the canonical text, but is only a vehicle for its recovery. There is no extant canonical text."[22] Acknowledging the difficulties of ascribing authorship for the book of Job, and admitting the theological temptations and in some cases justifications for "improving" the book of Job by rearranging it, we are following Childs, using the canonical order and structure of the book of Job as it is found today in most translations. The Masoretic Text is widely used as a basis for translations of the Old Testament in Protestant and Roman Catholic Bibles as well. For most scholars, it is consulted often to obtain the best text for translation of Job.

While the Masoretic Text is a "vehicle" for recovery of a so-called canonical text, the vehicle has found numerous roads on which to guide the rearrangement of Job. It seems clear to many commentators that speeches ascribed to various of the friends and to Job in this last grouping of the third cycle could not have been spoken by those speakers, given the theology and/or poetic imagery of their previous speeches, and that the third cycle was purposefully

20. Robert Gordis, *The Book of Job: Commentary, New Translation, and Special Studies* (New York: Jewish Theological Seminary of America, 1978), 534.
21. Leo G. Perdue, *Wisdom Literature: A Theological History* (Louisville, KY: Westminster John Knox, 2007), 116.
22. Brevard S. Childs, *Introduction to the Old Testament as Scripture* (Philadelphia: Fortress, 1979), 100.

rearranged by scribes in an attempt to clean up some of what was thought to be more than marginally heretical theology. Thus, Pope argues, the scribes made "deliberate attempt to refute Job's argument by confusing the issue."[23] Given these incongruities, the assumption is that the arrangement has been lost, mistranslated, and garbled over the long history of the book's transmission. While suggestions have been made for rearranging some material from each of chapters 21–27, the majority of proposed changes have centered on chapters 25–27. The table below gives some of the proposed "corrections" to chapters 25–27. Publication dates give some indication of a more recent shift away from rearranging texts; * = no change/rearrangement from NRSV.

	BILDAD	JOB	ZOPHAR	DATE
Perdue	25:1–6; 26:5–14	26:1–4; 27:1–23	None	2007
***Balentine**	25:1–6	26:1–27:25	None	2006
Newsom	25:1–6; 26:5–14	26:1–4; 27:1–2	None	1996
***Wolfers**	25:1–6	26:1–27:25	None	1995
***Good**	25:1–6	26:1–27:25	None	1990
***Janzen**	25:1–6	26:1–27:25	None	1985
Habel	25:1–6; 26:5–14	26:1–4; 27:1–12	27:13–23	1985
Pope	25:1–6; 26:5–14	27:1; 26:1–4; 27:2–7	27:8–23; 24:18–24	1979
Gordis	25:1–6; 26:5–14	26:1–4; 27:1–12	27:13–23	1978
Dhorme	25:1–6; 26:5–14	26:1–4; 27:1–12	27:13–23; 24:18–24	1967
Terrien	25:1–6; 26:8–13	26:1–7, 14	None	1957
Driver	25:1–6	26:1–14; 27:11–12	27:13–23	1921

---

23. Marvin H. Pope, *Job*, Anchor Bible (New York: Doubleday, 1965), xxvii.

Balentine concludes that though each of the above proposals has both merit and flaw, "None can be verified by any external evidence."[24] To the extent that interpreters prefer one or more of these proposals to the text that we have, they must concede that they are working from "a text made, not found."[25]

From the table above the pendulum seems to be swinging back, slowly, in favor of an interpretive strategy based on the canonical approach proposed by Brevard Childs. Good, for instance, after referencing the scholarly work of rearrangement, writes tersely: "Thinking such rewriting unnecessary, I will make no gestures toward it."[26] Balentine aptly sums up and justifies the position we will pursue: "None of the proposed reconstructions is fully convincing. Moreover, although it is *possible* that the text has suffered some disturbance in transmission, there is *no evidence* that this is so. The earliest translations of the book (the Aramaic Targum of Job from Qumran [11QtgJob] and the LXX) show the same sequence of speeches as the Masoretic Text. A better approach is to wrestle with the text that we have instead of rebuilding a text that conforms to a pattern that may never have existed."[27]

It is possible to understand the breakdown of the texts and the disarray of the speeches as an interpretive clue that the dialogue between the friends has itself also finally broken down. Doing so does justice to the mastery and integrity of the poet and adds depth, subtlety, and unexpected twists to Job's growing understanding of the relation between divine justice, power, and action, and to Job's questions about what human beings are in relation to the Creator of the world (cf. 4:17; 7:17; 15:14; 25:4 with 38:2: "Who is this?"). Keeping the chapters and verses of Job in the order in which we have them today forces the reader to go deeper with Job into his suffering, to track with Job along a way unfamiliar and treacherous, and to question our own assumptions about our relations, prayers, and actions regarding both suffering and God.

---

24. Balentine, *Job*, 382.
25. Terrence W. Tilley, *Evils of Theodicy* (Eugene, OR: Wipf & Stock, 2000), 90.
26. Good, *In Turns of Tempest*, 282.
27. Balentine, *Job*, 381.

25:1-6 *Bildad: A Little Lower than God*

Bildad's third speech is made of two components, verses 2–3 and
4–6. In the first verses, Bildad takes up Job's challenge to prove him a
liar (24:25). The first line asserts that it is God's prerogative to decide
who will be on top and who underneath. Job had protested that the
current ordering of society is illegitimate. Bildad, responding to that
claim, states what to him is obvious: "Dominion and fear are with
God; [God] makes his peace in [the] high heaven" (v. 2). "Dominion" (*mushal*) points to God's sovereignty on earth and within the
entire cosmos, while the "fear" (*pahad*) Bildad refers to is to be taken
in the sense of "dread" or "terror" (cf. Exod. 15:16; Isa. 2:10, 19, 21).
The second line (v. 2b), as Wolfers has written, "refers to the subjuga-
tion of God's celestial rivals recorded mainly in Akkadian mythology
but also fully integrated into the book of Job. The implication is that
God has proved His statecraft in a harder school than earth, justifying His assumption of the power specified in the first line."[28] In other
words, God has, and has had, bigger fish to fry than lowly Job.

Divine sovereignty and power, as Bildad reminds Job, are inescapable (v. 3a). This is no news to Job, who has complained over
and over that the relentless all-seeing eye of God gives no peace. Bildad goes on to compare divine sovereignty unfavorably to Job, who
is a simple "mortal" (*enosh*), subject to "maggots" (*rimmah*, v. 6a),
a "human being" (*adam*) destined only for "worms" (*tola*, v. 6b).
These Job and the reader have heard before. Against Bildad, Perdue,
who looks at the book of Job through the lens of Hebrew Wisdom
literature, sees Job as a human hero in revolt or even in revolution
against God. In his sinlessness, Job is convinced that he is in a position to temper the sovereignty of God's terrible power on a balance
point of justice. But Bildad throws out the main argument against
any possibility of this happening: "How then can a mortal be righteous before God? How can one born of woman be pure?" If Job is a
human hero it is in part because he has survived the terrible consolation of his friends.

As if it were not enough that human beings are neither pure

---

28. Wolfers, *Deep Things*, 242.

nor righteous enough to peer into the complexities of governing the cosmos, Bildad also describes the divine sovereignty over not only the earth, but over the heavens, the underworld, and the cosmic ocean. Describing God "setting up the sacred canopy over the abyss, thus signifying control over the power of chaos, assuming his royal throne, and issuing decrees that govern the cosmos,"[29] Bildad uses his theology of transcendence in an attempt to humiliate, crush, and, demoralize Job. In the process he warns Job of any foolish, revolutionary plot he might be planning against YHWH.[30] Job's new, emerging theology is so disturbing to Bildad that

> If we are honest, I think we have to admit that we will likely try to sabotage any movement toward true freedom. If we really knew what we were called to relinquish on this journey, our defenses would never allow us to take the first step. Sometimes the only way we can enter the deeper dimensions of the journey is by being unable to see where we're going.
>
> Gerald G. May, *The Dark Night of the Soul: A Psychiatrist Explores the Connection between Darkness and Spiritual Growth* (San Francisco: HarperSanFrancisco, 2004), 72.

he can only perceive it as an unrighteous heresy, a plot to overthrow Bildad's sovereign God. We might ask, if Bildad is so concerned about Job's ability to breach the divine fortress of power, what is so unsettled in Bildad's mind about his own doctrine of God that would cause him to harass so relentlessly the bag of skin and bones still cast out of the city, sitting on a dung-heap?

That the third cycle breaks down structurally is a vivid artifice by the poet that signals the breakdown of the arguments and theology within the cycle itself. The route to sorting out law and guilt is like a long hallway with many, many identical doors behind which may or may not be anything like the just resolution to Job's dilemma that Job seeks, even demands. But Job will have to choose if he is to move forward. Whatever Job chooses, what has come before alerts the reader that something new is forming on the Hebrew theological landscape.

29. Leo G. Perdue, *Wisdom Literature: A Theological History* (Louisville, KY: Westminster John Knox, 2007), 117.
30. See ibid., 117–18.

26:1–14 *Creation Collapsing into Chaos*

Chapter 26 has always puzzled readers because, rather like chapter 28, there is no attribution to a particular speaker and the chapter seems on the surface to be a hymn to wisdom unconnected with surrounding material. The first two verses clearly do belong to Job, recalling Bildad's general abuse of their friendship, sarcastically adding that in any case Bildad's counsel is worthless, lacking in "wisdom" (v. 3a), adding finally that he would be better off without Bildad's "counsel" or "advice" (v. 3) and that collectively, the friends' silence would be the better part of their wisdom. Verse 4 moves into the arena of what one commentator calls the "sinister":[31]

> With whose help have you uttered words,
>   and whose spirit [*neshamah*, "breath"]
>   has come forth from you?

Job is in part referring to a certain plagiarism on Bildad's part for having used Eliphaz's words from chapter 25. But this verse goes much deeper than that. The insinuation that Bildad is alluding to and actually quoting Eliphaz can be traced back to 4:12–16 and Eliphaz's claim of a vision that came to him in the middle of the night and that was told to him by a "spirit" (*neshamah*). As Wolfers comments, "Now, when Bildad delivers the same message, Job is asking him in the nastiest way, which spirit dictated the message to him! Job did not appreciate this message—that all men are sinners in God's eyes—the first time he heard it. Now he is truly enraged at having it forced upon him for the third time."[32] What makes this verse potentially "sinister" is that with the second-person singular verbs, just to whom the verse is directed is unclear. It could certainly be directed to Job, in which case it is indeed sarcastic and nasty. Or it could be directed at God, in which case it is Job who is in effect cynically asking the silent God, "From what nonspirit comes your nonspeaking?"

Job's speech in chapter 26 is a wisdom poem that questions the power of the Creator to keep chaos under control. Job has

31. Good, *In Turns of Tempest*, 284.
32. Wolfers, *Deep Things*, 243.

undergone such a radical change in relation to his God that, given Job's situation and his friends' commentary on it, he has moved theologically to a point where he questions the power of God over the forces of chaos. His cosmological outburst is clearly something other than a positive doctrinal statement. There are references to chaos or death throughout verses 5–17 that are unfamiliar or easily missed. In order to understand what Job is saying about creation and about ongoing divine power and justice within it, it is helpful to sort out these references, remembering that in every case they are referred to as "enemies" of God.

> I am growing nervous (how you will laugh!)—but it is true,—really, wretchedly, ridiculously, fine-radically nervous. . . . I can neither read, write, or arouse myself, or any one else. My days are listless, and my nights restless. . . . I don't know that I sha'n't end with insanity, for I find a want of method in arranging my thoughts that perplexes me strangely.
>
> Lord Byron, "Letter to Francis Hodgson, October 13, 1811," in *Letters and Journals of Lord Byron*, ed. Thomas Moore, vol. 2 (London: 1830), 111–12, http://lordbyron.cath.lib.vt.edu/monograph.php?doc=ThMoore.1830&select=AD1811.27.

The important metaphor in chapter 26, illustrated by the references to death and chaos, is conflict. God has gained and continues to maintain divine rule by the real and threatened use of fear-evoking power. "Dominion and fear are with God" (25:2): divine rule is based on fear, not justice. The friends have previously described the Hebrew deity as a being well beyond human understanding, as being transcendent in power, control, and justice, but nowhere have they described God in such powerful terms as does Job in verses 5–13.

In Job's vision, Sheol and Abaddon stand naked before God's sight, a sign of their weakness and humiliation before the Creator. The cosmos, according to Job, is under the thumb of a cruel, harsh tyrant. The "shades" (the dead) "writhe in agony" (v. 5a, *huwl*; "tremble," NRSV) even in the shadows of Sheol. This is God as tormentor and oppressor, a God that neither Bildad nor the other friends have given voice to nor understood. And Job is just getting started. The entire universe lies passive under this divine rule (vv. 7–10) as God stretches, hangs, binds, covers, overspreads, inscribes circles around, and sets boundaries as the "pillars of heaven tremble, and are astounded at his rebuke" (v. 11). Creation then cowers under the heavy reproving, reprimanding, and censuring hand of God: it is hardly a picture of the first creation story of Genesis, where all that was created was declared "good."

And still Job is not finished. Why would God blow away the pillars of heaven, cause them to tremble "stunned by his blast" (v. 11a, Good)? Why through God's "power" and "understanding" (v. 12) would God still the "sea" and "strike down Rahab" (v. 12)? Why pierce the "fleeing serpent" (v. 13)? And why overcome the "sky" (v. 13a; "heavens," NRSV)? In no myth in the ancient world does any deity successfully displace a sky god in combat.[33] We could say that Job is wildly concocting new mythic themes, depicting a universe tyrannically controlled by a divinity interested only in a sadistic, troublesome use of dominion, sovereignty, and power over a creation once declared "good" but now manageable only through force.

An easy way out of this remythologized divine tyranny is to revert to an earlier proposal that they are in fact the words of Bildad and as such conform to Bildad and the friends' "understanding" of divine forces in creation. But we have chosen not to pursue this route and, in any case, what is said about the Creator in chapter 26 is of a completely different order of magnitude than the tepid comments of Bildad describing the "dominion" of the Creator in chapter 25. Once again, as Job's words, the descriptions of divine control in creation over death and chaos and destruction are breathtaking. In them we hear Job's terror-driven quest to confront God face to face merge with Job's venomous sarcasm.

The friends trivialized and domesticated the transcendence they so readily ascribed to God. Job is on a mission to magnify divine transcendence: "Oh, that I knew where I might find him, that I might come even to his dwelling!" (23:3). "Would he contend with me in the greatness of his power? No; but he would give heed to me" (23:6). The friends have pushed up against the limits of Job's patience and of his theology. They trivialized and domesticated the God that "made my heart faint; the Almighty has terrified me; If

33. See Good, *In Turns of Tempest*, 285.

only I could vanish in darkness, and thick darkness would cover my face!" (23:17). Job's suffering brings a new ability to balance opposites—to pray that he might come to God's dwelling at the same time that he admits that the Almighty terrifies him. It is *coincidentia oppositorum* that brings new clarity for seeing God's real power in God's ability to control God's own inclination to control. Job is newly balanced in other ways as well, vehemently condemning the friends even as he is awakening to a new vision of God's raw power, God's terror, and God's wonder.

In effect Job is releasing the false surety of a too-easily domesticated God: Job is raw to the bone and inching ever closer to the kind of emotional theological condition that is often the predicate of a divine showing, and divine showing never leaves the person as the person was found.

The final verse echoes an earlier claim and anticipates what is yet to come. Verse 14 is in many ways not unlike the divine power Job describes in chapter 26; in "whisper" we hear little of God, in "thunder" we hear too much: who can understand? The NRSV reads:

> These are indeed but the outskirts [*qatsoth*; "fringes"]
>> of his ways;
>> and how small a whisper [*shemets*] do we hear of him!
> But the thunder of his power who can understand?

The verse looks back, reflecting Eliphaz describing the way his night message came to him:

> Now a word came stealing to me,
>> my ear received the whisper [*shemets*] of it.
>> (4:12)

The re-presentation of Eliphaz's vision is brought to the reader's attention through the whispering of a word. Such are the threads weaving through this poetic cloth of power and terror, of whisper and thunder. But how different the threads are: the whisper from Eliphaz's spirit-counselor tells him all he needs to know; Job's small whisper is only tantalizing, drawing attention but explaining

> And one feels slipping into the
>   dark spiral
> Of the abyss where Job,
>   Thales, Epicurus have fall'n,
> Where one goes agroping for
>   someone in the pit,
> When man says, Answer! and
>   God is not able.
>
> Victor Hugo, cited in Samuel Terrien,
> *Job: Poet of Existence* (New York: Bobbs-
> Merrill), 167.

nothing. And another slight tightening of this thread linking Eliphaz, Bildad, and Job through spirit, word, and whisper occurs: nowhere else in Scripture does the word for whisper, *shemets*, occur but in these two instances in Job, one complete in its smallness, one overwhelming in its thundering.

The thread also runs forward through the narrative into a future not yet revealed, but suggested. As Balentine points out, Job's "description of the mystery and power of divine governance in the world (26:5–14) foreshadows what God will subsequently spell out in more detail for Job in chapters 38–41."[34]

In an even deeper discernment of divine activity, Job refuses to accept that this is the full sum of what God intends to reveal. Here in chapter 26 God seems to have revealed to Job—whether by "accident" or by "whisper" or by wisdom—that the divine power is fierce and ever vigilant and were this not so, darkness and chaos would swallow all the "good" heretofore created. In this chapter Job has been contemptuous to his friends, but he is also acknowledging, through praise, the divinity with which he is much more concerned. He concludes with the question, "Who can understand the thunder [*ra'am*] of God's power?" The thunder of God's power is what Job has been describing, but who can understand it? His friends apparently already have the answers: in their minds they need search no longer; their questioning is finished. Job will "match God thunder for thunder until he has had his full say. Only then can the answer to the question he anticipates from God in response be fully adjudicated: 'Can you thunder (*tar'ēm*) with a voice like his?' (40:9)."[35]

---

34. Balentine, *Job*, 382–83.
35. Ibid., 383.

27:1–23

Job's Response and Interlude: Terrors Overtake Them

Chapter 27 *Paradox and Beauty*

Another beautiful piece of poetry, the end of the third and final dialogue cycles is paradoxical and controversial, and it ends asking more questions than it solves. Because of its seemingly redundant images and theological claims, some might wish the dialogue had ended much before chapter 27. Others find chapter 27 a fitting place to pause, to catch one's breath (*ruach*) and, resting in the quiet, to assess where Job, God, the friends, and especially the reader have been, ponder what the mystery and terror of God's silence entails, consider the thorny meaning of justice in the world, and find parallels in one's own life to the slow evaporation of Job's hope. Still others have claimed that the book should in fact end at chapter 27. But many will want to marvel and absorb what David Wolfers has called "a landmark in the history of ideas: [the] development of moral philosophy."[36] Good summarizes chapter 27 as a piece of writing that "completely redefines the debate, in effect, redefining its protagonists."[37]

The controversy and the questions begin at the structural level. As we have seen, many commentators give a good portion of this chapter over to Zophar, others claim substantial portions of the third speech cycle are missing, especially here in chapter 27, and others do follow the earliest sources of the text in attributing the entire speech, as we have it today, to Job. There is a certain amount of vitriol among commentators on opposite ends of the spectrum. But, if the reader is able to accept paradox, able to find a certain comfort in ambiguity, and willing to suspend Western logic and its need for closure, the poem becomes exponentially richer, evocative, and even disturbing when read in its entirety as an utterance of Job both to his friends and to God.

---

36. Wolfers, *Deep Things*, 286.
37. Good, *In Turns of Tempest*, 287.

Seeing all of chapter 27 as a speech of Job, we will emphasize the paradox and the mystery—especially of the divine-human relationship—that Job himself highlights in this speech. Beginning the chapter, Job gives a series of oaths declaring his innocence and by implication God's guilt; in doing this he also claims that his conscience is clear (vv. 1–6). The basis of Job's claim to truth is his own experience, and he dares to invoke an oath against any "enemy" who would contradict him (vv. 7–10). Job also has something significant to teach his friends about the "hand" that wields the divine power that "encloses" him (vv. 11–12). Job's speech ends by describing the punishments a righteous God must inflict on the wicked (vv. 13–23). These final words sound suspiciously like what we would expect one of the friends, especially Zophar, to speak. As Carol Newsom writes, "These are persons who finally have no more to say to one another and no desire to hear one another any longer."[38] This may be true in part, but by the end of the book, Job will experience a complete upheaval in how he experiences his moral and spiritual world and in the way humanity and God understand and are in relation with one another.

FURTHER REFLECTIONS
Job's Mashal (Discourse)

The first hint that Job has turned a spiritual and theological corner is the way he opens this speech. In every previous speech of Job's, the writer/editor has Job begin, "Then Job answered." In 27:1 this changes and Job opens with a fresh, formal introduction: "And Job again took up his discourse" (mashal; "proverb, parable"). This seemingly simple alteration is a first clue that, while the dialogue between the friends and Job is disintegrating rapidly, Job is preparing himself for a deeper conversation or "discourse."

The term mashal refers to a variety of literary forms, most of which have to do with the wisdom tradition. Balentine notes that,

---

38. Carol Newsom, "Job," in *NIB* (Nashville: Abingdon, 1996), 4:522.

"The etymology of the Hebrew word [*mashal*] suggests two related ideas: comparison (from *mšl* 'to be like') and authoritative word (from *mšl* 'to rule')."[39] Both ideas are at work in the literary form of a proverb or parable that brings together two things for comparison so that one or both may be more fully understood. The *mashal* as a proverb may then have the power of an authoritative word that rules human (or as Job hopes, divine) behavior, or helps one grasp the truth of life.[40] Balentine adds that, "If [Job's] enemy could experience what it is like to be treated as one of the wicked, then perhaps he would have more compassion for Job."[41]

One of the reasons for Job's turn to the proverb or parable form of a *mashal* is a rising sense of disjunction and confusion concerning the relation between the righteous and the wicked. Though Job once again states clearly in this chapter that he considers himself to be righteous and innocent, he nonetheless is experiencing suffering in a way that has meaning for him only in the context of punishment justly inflicted on the wicked. The intriguing question in the midst of Job's *mashal* in chapter 27 is: who for Job is the real "enemy," the truly wicked, the one deserving of punishment and suffering that Job himself is experiencing? To this point the answer is ambiguous. One possibility is the friends, but if the comparison in his *mashal* is intended for the friends, there is little evidence that as the wicked they are much affected by unrighteous suffering. If the comparison is meant for Job, the *mashal* does not clarify anything for him. Could the comparison possibly be meant for God? Balentine concludes, "Only then [in chapters 29–31 when Job once again takes up his *māšāl*] will we know more certainly who Job thinks his enemy is, how Job expects this enemy to respond to what he has said, and what is at stake if the dialogue about the enemy and the wicked really has dead-ended."[42]

---

39. Balentine, *Job*, 399.
40. Cf. Habel, *Job*, 379, on the comparative quality of the *mashal* and the idiom, which Job himself uses, of "to take up a *mashal*."
41. Balentine, *Job*, 399–400.
42. Ibid., 400.

27:2–6 *Job's Oath of Innocence*

Habel is the primary (though by now not the singular) advocate of
the theory that the book of Job is structured according to the metaphor of "trial." Legal language describing God and people as litigants in trial occurs frequently in the Hebrew Bible. Normally God
is depicted as the plaintiff (and judge) in such cases and God's adver-
saries (individuals, Israel, foreign nations) are the defendants. Prophetic pronouncements often are formulated according to this trial
metaphor in which God indicts, examines, and ultimately judges
Israel for failing to obey the covenant.[43] It is not surprising, then,
that Habel interprets verses 1–12 in terms of the trial metaphor.

Habel then makes the case that the adversary is God. This is a rare
and bold contention. In the Hebrew Bible, God as adversary occurs
elsewhere only in Jeremiah, who dares to imagine that he will reverse
the process of the trial metaphor and become the plaintiff who summons God into court to answer charges that it is God, not Jeremiah,
who is guilty of injustice (Jer. 12:1–4). But what was for Jeremiah
a fleeting thought becomes for Job a primary objective. Identifying
God as the enemy and insisting on his right to call God to court is
bold, rare, a reversal of Job's moral universe . . . and dangerous. The
verses are pivotal and transitional for several reasons: (a) they look
back to the prologue and especially to Job's protests that he is a man
of integrity (*tummah*), which echoes God's own testimony about
Job in the heavenly court; (b) they formally close the speeches with
the friends; (c) they introduce the formal testimony of chapters
29–31, which are, in effect, an elaborate testimony of Job's integrity;
and (d) they look forward to the theophany, in that they are the one
public statement of Job to which God makes reference (cf. 40:8).

Once again paradox and ambiguity pervade this chapter: Job
seeks a comprehensible God who is in fact incomprehensible. Job
dares to swear an oath to God. As Habel has written, "Job's oath . . .
is not just another verbal outburst . . . but a catalytic action in the
narrative plot which is designed to initiate action from God."[44] Job

---

43. See Habel, *Job*, 54–57; cf. Balentine, "The Trial Metaphor in Job," in *Job*, 165.
44. Habel, *Job*, 380.

has no idea whether the action he calls for will itself be catalytic. But Job has already summoned God to court or confessed his wish that God would summon him (13:22). He has issued challenges (13:19), made accusations (9:22, 28), protested his innocence (9:20–21), summoned the earth as a witness (16:18), hoped for a mediator to intervene (19:25), cried out in anguish against God's fury (16:9–17), and sought to find God's abode (23:3). But in all this, God "has taken away my right" (v. 2a, *mishpat*; "judgment, case, litigation") and embittered (*marar*) "my soul" (*nefesh*, v. 2b). Job's oath is a final, desperate act, the paradox being that Job "now rests the full weight of his claim to innocence on this conflicted God, his persistent adversary and his chronically absent advocate."[45]

Job's oath is that he will speak the whole truth and nothing but the truth. Job states the substance of his oath in verses 4–5 with three "if" (*'im*, not translated in NRSV) clauses: if his "lips" should ever "speak falsehood"; if his "tongue" should ever speak "deceit" (*remiyah*); and if he should ever soil his "integrity" (*tummah*) by saying the friends are right, then may God declare Job guilty. Job's expression "far be it from me" (v. 5a) is a formulaic expression introducing a serious declaration that carries with it a self-imprecation or self-curse. In effect, Job is saying, "May I be damned if I declare you in the right." And Job's declaration of personal righteousness is at the same time an implication that God is the guilty party.

As noted above, to take an oath on an unjust God might seem a contradiction in terms, but throughout the narrative Job's moral and legal opposition remains intact on the basis of his own integrity. God has turned away his case and embittered Job's soul, yet this opening oath of Job's presents a duality between Job's truthfulness and the deity's injustice. About this intriguing duality one commentator writes, "What is so fascinating about the remainder of this speech is the way it completely redefines the debate by, in effect, redefining its protagonists. In order to maintain his moral rightness, Job inverts the terms of the prior discussion, thus standing the entire moral universe upon its head. The only factor that remains stable throughout this

---

45. Balentine, *Job*, 401.

> In Job's complaint as such we cannot distinguish between right and wrong in such a way as to fix on any of his utterances and say that this is right or this is wrong. . . . Inextricably intermingled are the glorious sincerity with which he strictly refuses to see white or grey where there is only black, to transform God in this incomprehensible form into God in a comprehensible form, and on the other side the shamelessness with which he does not even request but demands as a right that God should put off this alien form and make Himself comprehensible, as though He were not his God even in this form. He rightly maintains as God's partner the cause which he has never abandoned but consistently championed. He rightly maintains his righteousness before God.
>
> Karl Barth, *Church Dogmatics*, IV/3.1 (Edinburgh: T & T Clark, 1961), 406.

redefinition is what Job, unknowingly following Yahweh's lead, calls his 'integrity' (*tummah*, cf. 2.3)."[46]

Twentieth-century theologian Karl Barth also speaks of this "integrity" as the crucial stabilizing influence in the book. Barth's insight is found not in a commentary on the book of Job, but in his *Church Dogmatics*. There, amid a larger discussion of the mystery of the incarnation, Job becomes for Barth a "true witness" to Christ. For Barth, Job's integrity is witnessed throughout the suffering, the mystery, the shredding of his moral universe, and by the idea that he "maintains [himself] as God's partner."

A final irony is found in verse 3 of this opening oath. The verse on the surface states simply that Job will adhere to his oath as long as he lives. But buried in the two short lines lies an irony of the power of creation held in the same "hand" as the justice that defines the moral configuration of individual, community, and creation itself. Job resolves to stick to his oath as long as he has breath still in him: "as long as my breath [*neshamah*] is in me and the spirit of God [*ruach eloah*] is in my nostrils" (v. 3). This sounds simple. To have "breath" (*neshamah*) is to be alive. But his pledge to speak the truth as long as he has "spirit of God" (*ruach eloah*) in his nostrils hints at something deeper and, once again, ironic, paradoxical, and even chilling should Job misstep. Job's life

46. Good, *In Turns of Tempest*, 287.

is a manifestation of God's spirit within him that is itself the divine life force given at the beginning of creation as the *ruach 'elohim* (Gen. 1:2, "spirit") hovering over the waters. In this oath of innocence, grounded in Job's "integrity" and "righteousness," he swears his innocence and implies divine guilt even as he holds the divine breath or spirit of that guilt as *the* vital force "within his nostrils." When God formed the first human "from the dust of the ground, and breathed into his nostrils the breath [*neshamah*] of life" (Gen. 2:7), "God set in motion a journey that would inevitably lead one day to someone named Job speaking *to* God, even *against* God, with God's own 'breath' and 'spirit.'"[47]

27:7–12 *Seeking Relationship, Losing Hope*

Having sworn an oath of innocence both *against* and *to* his God, Job now moves to redefine what it means as a human to be in relation with God. In these verses Job redefines his standing before God and in so doing redefines the moral order under which he has been laboring. "Wickedness" and "righteousness" are standard opposites in the Hebrew Bible. It is therefore appropriate that Job, the man of "righteousness" (v. 6a), begins by comparing his enemy to the "wicked" (*rasha*).

But who is the "enemy": the friends, God, someone from the divine court? As a *mashal* used in the comparative, metaphorical sense, Job offers a comparison between the "wicked" (v. 7a, *rasha*) and "my enemy" (v. 7a, *'oyebi*), "my opponent" (v. 7b, *mithqomemi*) and the "unrighteous" (v. 7b, *'awwal*; "unjust, vicious"). The "enemy" and "opponent" are singular, while the friends who are obviously addressed in verses 11–12 are referred to in the plural. Grammatically, then, it becomes apparent that God is the "enemy." Previously, Job made pointed though still implicit suggestions that God is his adversary and enemy: God is the foe (*shar*) who attacks Job viciously (16:9). God is the field commander who besieges Job as if he were God's own foe (*shar*, 19:11–12). And Job has wondered why God should treat him *as if* he were his "enemy" (*'oyeb*, 13:24; cf.

47. Balentine, *Job*, 404.

33:10). But Job now combines these ideas: Job's enemy who attacks him (chaps. 16, 19) he now dismisses as "wicked" and "unrighteous." Job's adversary at law, his adversary against any kind of peace or hope, his adversary against all he had previously assumed would be his as a righteous man, and the adversary whose agents include Job's friends and creation itself, is God.

Another literary subtlety of the poet arises here: Job still does not say that God is wicked, but that he is "like" the wicked or that God behaves "as if" God were wicked. There is a theological reason why Job does not say "God is wicked," but it is not that Job at this point has any scruples against doing so. As we might expect from this poet, it is a bit more subtle. God has caused Job to suffer "as if" Job were wicked: theologically the issue is one of innocent suffering. Thus regardless of divine guilt, Job would like God to experience suffering in the way that Job has, suffering that cuts all the deeper because it is inflicted on the innocent. As we have noted in this chapter, Job is turning what it means to be a child of God on its ear: he wants God to experience the same calamities that the innocent suffer. Job says God is "like" the wicked, but he would like God to experience suffering as an innocent.

As a new dimension to the divine-human relationship develops between Job and God, there are two experiences Job would particularly like God to experience: (1) having all "hope" (v. 8a, *tiqvah*) vanish as a result of being "cut off" (v. 8a, *batsa*; "gain by violence") from God as God "takes away" (v. 8b, *shalah*; "draws out, extracts") Job's life; and (2) having to "cry" (v. 9a, *tseaqah*) out to God continuously, imploring the favor (v. 10a, *anog*) of God, and "calling" (v. 10b, *yikra*) continuously. In both cases he wants God to experience them in Job's context, that of righteous suffering. Of course God will not experience these, but will God answer? God has not to date, and the question lingers, the silence accumulates.

In lament form, Job's prayer is little different from Moses' prayer of intercession to God on behalf of his people. The exception is that in Job's case God neither responds with compassion (the old relational model) nor does God respond out of a covenantal promise (the new relational model). And these are *not* passive constructions:

Eloah drains Job's life away; El will not hear his cry; he implores Shaddai; he calls on El continuously.

We are nearing the end of the dialogues. In suffering Job has lost all hope. In seeking peace, seeking justice through prayer, Job receives only silence. Job describes himself as afflicted with the sufferings of a person in "trouble" (v. 9b, *shara*); he wants God to experience the same as if God were a godless person without hope.

We have seen the "hand of God" (v. 11, *yad 'el*) before. Job has taught the friends that the "hand" of God is the hand of Job's relentless foe (cf. 19:21), that God's "hands" have fashioned him as an object targeted for destruction (10:8), that God's "hand" has terrified him (13:21), and that God's "hand" has touched him nearly to death (19:21–22). But Job concludes that to speak further to the friends would be a waste of time. More than a waste of time, it would be senseless in ways that the poet has already prepared us for and that the NRSV does not quite capture with its translation as "vain." "So why talk nonsense" is the blunt, interpretive translation of the JPS. The phrase is *hebel tehbalu*, literally to "blow empty wind," or, as translated even more literally in a way that is pregnant with resonance from earlier chapters in Job and as Job's final judgment of his friends: "Why do you puff a wind-gust?" (v. 12, Good).

27:13–23 *"The east wind lifts them up and they are gone"*

Once again, in this section Job speaks in beautiful, concrete, and poetic images of the fate of the wicked. But the fact that the images are concrete and the poetry recognizably true, in the way that only the creative imagination can be true, does not lessen the mystery of what he says. The poet of Job is not a person interested in Western logic so much as in the mystery of God. In following Job we find we are on a journey not of answers, but of movement ever deeper into the mysterious, even incomprehensible ways of God. What Job finds in the mystery is not what the comforters themselves have been saying ad nauseam about the fate of the wicked, but something entirely *new* and provocative: there is a sense in which in divine mystery, God too is wicked, or at least complicit in some way in evil. Job will find that at the very least God plays with chaos (Leviathan and Behe-moth), and it is never clear if God created that chaos represented by the monsters or if God even has control over them.

One of the primary arguments that these verses belong in the mouth of a friend, particularly Zophar, begins with verse 13. With only a slight alteration, the verse is a recitation of the last words of Zophar (20:29). More important, however, than the repetition are the slight alterations. The following comparison highlights the pri-mary alteration:

Zophar (20:29a): "This is the portion of the wicked *from* God
                [*me' elohim*]."
     Job (27:13): "This is the portion of the wicked *with* God
                [*'im 'el*]."

A preposition may make a great difference. Zophar's "portion of the wicked" is received "from Elohim," and it is punishment. Job's "portion of the wicked" is received "with El," in "the presence . . . of the deity, and it is reward."[48] That is, humankind receives its "portion" to the extent that it matches God's portion. In the second half of verse 13 the prepositions return to match, Job saying "*from* Shaddai" (27:13b) and Zophar saying "*from* El" (20:29b). Balentine elabo-rates on this important prepositional difference: "The normal mean-ing of this preposition (*'im*) is 'accompaniment' or 'addition,' hence Job appears to be speaking of the punishment the wicked deserve '*along with*' or '*in addition to*' God. Given this meaning, his objective would be not only to describe the just rewards of the wicked, but also to suggest that inasmuch as God, his 'enemy,' behaves 'like the wicked' (v. 7), then God deserves to experience the same fate as the wicked."[49] Calling on a possibly wicked God to judge God makes many commentators uneasy; they often suggest that the preposition "with" in 27:13 be emended to "from," bringing it in conformity to Zophar and in comfort with their own theology. But we can let Job

---

48. Good, *In Turns of Tempest*, 289.
49. Balentine, *Job*, 409.

say what he really says in the text: he *is* calling on God to judge God and he *is* implying that God, as Job has experienced God, *is* wicked. It is better that we wrestle with this seeming paradox as Job himself is forced to do than to change the text in the name of conformity or comfort.

Theologically, as long as Job must live with that same "spirit of God in my nostrils" (v. 3b) who terrifies him and who "has taken away my right" (v. 2a), Job here continues to stand firm on his "integrity" (v. 5b): he "cries" (v. 9a) for justice to be applied to the Judge of heaven in the same way he has experienced justice here on earth, and he "calls" (v. 10b) for peace. Job opens up a dark place in the divine justice and invites us into the paradoxical mystery of divine injustice as it plays out in human lives. Unlike logic, Job's poetic invitation gives permission to dwell in paradox and incomprehensibility, to open our own dark places, to call a wicked God to task, and to experience the same silent response that Job experiences as we ourselves cry for justice and as we make our own hopeless calls for peace. In fact, Job's view has reached a new level from that of his friends; Job begins to see a deeper, spiritual fate of the wicked that is not to be *envied*. It is true that their fate cannot be denied: many of the wicked, individuals as well as communities, do prosper in this life. At least they prosper materially, and if the values of a culture are based on material acquisition, there is a sense in which they do prosper. But to see this as "prospering" is to miss the true point of the punishment that is so sharply distinct from Job's sense of punishment. There is no denying that Job suffers righteously

In tests of convergent thinking there is almost always one conclusion or answer that is regarded as unique, and thinking is to be channeled and controlled in the direction of that answer.... In divergent thinking, on the other hand, there is much searching about or going off in various directions.... Divergent thinking ... is characterized ... as being less goal-bound. There is freedom to go off in different directions.... Rejecting the old solution and striking out in some new direction is necessary, and the resourceful organism will more probably succeed.

J. P. Guilford, "Traits of Creativity," in *Creativity and Its Cultivation*, ed. H. H. Anderson (New York: Harper, 1959), 151, 157, 160–61.

and in many, many ways. But Job's point is that the wicked who do "prosper" are not to be *envied*, but rather pitied for what they lose. As Wolfers writes, "The penalty for a life of evil is the loss of something infinitely more precious than any that has yet been taken from Job— the right reserved for upright men(13:16; 23:7; 27:9) to approach God, the certainty of continuity through the ages for his posterity, and the embrace of death as a friend."[50]

This indeed is something new. There is something of a spiritual nature that supersedes the apparent material prosperity of the wicked: a reciprocal relationship with God, the promise of continuity and cohesiveness for his posterity, and peace (*shalom*) even in death. Job has none of these things at this point, but he is moving toward a new position from that of his friends, in which he finds that whatever prosperity the wicked do enjoy is not worth the loss of a working partnership with God, a sense of justice, a sense of peace. The irony is that for those who know the final outcome of the book of Job, Job has hit on something that is indeed the fate of the just. He is seeing that the wicked do not really prosper as they might seem; he is intuiting that the righteous might have something *enviable* regardless of their present fate, though he as yet does not see it clearly. Beyond the material and social wealth that often seems the reward of the wicked, there is something intangible but real in the faith of the righteous that the wicked miss: divine relationship, posterity, peace, and hope.

The dialogue has run its course. While Job is contemplating what might be *enviable* among the righteous, even in suffering, with the dialogue dead there is silence. We may want to pause with the silence that comes at the end of chapter 27. The wind hurls its power against Job without pity (v. 22), it claps its hands at him as if urging him to arouse himself from his dreams (v. 23a), the wind in the desert "hisses" (v. 23b), a mocking nothingness in the silence. Job sits yet in the hissing silence.

---

50. Wolfers, *Deep Things*, 251.

28:1–28

Wisdom: The Hidden Observed

Where Shall Wisdom Be Found?

Chapter 28 gives us one of the most alive, gemlike pieces of poetry in all of Scripture, in all of literature. The theme of the poem is how and by whom wisdom can be found. As such the poem may seem at first a puzzling interruption in the overall story of Job. But the answer to the question of where wisdom is to be found is itself puzzling: it is a pause in time, a rest in place; it is also movement, a search in time for a way to a place for the acquisition and probing of a design, of a structure. For humans wisdom is often puzzling and obscure, and so for the sake of humans the poem ends with a simple, concrete answer to the meaning of this wisdom pause (v. 28).

But true wisdom is not a thing: it is, as we have implied, a place, a source, a discovery, an acquisition, a way, a probing, a doing. And unlike Proverbs 8, wisdom in Job 28 is not a personification and a beloved assistant in creation. Wisdom in this lovely poem is at once more primordial, more ephemeral, more provocatively mysterious even than that. In Job wisdom seems not to be a natural attribute even of God, but something acquired and found by God. Specifically, wisdom is acquired by God in the process of creating the universe. Wisdom is thus a principle and design guiding the very activity by which she is known. For humans wisdom is a form of piety (v. 28). But to the extent that the mystery of divine wisdom is revealed in Scripture, the hint is that the possibility exists for humans to discern wisdom in the *act* of creating, in the *doing* of righteousness, in, for instance, the *way* and *place* of prayer.

Chapter 28, as a creative piece of writing, is thus a way of wisdom, the reading, praying, and assimilation of which is a way of understanding the designs and functions and movements of wisdom itself. The poem twice asks, in effect, "Where shall wisdom be found?" (vv. 12, 20). It ends with a direct answer (v. 28) that is at the same time an admission of wisdom's hiddenness within governing principles and contours of creation. The hidden/revealed nature of wisdom finds a parallel in the divine nature: discerning or knowing wisdom

is for humans one thing while for God it is something quite different. We can say that humans are participants in wisdom as an act
of divine creation. We can say that for YHWH wisdom is an active
agent in the fabric and design of creation itself. In the language of
the poem, the integrity and truth through which we search for wisdom is expressed in terms of some of the finest, most difficult-to-
obtain aspects of creation—for instance, onyx, sapphire, gold, coral,
crystal, rubies (vv. 16–18). But while it is clear that these are divine
creations, for humans they are poetic symbols of the obscurity, rar-
ity, and value of wisdom, of what we are likely to find in our search
for wisdom. Gems are precious to be sure, difficult to acquire. And
wisdom is hidden, even more inaccessible than gems.

If this sounds incomprehensible, it is meant to be: in chapter 28
we are brought, through the suffering of Job, into an encounter with
wisdom that is at the same time an encounter with mystery. The core
theme of chapter 28 becomes the nature, mode, and measure of continuity between humanity and God along this axis of wisdom played
out in the mystery of creating. It is an invitation that in another context was described by the twelfth-century mystic Richard of St. Victor as a contemplative wisdom journey "into the secret places of
divine incomprehensibility." With Richard of St. Victor, the author
of this poem in Job will insist that the secret to finding wisdom is in
the *doing*: in *doing* righteousness, in *doing* justice, in *doing* a turn to
God, in *doing* creation.

FURTHER REFLECTIONS
Wisdom in Job

Chapter 28 is a pause in the story of Job. It is an odd sort of pause,
in that it speaks of the search for wisdom as a near equivalent of a
search for God; at the same time it must be read and understood
through the reality of Job's ongoing suffering. This narrative pause,
meditative and beautiful and restful as it is, has embarrassed, even
irritated, many commentators. Not only does it seem to many readers to be out of place, even interruptive, in the story of Job, it is also

unclear who is speaking the poem, to whom it might be addressed, and how the search for wisdom described in the poem might be connected to the issue of suffering or of evil.

The chapter is a refreshing pause about which there is much disagreement. Habel presents an impressive list of commentators with their objections, puzzlements, and suggestions for "improving" the poem by placing it elsewhere in Job or deleting selected lines.[51] Stephen Mitchell's otherwise lovely rendition of the poem even omits chapter 28 altogether.

Whatever might be an objection to the poem as an intrusion, an early lyrical creation of the poet placed with no reference to the rest of Job, an interlude, a look at the lack of wisdom in the earlier part of the poem, a misplaced bridge, or simply disposable, the poem itself is among the most beautifully rendered in the Hebrew Bible. That in itself is hardly a justification for its presence in the story of Job or for its presence in Scripture at all. But there are as many reasons to treasure the poem as and where it is as there are for objecting to it: the poem does make an obvious and direct connection to Job 1:1; its themes of "searching" and "seeking along" a "way" or "path" in the darkness and gloom are also presented metaphorically throughout the book of Job; the all-seeing eye of a divine Creator in the poem is experienced by Job throughout the book, at times as a comforting presence, at times as an intolerable presence; the poem is itself an example of what it describes; as an interlude it forces us to meditate on the relation between suffering and wisdom; though it anticipates the speeches of YHWH in the whirlwind, it does so only as tantalizing hints; the idea that YHWH sees, names, establishes, and searches out wisdom only in the act of creation is a haunting rumination on both the comprehensibility and incomprehensibility of God. Finally, and only in its final verse, the poem hints at wisdom as a way for Job himself to see, name, establish, and search out the face of God and to live once again a way of righteousness on a path that turns from evil (Job 1:1).

51. Cf. Habel, *Job*, 391–92.

The poem of chapter 28 is itself a creative act, a creative act that, according to the poem itself, is the only path or place or way of *doing* wisdom. In that sense it is a synopsis of Job's own journey, a transformative act placed in the *doing* of suffering. The question then becomes: is suffering a creative act out of which wisdom emerges from the secret places of divine incomprehensibility? The question may be unanswerable, but what the book of Job does show us is a man who points to a way that assists us in pausing and settling into our own suffering. Settling into suffering is something that for the most part we try to avoid. We know of and entertain joy: we have heard of it, we have seen it (42:5), we have experienced it. We have heard of suffering, seen it, but prefer blindness to our own and to others' suffering: if the onyx, sapphire, gold, coral, crystal, and rubies are symbols of suffering, we prefer to leave them in the dark, in the hidden places. The images of mining for precious gems and metals in chapter 28 are in turn images of mining suffering. As Carol Newsom has written, the chapter "serves as a sort of meditative interlude, reflecting on the dialogue that precedes it, and preparing for the final section of the book. . . . The important issue is not whether chap. 28 belongs where it is placed, but what role it plays."[52] The chapter, as does the entire book of Job, provides the needed "technology" for mining suffering.

28:1–11 *Of Precious Metals, Seeking, and Human Ingenuity*

The first section of the poem (vv. 1–11) describes the most precious metals and the heroic effort required to mine them. Job's friends refer to and think of themselves as sages, but they never claim to be wise. Job once enjoyed the respect of a man of wisdom, but Job likewise never claims to be wise. Chapter 28 also does not mention wisdom in these opening verses. It instead describes the mysterious origins of precious metals and the human ingenuity involved in finding, extracting, and acquiring them.

---

52. Newsom, "Book of Job," 528.

Even before wisdom has been mentioned, humans are portrayed in a flattering way. They recognize the value of precious metals. They know their "source" and their "place"; they know the process of extracting, refining, and smelting. They can transform what is precious into items of even more value; they can develop technology to overcome what initially shows itself as chaos. They know how to seek out such metals and as they do so "penetrate," almost like gods, the extremities and limits of darkness, deep chaos, and sinister, death-like gloom. In their search the miners are willing to work far from other humans, as if solitude were also a prerequisite of this seeking, penetrating, and extracting. Knowing the "place" and the "source" and the "path" to these metals, they are superior to other creatures, even those who have been endowed with sharper eyes or particular cunning. They are little less than gods: tearing up mountains "by the roots," carving through rock and damming up rivers, seeing what birds of prey do not see, finding the deep sources of things, and in their ingenuity and intelligence bringing hidden things to light.

In these few verses humans are illuminated and enlightened such that they contrast with Job's pitiable hiddenness. They are creations of many wonders: they are resourceful, cunning, persistent, and courageous; they know of sources, places, paths, and the nature of seeking; what they may lack in perceptual acuity they easily make up for by sheer intelligence and understanding; they are like gods in many ingenious ways and with their ever-evolving technology they can tame chaos, darkness, and fear; they know what is precious and beautiful and valuable.

Only after this precise, flattering account of the blessings of humanity come the questions: "But where shall wisdom be found? And where is the place of understanding?" (v. 12).

28:12–27 *"God understands the way to it and knows its place"*

The second section of the poem (vv. 12–28) describe the inability of humans to find wisdom: humans are not so adept at finding wisdom, in contrast to precious gems; God finds wisdom. Verse 12 asks where "wisdom" (*hokmah*) can be found? In asking about wisdom's

"place" (*maqom*) and its discernment (*binah*; NRSV "understanding"),[53] the poet suggests a formal parallel that will accentuate the
difference between humanity's impressive ability with metals (vv.
1–11) and God's infinitely more incomprehensible ability to know
wisdom. Already here in verse 12 the question revolves around
where wisdom can be "found" and the "place" of discernment. Seeking and finding, place and way have already been established as pre-
conditions to humanity's acquisition of precious metals; in the same
way, wisdom is immediately conditioned by finding, place, and way.

The next verse admits that mortals can seek and find a place and a
way, but when it comes to wisdom, "Mortals do not know the way to
it, and it is not found in the land of the living" (v. 13). In verses 2–3
and 6–8 referring to metals, mortals in the land of the living do know
the way and the "path"; they "search" and they find what is hidden,
they acquire and extract. The same cannot be said of wisdom. Even
the powers *beyond* the land of the living are helpless in the search
for wisdom: personifications of the primordial "Deep" (*tehom*; "sea,
abyss, confusion") and the watery chaos of the "Sea" (Yam) chant
of wisdom: "it is not in me" (v. 14). This denial of access to wisdom
is later echoed by Abaddon, a common name for Sheol, meaning
literally "destruction and death," and by "Death" (*maveth*) itself, who
together say only: "We have heard a rumor of it with our ears" (v.
22), literally "we have heard a hearing of it with our ears"; but of
wisdom they know not the way or the place.

In the context of the poem, only the miner can find or knows the
way to precious metals and gems. The way to wisdom is in effect
the path or way of the "inner miner." But for the inner miner seeking wisdom, the way is blocked by those primordial personifications
who themselves know nothing of wisdom: the Sea, Abaddon, Sheol,
Death. Job as an inner miner has been suggested in earlier verses: in
3:21 he makes an analogy between his longing for death and those

---

53. NRSV translates *binah* as "understanding" throughout this poem. *Binah* also has the
connotations of keen discernment, sharp intellect, correct judgment, and the experience
of seeing or hearing correctly. In light of the primary theme of wisdom in the poem, I
believe "discernment" to be the more nearly correct word; it is more naturally associated
with wisdom in theological and spiritual traditions than is "understanding." I will thus use
"discernment" for the rest of this chapter.

who dig for hidden treasures; in 10:22 Job characterizes the under-world as a land of darkness, gloom, and deep darkness without stars or God's light; and in 12:22 Job accuses God of uncovering deeps out of darkness in order to bring to light deep darkness.[54]

Verses 15–19 add another aspect to the inaccessibility of wisdom. First note that the question of locating wisdom (vv. 12–14) precedes the consideration of its value (vv. 15–19).[55] Secondly and more importantly, according to chapter 28 wisdom cannot be purchased at any price, even with any rare gem recovered by humans. Habel writes, "The higher Wisdom of this poem is not only more valuable than any precious stone or metal, but these costly materials are worthless for those who wish to acquire Wisdom. This higher level Wisdom cannot be bought; [it] is totally inaccessible by any normal human means of acquisition."[56] To emphasize this point, the poet packs these verses with the names of precious gems and gold as if such a conglomerate of wealth could somehow purchase at least a portion of the commodity of wisdom. Within the verses, five separate words for gold are used, the nuances of which are not discernible in English translations. Beginning by saying simply that wisdom "cannot be gotten for gold" (v. 15a), these verses pile up precious metals and stones like a heap of treasure, only to end in saying that wisdom cannot be bought (v. 19b).

Abaddon and Death have only heard "a rumor" of wisdom, but "God understands the way to it." Both the word "God" (*elohim*) and "he" (v. 23) are in emphatic positions in the sentence, setting the clear contrast between God and humanity: God knows the way to wisdom; humanity does not.[57] As we have seen, the "way" and the "place" are major motifs in Wisdom literature, and in verses 23–24 God "looks to the ends of the earth" and "sees everything under the heavens," finding the ways and the places. Still these verses do not describe God's relation to wisdom. Instead the poet hints at what

---

54. Cf. Gerald J. Janzen, *At the Scent of Water: The Ground of Hope in the Book of Job* (Grand Rapids: Eerdmans, 2009), 194.
55. Cf. Habel, *Job*, 390.
56. Cf. ibid., 399.
57. Habel notes that certain deities of the ancient Near East were also closely associated with wisdom as profound knowledge and the capacity for discerning hidden realities. See Habel, *Job*, 399.

wisdom is *not*: it is not an eternal, innate attribute of God; and it is something God too must in some way seek to discover and acquire.

What wisdom is in relation to God is finally revealed in four *creative* activities: seeing, establishing, declaring, and searching out (v. 27). YHWH is all seeing, in fact YHWH sees to the ends of the earth and everywhere under the heavens (v. 24), but it is only in those creative activities (v. 27) that YHWH "then" encounters wisdom. Wisdom's place in God's creative activity is theologically startling; God too must find the place where wisdom exists. Theologically, the poet of chapter 28 associates the divine knowledge of the way to the place of wisdom with the divine activity of creating the cosmos itself. The all-seeing YHWH must, according to the poet, search within the act of creation itself in order to find wisdom as something primordial, hidden, and in an important way external to God.

"When" God does something and "when" God does something else, "then" God sees wisdom. This "when . . . when . . . then" is typical of many creation stories of the ancient Near East.[58] Genesis 2:4b–7 and Proverbs 8:24–31 show this same grammatical structure. In the latter, for instance, we find: "When there were no depths I was brought forth. . . . Before the mountains had been shaped. . . . when he assigned to the sea its limit, . . . when he marked out the foundations of the earth, then I was beside him." In each case, and here in verses 25–27, the main clause, introduced by "then," contains the crucial conclusion.[59]

And what is the crucial conclusion concerning wisdom; where shall it be found? Wisdom in Job 28 is not, as in Genesis and most other Near Eastern creation stories, a "then" that follows after creation. Chapter 28 is also not like Proverbs, which plays the wisdom tradition against itself, portraying wisdom as the "when," abiding before, with, and as a helpmate of God in the process of the "then" of creation. Job 28:25–27 does something different, setting up a condition in which wisdom is to be found neither before as a helpmate of creation, nor after as a product of creation, but rather as an entity temporally simultaneous with creation and spatially

58. See ibid., 398.
59. Cf. Newsom, "Book of Job," 532.

coordinate with creation. Thus wisdom emerges in the act of creation itself. In giving measurement, order, and control to creation, God perceives wisdom. In giving order to the formless and the dark, YHWH encounters wisdom: the "wind" instead of breezing through chaos is given "weight," and in this is wisdom found; the unbounded "waters" of darkness are given boundary and "measure," and therein is wisdom seen; the rains are given "measure" (*hoq*, literally "law, statute"; NRSV "decree"), and within the rain's limits and bounds, wisdom is established; and in giving "thunderstorms" their "way" (*derek*), in following his "way" in the process of creating, wisdom is searched out and found. Thus in the process of bounding, measuring, controlling, and setting free creation, wisdom is found.

This unexpected depiction of wisdom is difficult to put into language, and the description of God's encounter with wisdom in verse 27 is understandably made up of verbs difficult to translate. The verbs are, after all, the fundamental metaphorical expressions of the divine relationship with wisdom (a relationship that to this point humanity is not privy to): it is no wonder they are difficult, but the four used in verse 27 are deftly chosen by the poet. "He saw it" is easy enough. But what of the other verbs? The NIV translation "attempts to bring out nuances of the verbs that would support the metaphor of wisdom as a jewel tested and confirmed as without flaws."[60] Gordis suggests that the Hebrew words "innumerable" (*'en mispar*) and "unsearchable" (*'en heqer*), elsewhere used of divine wisdom (Ps. 145:5; Isa. 40:28), are related to the verbs used here, "declared" (NRSV) or "appraised" (*sapparah*) and "searched out" (*haqarah*).[61] Habel suggests that the final verb, "searched out" (NRSV), could be translated as "probe, explore, or penetrate" and finds a parallel with the opening verb of the verse, "see," in the use of this verb early in the poem (v. 3).[62]

God's relation to wisdom can only be described in inscrutable ways, searched out, declared, probed, and seen by God, but not in ways amenable to the constraints of human language. Wisdom is a

---

60. Ibid., 532. Newsom notes that this approach is appealing on the surface but does not believe that the Hebrew really has that precise a connotation.
61. Gordis, *Job*, 311.
62. Habel, *Job*, 400.

doing more than is sayable, and even in the doing it is not the final product. Wisdom can be searched out, probed, declared, and seen only in an act of creation. It is a "faculty of the maker, and yet that wisdom is also worked into every aspect of the thing that is made.... [Wisdom may make crafting possible] but is only known in the skill."[63]

Chapter 28 stands as a statement of humanity's limited powers to seek out, find, and acquire wisdom. It is also a unique declaration of the capacity of God to see, declare, establish, and search out wisdom in the process of creation. Creation and wisdom are born together. Wisdom is creation's design and structure, while creation is wisdom's source and path.

28:28 *A New Look at Wisdom: Piety and Moral Order*

Wisdom is a treasure mostly inaccessible to humans, even more so than diamonds hidden deep in the earth. Wisdom is accessible to God, but here in Job, only in the process of the action of creation. Chapter 28 has made a beautiful case for both these assertions. Then we come to verse 28, which seems to overthrow all that has come before: the Lord "said to humankind": "fear of the Lord, that is wisdom; and to depart from evil is understanding." After what has preceded it, this is too much for many commentators: it is considered spurious and is often omitted, an unfortunate capitulation to rational consistency over poetic truth. A few things can be said about the verse before making a case that its presence enhances rather than detracts from the subtle work of the poet.

At first glance the verse is indeed surprising and seemingly at odds with the rest of the chapter. A second consideration is that "fear of the Lord" as the beginning of wisdom is common in biblical Wisdom literature. In this context "fear" (*yirah*) is not to be taken as a distressing emotion aroused by impending danger, evil, pain, or divine anger or revenge. Rather "fear" is best understood in the sense of piety, reverence, a sense of being in an awesome presence, or as Rudolph Otto defined the numinous, as being in the presence of

---

63. Newsom, "Book of Job," 533.

mysterium tremendum. At the same time "turning from evil" refers to the moral order and is generally conceived as an action: thus "turning from evil" is *doing* righteousness or *doing* justice. The use of the word *adonai* (Lord) is otherwise unattested in the book of Job, adding once again to the verse's unique quality.

Two major interpretations accept verse 28 as a legitimate portion of the poem: (1) a distinction must be made between the wisdom of a higher order that is accessible only to God, and the wisdom of the final verse, which refers to the piety or practical wisdom that humans can attain; and (2) distinctions focus not on the different types of wisdom but on the different modes in which it may be acquired: God acquires wisdom by immediate personal discovery in the process of creation in the past and in the process of sustaining creation in the present and into the future, while mortals acquire wisdom indirectly through the revealed path of the Lord of wisdom. These two positions are complementary and reflect the dual tradition in Israel of wisdom as a mystery of God acquired and employed by God in the ordering and organization of the universe and as the path for humans in understanding their God, creation, society, self, and family.[64]

With this perspective on verse 28, we can return to the question of why this traditional statement about wisdom is in chapter 28. The verse is irrefutably linked to Job 1:1, which declares that Job is "one who feared God and turned away from evil," thus attributing to Job the attributes of an ideal wise man. If this is the final solution of the dilemma of Job, it preempts the answer of God to Job in the whirlwind and certainly provides him no wisdom for facing the trials and crises that have enslaved him. "Turning from evil" neither protected Job from being afflicted by God nor provided him with the discernment to understand his affliction. One possibility of the seeming incongruous nature of verse 28 is that in writing it the poet actually emphasizes that traditional, orthodox answers are no longer of use to Job. And Job is no longer seeking traditional answers through wisdom: he is demanding direct, personal experience and access to God. In this sense wisdom no longer serves as an explanation for

64. Cf. Habel, *Job*, 401.

Job. At the most, if there is any sense to be made by Job at all of this curious verse, it is that "fear of God" and "shunning evil" may be two modes of participation in God through which some manner of personal experience and access to God may be possible.

Regardless of what verse 28 may mean for Job, for the reader, and for the poet, the verse sets up yet another layer of conversation and dialogue within the poem that deepens the meanings of wisdom, piety, the moral order, and disciplines dedicated to participation in God.

29:1–31:40

Job's Final Summation and Laments

Remembrance and Vision

An aesthetically complex, illuminating, and beautiful hymn of wisdom passes. And in its passing, Job 28 becomes an echo of the silence of Job 2:13, in which for "seven days and seven nights . . . no one spoke a word." The silence of chapter 2 is a sister to wisdom, while chapter 28 is brother to meditation, offering wisdom as a new opportunity for silence. For the reader, for Job and the friends, no doubt for the writer, and perhaps even for God, chapter 28 is "seven days and seven nights" of attention and creative reflection on suffering and justice, righteousness and power, the "fear of the Lord" and the path that "departs from evil."

After the silence of chapter 2, Job "opened his mouth" (3:1) and the conversation began. In 29:1 Job again breaks silence by opening his mouth, not in answer, but in discourse: "Job again took up his discourse" (*mashal*). In this new "discourse"—his final words before the whirlwind—Job remembers blessings (chap. 29), laments suffering (chap. 30), and declares his integrity and righteousness (chap. 31). With fear and trembling but now without restraint, Job offers a discourse of prayer that is a petition that a heretofore silent, absent God might speak and appear.

In both chapter 3 and chapter 29 Job evokes a theology of the word born from the wisdom of stillness and silence. In chapter 29 Job uses images of silence to describe the attitudes of other people to Job's leadership and the "good old days when he got on well with life

Where too it is fitly added, They waited for me as the rain, and opened their mouth as for the latter rain (29:23). For the words of holy preaching we undergo as rain, when by true humility we learn the dryness of our hearts, that we may be watered by the draught of holy preaching. . . . He "gave the later rain," because He caused the mystery of His Incarnation to be preached in the last days. Which same mystery because Holy Church ceases not to tell forth day by day, she waters the mouths of her hearers' hearts as it were by "the later rain."

Gregory the Great, *Morals*, vol. 2, Library of the Fathers of the Holy Catholic Church, 20.5, 448–49.

and God and his fellows."[1] Both the rhetoric and the formal genre of the book of Job sear this nascent theology of the word into the listening ear of the reader. Nearly the entire book (all but portions of chaps. 1–2, 28, and 42) is conversation, dialogue, soliloquy, speech, a narrative under the direction and steady navigation of the spoken word heard in the reader's ear, the ear of the heart. Certainly, the varieties of religious silence in chapters 2 and 28 bracket and focus what the ear can hear. Yet it is the varieties of the word that bracket and focus most of the book of Job—the word spoken by Job, the friends, the *satan*, God, and by implication the varieties of the divine word spoken in and through all creation, composing together the incarnate, cacophonous, but stunningly awesome, terrifying beauty of all voices forming the varieties of "speech" of the Word. In the only direct address to the deity (30:20–23) in the entire three-chapter speech, Job claims:

> You lift me up on the wind, you make me ride on it,
> and you toss me about in the roar of the storm.
>
> (30:22)

But in the new word of chapter 29, there is a relative calm before the real whirlwind. On it Job floats for our consideration something like a gospel of Job, a Joban journey into the brisk wind of the beatitudes.

1. Edwin M. Good, *In Turns of Tempest: A Reading of Job with a Translation* (Stanford, CA: Stanford University Press, 1990), 294.

Chapter 29
Job's Beatitudes, a Speech of Remembrance

Using memory as a guide in the discernment process of examen of conscience in chapter 29, the poet utilizes poetic imagery and poetic theology that invoke memory of earlier passages in Job. This section looks at these images of remembrance and then at the pride and beneficence that the use of these symbols implies about Job's own theological self-identification.

Job recalls the days when as a righteous, just man he used "light" to extinguish "darkness." These first memories (vv. 3–6) on one level evoke a time for Job of a rich and harmonious relationship with God, "when I was in my prime" (v. 4a), and serve as symbols of divine blessing and protection. At this point Job remembers when a "lamp shone over my head" and by God's "light I walked through darkness" (v. 3). These images of light and darkness recall the same images with which Job began his conversation in chapter 3. In chapter 3, however, light and dark are already perverted; for Job they are a curse (see 3:1–10, 20, 23) by which he expresses his wish that the light of day would never have witnessed his birth nor the dark of night the joy of his conception.

Another multivalent image used by Job in chapter 29—an image with both theological and spiritual resonance—is water. Like the image of light, water is linked poetically to theological issues throughout the book of Job. A passage in chapter 29 has striking theological roots in an earlier chapter. Job remembers and laments:

> My roots spread out to the waters,
>> with the dew all night on my branches.
>> (29:19)

Chapter 14 used similar images, but there they depict Job's complete abandonment by and of hope: "For there is hope for a tree, if it is cut down, that it will sprout again, and that its shoots will not cease . . . yet at the scent of water it will bud and put forth branches like a young plant. But mortals die" (14:7–10a). Other images of water become memories for Job of a time that is no more, in which he was permitted to offer solace to the people and to bring economic and spiritual comfort. The lament is past tense: "They listened to me, and waited, and kept silence for my counsel. After I spoke they did not speak again, and my word dropped upon them like dew. They waited for me as for the rain; they opened their mouths as for the spring rain" (29:21–23). As with reference to the light, this expresses the loss of Job's essential vocation.

Throughout this chapter Job also develops a theology of embodiment. It is the healing of the body—as body that encompasses soul and mind—that Job remembers in lament. His righteousness and justice together have been in the past a kind of medicine to the poor, the widowed, the oppressed. In verses 7–10, Job recalls that the body of his townsfolk responded to the benevolent medicine of Job's presence. The eyes, the ears, the feet, the mouth and the tongues, and the tears are, strikingly, the embodied recipients of Job's former glory and agents of his healing. It is clear in these images that Job has touched the lives of the people. To this theology of embodied justice, Job announces a new metaphor that summarizes the lost grace of this ministry: that of clothing. At the heart of a wide array of allusions to parts of the body Job announces, quite fittingly, that he is robed in righteousness and justice:

> I put on righteousness, and it clothed me;
> my justice was like a robe and a turban.
>
> (v. 14)

But what do Job's memories and images of light and water and body mean? Is this chapter a "provocative speech of remembrance"[2] through which, in his pride, Job somehow attempts to make himself appear to be the equal to God? Or is the chapter a compassionate memory, evoked in light, water, and body, of Job's most fundamental grief and of those most personal of losses initiated by his God? Job is in effect asking: What are the most devastating, personal losses we

---

2. Norman C. Habel, *The Book of Job: A Commentary*, Old Testament Library (Philadelphia: Westminster, 1985), 406. Many commentators claim that in chapter 29 Job has the audacity to make himself appear to be, in many ways, equal to God.

can experience? Do they have something to do with stripping a dedicated man's capacity to do what is right and what is good, depriving a person of the means to promote justice, cutting off the paths that lead to practicing righteousness and justice, to assisting the poor, the broken, the widow, and the orphan?

The theology of social justice laid out in 29:11–17 can be read in two ways. In the way championed by most commentators, Job's overall speech in chapter 29 is a final, desperate litany of self-praise. In this reading "my glory" (v. 20; *kabowd*) is interpreted as "my pride,"[3] and all that Job says in chapter 29 reflects this pride. This provocation then is read as a challenge to God.

This way of reading chapter 29 is plausible, even ingenious, and adds richness to the story of Job. But it fails to capture Job's complete, abject, and unrelenting loss, the grief of which is an emotional scar much more painful than false self-righteousness. What is Job's most lacerating wound? Certainly the loss of material goods is lamentable. The death of his children is unspeakable. Abandonment by his friends and his community is stifling, wilting. Physical torment that draws him close to death is terrifying. The absence of his God is unfathomable. But what drives Job to the pile of ashes outside of town and keeps him there? Perhaps another reading of Job's memory of divine glory and acts of personal compassion gets to the real source of Job's loss: he has been "fenced" (1:10; 3:23) out from what had been his calling, his vocation, ministry, his discipleship; these acts giving meaning to his life were derived from acts of compassionate love. What is the theology behind being "fenced off" from any hope of being a "father to the needy" (v. 16a) or from a life in which "I broke off the fangs of the unrighteous" (v. 17a)? There may be no theology for one "fenced off" from doing the good one is born to do. But that is Job's deepest wound: Job has been denied the blessing of healing another, fenced off from compassion toward others, jailed in a prison in which the only good he is permitted is the memory of the good he can no longer do.

---

3. Raymond P. Scheindlin, *The Book of Job* (New York: W.W. Norton, 1998), 120, reflects this hermeneutical bias even in his translation, rendering verse 20: "My *pride* constantly renewed for me . . ."

This more complete interpretation takes into account Job's present inability to arbitrate justice, to be the eyes of the blind, to bless the wretched, to champion the cause of the needy, to break the fangs of the wicked. Often the most debilitating effect of loss is not only material, familial, social, or cultural, but spiritual (where "spiritual" incorporates all these losses as well), in the sense that one loses the capacity and power to reach out to others and to assist them, regardless of their particular need. To read into or interpret Job's memory of compassionate ministry as a self-righteous litany of pride is itself a reading grounded in pride. Job may believe he is gathering strength for a litigious courtroom battle with God, but what he gathers instead are memories that have nothing to do with pride and everything to do with sapping what little resources he has left, resources formerly accumulated for the sake, benefit, and healing of others. It is from these life-sapping memories that Job builds an early beatitude.

FURTHER REFLECTIONS
Job's Beatitude

There are many parallels between Job (and Adam) and Jesus Christ as Christ is depicted in the New Testament. Job has been described as a prefigurement of Jesus Christ by writers as diverse as Gregory the Great, Thomas Aquinas, and John Calvin. One obvious parallel is the absolute righteousness and sinlessness of Job and Christ (regarding Job, see 1:1; 1:8; 1:22; 2:10, where both the narrator and YHWH confirm Job's righteousness, and 42:7, in which YHWH affirms all that Job has said about Job's righteousness). The second obvious parallel is the innocent suffering endured by both Job and Jesus Christ.

The parallels are so striking that we can begin to contemplate the possibility of a "gospel of Job." One aspect of such a gospel reading of Job would include the Joban beatitudes of chapter 29. Read the Beatitudes (Latin for "blessings") spoken by Jesus from the mountain in Mathew 5:3–12 and from the plain in Luke 6:20–23. In Job 29 Job remembers his own "beatitude," a time when he was blessed in giving blessing.

Job's beatitudes include a time when Job was blessed by God:

> As in the days when God watched over me;
> when [God's] lamp shone over my head,
> and by [God's] light I walked through darkness;
> when I was in my prime,
> when the friendship of God was upon my tent;
> when the Almighty was still with me,
> when my children were around me;
> when my steps were washed with milk,
> and the rock poured out for me streams of oil.
> (29:2b–6)

And there were those times when Job blessed, when Job was the beatitudes:

> I delivered the poor who cried,
> and the orphan who had no helper.
> The blessing of the wretched came upon me,
> and I caused the widow's heart to sing for joy.
> I put on righteousness, and it clothed me;
> my justice was like a robe and a turban.
> I was eyes to the blind,
> and feet to the lame.
> I was a father to the needy,
> and I championed the cause of the stranger.
> I broke the fangs of the unrighteous,
> and made them drop their prey from their teeth.
> ....
> I chose their way, and sat as chief,
> and I lived like a king among his troops,
> like one who comforts mourners.
> (vv. 12–17, 25)

Many of the church mothers and fathers saw in Job a man worthy of the apostles or even of Christ. In his *Commentary on Job,* John Chrysostom writes, "See how these miracles are worthy of the

apostles." Job, before the onset of his trials, was an apostle of beatitude, in compassionate service to healing.

Chapter 30

Abasement and Injustice

The tone of Job's complaint shifts radically from a lament of memory
in chapter 29 to a present tense, ongoing claim of abasement and
injustice in chapter 30. Instead of a lost capacity to administer justice and peace, Job now describes a personal experience of present
loss and additional assault and injustice that he traces to the hand of
God. As he moves from memory to reflection on his present situation, Job also shifts from self-analysis to lament of community abuse
and finally to God's apparent implication in human suffering. As if to
contrast even more sharply with the memory Job invokes in chapter
29, the soliloquy of chapter 30 on the present moment is peppered
with the phrase "and now" (*we'attah*, vv. 1, 9, 16), which draws the
reader from reflective memory to active participation in Job's ongoing, present lament.

This chapter of present lament and abasement can be divided
into four overlapping sections, each of which is linked to an image
that was, or is to become, a powerful metaphor in the literature of
spiritual journey or spiritual theology. The first section, organized
around the image of the desert (vv. 1–11), includes the enemies of
Job and the fears and uncertainties of wilderness spirituality. In the
desert spirituality, one is purified and finds clarity through hard-
ship: "want and hard hunger" (v. 3a), "gnawing the dry and desolate
ground" (v. 3b), "picking mallow . . . and to warm themselves the
roots of broom" (v. 4), "driven out from society" (v. 5a), "in the gul-
lies of wadis they must live, in holes in the ground, and in the rocks"
(v. 6). Job describes the life of a desert saint.

The second section is organized around the image of the spiritual road or journey (vv. 12–19). In Job's case the way now becomes
relentlessly blocked and impassible. Job's path is so barricaded
against any kind of progress that his "soul [*nefesh*, often representing the entire person in Hebrew literature] is poured out" (v. 16)

or, as Gordis suggests, Job "pours out the heart in prayer or in grief."[4] As with the image of the desert, the blocked road or path organizes and focuses Job's lament: his "right hand" is blocked where the "rabble rise up" and "build roads for my ruin" (v. 12), his enemies "break up my path" (v. 13a), and as they do so they pour in at him: "through a wide breach they come" (v. 14a) as though a tide of evil and abasement. Formerly on a path of prosperity and justice, now "terrors are turned upon me," his way becomes a "wind" and his spiritual path no more than a "cloud" (v. 15). Ashes to ashes, dust to dust, for Job "[God] has cast me into the mire, and I have become like dust and ashes" (v. 19).

> "I have become like dust and ashes," that is, I have been rendered contemptible to them as if I were dust, and I appear to be similar to vile mud. Emmanuel too, even though he was God, was thoughtlessly considered to be unworthy when he was clothed with flesh, so that some said, "Even though you are a man, you make yourself God."
>
> Ephrem the Syrian, *Commentary on Job* 30:19, *Sancti Patris Nostri Ephraem Syri Opera Omnia*, 2:13, in ACCS, 155.

A third section opens the lament directly to God in a second-person singular construction (vv. 20–23). These are the only verses in chapters 29–31 that directly address God. In this section the spiritual focus is on YHWH, and in particular on YHWH's justice. Job reiterates his earlier demands for justice and litigation and complains that God ignores these pleas: "When the poor 'cried out' for justice Job delivered them from their distress (v. 24; 29:12). When Job 'cries out' in his distress God stifles him with afflictions."[5] Job also reminds his God once again, in a wrenching way, of the divine silence and absence:

> If I cry out to You, You do not answer me;
> if I remain silent, You pay me no heed.
>
> (v. 20, Gordis)

---

4. Robert Gordis, *The Book of Job: Commentary, New Translation, and Special Studies* (New York: Jewish Theological Seminary of America, 1978), 334.
5. Habel, *Job*, 418, 419.

This silent response to Job's pathetic cry is the answer of death:

> Yes, I know that You will bring me down to Death—
> to the meeting-place of all the living.
>
> (v. 23, Gordis)

In this verse, *ki yada'ti movet teshiveni* is literally, "For I know that you will bring me back to the realm of nonexistence."[6]

The fourth and final section of chapter 30 (vv. 24–31) is a synopsis of Job's present, intractable condition of suffering and also alludes to previous images in the Joban poem that now resonate in new and newly terrifying ways, summed up in Job's phrase, "But when I looked for good, evil came; and when I waited for light, darkness came" (v. 26). Job once believed that justice would be rewarded, that within the tight confines of the doctrine of retribution the righteous could expect goodness and light. Repeating his claims of chapter 29 in two short verses (vv. 24–25), these concrete examples of righteous actions, of "good" (*tob*) and "light" (*or*), are now only hollow and meaningless sport (cf. v. 1): the cause and effect of "evil" (*ra'*) and "darkness/gloom" (*ofel*). Beyond restless, it is not only Job's soul that is poured out within him (v. 16); his body is stretched and torn and nearly as lifeless as his mind and emotions.

Chapter 31
Trial Redux: I Am Innocent

One of the best *literary* biblical scholars to work on the book of Job, Robert Gordis, is more than a little impressed with this, the final prolonged speech by the man from Uz: "This Code of a Man of Honor is the noblest presentation of individual ethics in the pages of the Bible. . . . The fervor and moral passion of Job's confession and the richly textured literary structure in which his thoughts are couched make this chapter [31] one of the great literary utterances in the Bible and without."[7] What of chapter 31 makes for such an

6. See Gordis, *Job*, 336.
7. Gordis, *Job*, 542, 546.

exemplary code for any man of honor, and what is behind Job's "fervor and moral passion" in his last speech, which makes the chapter so ethically and theologically compelling?

Two essential qualities—beyond the literary genius itself—contribute to the moral tension and passion of this chapter. The first has to do with the way Job describes so deftly what it means to be a moral human being; the second is grounded in the series of curses that are designed to prepare the groundwork for what Job intends will be his trial with God.

In Job's description of the moral person he implies that he, himself, is and has been the embodiment of just such an ethical man. Recalling what it means throughout the book of Job to be "scrupulously moral," Edwin M. Good writes,

> Both inwardly and outwardly, this speech lends credence to the first characterization of man we saw: *tam wᵉyašar*, "scrupulously moral" (1.1, 8; 2.3). The narrator said it, the god said it, Job himself has claimed it in passing before. Now he describes in detail just what it means, both in outward act and inward thought, to be *tam wᵉyašar*.[8]

This "scrupulously moral" human being is portrayed as righteous, in effect without sin. In a manner similar to earlier ancient Near Eastern "negative confessions," in chapter 31 Job goes out of his way to list the sins he has *not* committed; the chapter is almost entirely a list of wrongs Job has not done. The list cited most often by scholars as a similar example is the "negative confessions" from Egyptian texts gathered under the title the Book of the Dead, which "show the prayers of a dying person when he presents his soul before the throne of judgment."[9] In that book we find a catalog in which "the deceased affirms his virtue before Osiris and forty-two judges."[10] Here is a representative example from the Egyptian Book of the Dead:

> I have come to thee, my Lord . . . Lord of Justice . . .
> I have not committed evil against men.

8. Good, *In Turns of Tempest*, 313.
9. Yair Hoffman, *A Blemished Perfection: The Book of Job in Context* (Sheffield: Sheffield Academic Press, 1996), 160.
10. See Gordis, *Job*, 546 on "parallels in Oriental literature" to Job 31.

I have not mistreated cattle.
I have not committed sin in a place of truth.
I have not known that which is not.
I have not seen evil . . .
I have not done violence to a poor man.
I have not done that which the gods abominate.
I have not defamed a slave to his superior.
I have not made (anyone) sick.
I have not made (anyone) weep.
I have not killed.[11]

Though Job's own catalog of offenses is as important for what he omits as for what he includes, the resemblances between the Book of the Dead and Job 31 are immediately noticeable. There are fourteen sins in Job 31 of which Job insists he is innocent:

—lust (vv. 1–2)
—cheating in business (vv. 5–6)
—taking the property of others (vv. 7–8)
—adultery (vv. 9–12)
—unfairness toward slaves in the courts (vv. 13–15)
—callousness toward the poor (vv. 16–18)
—lack of pity for the wayfarer (vv. 19–20)
—perversion of the just claims of the widow and the orphan
   (vv. 21–23)
—love of gold and confidence in wealth (vv. 24–25)
—worship of the sun and moon (vv. 26–28)
—joy in the calamity of his foes (vv. 29–31)
—failure to practice hospitality (v. 32)
—concealing sins because of fear of public opinion (vv. 33–34)
—expropriation of the land of others (vv. 38–40)[12]

Job, unlike the Book of the Dead, does not include in his list

---

11. J. B. Pritchard, ed., *Ancient Near Eastern Texts* (Princeton, NJ: Princeton University Press, 1969), 34–35, cited in Hoffman, *Blemished Perfection*, 160–61.
12. Gordis, *Job*, 542.

palpable crimes punishable by law like murder or theft, except adultery, which is punishable but also can be covertly practiced. In his negative confession, Job's series of litigious oaths are moral qualities pointedly focused, not toward his fellow human persons for judgment, but to the God of creation. The sins listed by Job "are not the crimes of the lawbreaker; at most they are the offenses of the law-bender."[13] Job's point of litigation as the just, moral man is that even his most heinous sins are minor if existent at all. Yet still it appears that it is his behavior, directly linked to his suffering, in which the "cosmic judge" finds fault.

Job's reaction as a potential defendant or even litigant is all the more striking given what he does deny even before a trial can begin. But something is even more unnerving about Job's negative confession. Denial of the fourteen sins is also, when taken in the context of Job's struggle with divine forces beyond his reckoning or understanding, direct accusation against God. The denials are accusations, even curses, against an "unseeing omniscience" of the cosmos whose all-seeing wisdom fails to see a man who has *not* committed any of the sins listed. His denial of sin is in the style of a liturgical confession. But what is Job confessing? Most obviously that the link between moral behavior and cosmic consequence is specious, that it is no longer valid either ethically or legally.

Thus in the name of preliminary litigation Job plays the Egyptian game before this judge of the universe by listing transgressions he has not done. Like his Egyptian counterpart, Job has not committed these sins. However, unlike other Near Eastern encounters with the judges of the dead, there is no declaration on Job's part of absolute innocence. "Nowhere does Job declare 'I have not done . . .'"[14] It is as though Job were waiting for YHWH to make the declaration of absolute innocence. In doing so Job is making YHWH the potential accused, accuser, and finally sentencing judge. The decision is now God's, and if God "will bring upon Job the punishments appropriate to these conditional sins, that will be a sign of Job's guilt; but if these punishments are not brought upon him, that must necessarily

13. Ibid.
14. Cf. Hoffman, *Blemished Perfection*, 161–62.

prove a divine recognition of innocence, and then God (in accordance with legal principles) will be forced to remove Job's unjustified suffering."[15]

FURTHER REFLECTIONS
Job's Trial Strategy

The character of Job's oath of purity in chapter 31 as a legal challenge highlights its function in the design of Job's speeches throughout the book. As Good writes concerning chapter 31, "We have seen before that Job wants a trial to establish his innocence, and the notion of an oath of clearance prior to the judge's appearance and the trial procedure would seem to make very good sense.... Yet we had reason earlier to wonder whether he might have dropped the idea":[16]

> I cry to you and you do not answer me;
> I stand [silent], and you merely look at me.
>
> (30:20)

Earlier, in an apparent struggle with the futility of litigation (chaps. 9–10), Job had said:

> Though I am innocent, my own mouth would condemn me;
> though I am blameless, he would prove me perverse.
>
> (9:20)

> I become afraid of all my suffering,
>   for I know you will not hold me innocent.
> If I shall be condemned;
>   why then do I labor in vain?
> If I wash myself with soap
>   and cleanse my hands with lye,

15. Ibid., 165.
16. Good, *In Turns of Tempest*, 309–10.

> yet you will plunge me into filth,
>> and my own clothes will abhor me.
>>> (9:28–31)

But finally in chapter 10 Job does decide on a plan to announce his legal suit (*rib*) against God:

> I will say to God, do not condemn me;
> let me know why you contend against me.
>> (10:2)

Later Job lets it be known that he is ready to argue the case he has prepared, regardless of the consequences (13:13–18); he then throws out his formal challenge, "Who is there that will contend [*rib*] with me?" (13:19a). Though Job is now ready to start the procedure immediately, as Habel comments, "It matters not to Job whether he or God summons the other party to court as long as the legal proceedings are conducted free of intimidation."[17]

After his dialogue with his friends, Job takes an oath that his testimony is free of perjury (27:2–4) and that he will not, a priori, acknowledge that his adversary may be in the right, but insists on maintaining his own innocence to his friends. Before his Creator, Job's refusal to humble himself through admission of guilt is fraught with danger of annihilation. But this integrity is the only way Job can see if the Creator, who is also the creator of his suffering, may be willing to break the silence and respond, and so again Job insists:

> Far be it from me to say that you are right;
> until I die I will not put away my integrity from me.
> I hold fast my righteousness, and will not let it go;
> my heart does not reproach me for any of my days.
>> (27:5–6)

But now with Job's final speech, Job decides to hold nothing back and gives what is in effect his testimony before the court. The

---

17. Habel, *Job*, 431.

culmination of this testimony is Job's oath of purity (chap. 31) containing formal plea for an arbiter and a written legal document from his adversary:

> O that I had one to hear me!
> (Here is my signature! Let the Almighty answer me!)
> O that I had the indictment written by my adversary!
> Surely I would carry it on my shoulder;
> I would bind it on me like a crown.
>
> (31:35–36)

Now, in Job's mind, it is up to God: God can come to make an appearance in order to deny or confirm Job's claims. As Job vows his innocence—"Here is my signature!"—again, in Job's mind, God has another option: remain silent thereby proving by default that Job is innocent; silent, God signals God's own guilt.

The trial motif is a unifying, even harmonizing, mimetic device used throughout the book of Job. However, it is important to keep the device in perspective: it is not a controlling device by any means, nor is it the paramount theological, moral, or literary device of the book of Job. Other themes and strategies have more comprehensive value, continuity, persistence, and, ultimately, unifying (if not harmonizing) integrity: moral turpitude versus moral coherence, suffering, death, justice outside the confines of a trial, wisdom, providence, immortality, doctrine of God, creation and the peace, righteousness, and political and moral qualities of creation.

Job's final words before God appears in the whirlwind to declare the glories of God's creation are of the earth and the earth's bounty and its use:

> If my land has cried out against me,
>   and its furrows have wept together;
> if I have eaten its yield without payment,
>   and caused the death of its owners;
> let thorns grow instead of wheat,
>   and foul weeds instead of barley.
>
> (31:38–40)

32:1–37:24

Elihu Chapters

Elihu Appears: Inspiration, Providence, and Creation

In a rhythmic and rhyming phrase that would serve well as the refrain of a song of seeking impossible answers, Carol A. Newsom captures the spirit of interpretive response to these six puzzling chapters in Job: "What to do with Elihu?" Newsom writes that this question "bedevils every interpretation of the book of Job."[1] There are very real issues of controversy in interpreting the speeches of Elihu: (1) difficulties having to do with literary-critical perspectives; (2) suggestions by some scholars that these chapters are written by the same author of the earlier dialogues, but much aged, a writer who has come to see suffering as less a matter of arbitrary innocence than a divine working of providence intended to form body, mind, and/or spirit.[2] Though important for many scholars, we can set aside historical-critical concerns, about which the writer was of course unaware and him or herself unconcerned. The second suggestion is also an important consideration and speculation about both stylistic issues and the developmental and spiritual journey of the writer, but is not the kind of suggestion that can ever be answered with any degree of assurance. Finally there is a third issue that has important implications for this book: (3) these include theological issues central to the book of Job. The Elihu speeches begin a shift in the writer's

1. Carol A. Newsom, *The Book of Job: A Contest of Moral Imaginations* (Oxford: Oxford University Press, 2003), 200.
2. Cf. Ann W. Astell, *Job, Boethius, and Epic Truth* (Ithaca, NY: Cornell University Press, 1994), 5–11. Astell shows that the epic form (in which she places the book of Job) explores three separate but mutually enhancing answers to the question "What is a human being?" (*Quid est homo?* or the answers given in epic formulations to the Delphic oracle, γνῶθι σεαυτόν.)

> Now it is said that we ought to judge prudently of him whom God corrects; for we must not conclude that each one is punished according to his offences. . . . Let us learn to hold ourselves as it were in suspense, until the truth may be known to us. . . . That is how, by the example of the friends of Job the Spirit of God warns us in the first place to be modest, in order not to quarrel too quickly against God: and then if we have been mistaken, even though we have not been obstinate, let us not persevere in the wrong but knowing our fault let us try rather to correct it. [Elihu's wisdom] in fact ought not to be received otherwise than from the school of the Holy Spirit.
>
> John Calvin, Sermon 15, "Righteous Indignation," on Job 32:1–3, in *Sermons from Job*, trans. Leroy Nixon (Grand Rapids: Eerdmans, 1952), 214, 217, 218.

perspective concering the theology of suffering. In the Elihu speeches we find advocacy for suffering that is not just or unjust, not divinely righteous or divinely unrighteous, not concerned with innocence or guilt, not oriented toward justification or redemption. The theology of suffering in the Elihu speeches is rather focused on suffering as formative and providential. In these chapters suffering is beyond human conceptions of good or bad, right or wrong, something certainly to be alleviated when possible, never condoned or perpetuated with malice, but somehow, in a transcendent, invisible, and unknowable way, suffering enters history and is immanent, visible, and knowable in and through creation. And in every case suffering is a formative, providential work of God, even if the eschatological dimensions of providence are to be "completed" in an afterlife.

Job has insisted that God explain God's self, that God is somehow knowable or, if not immediately knowable, at least God is just, and therefore if Job can only present his case in a heavenly court of law, Job will be vindicated. But creation begins to become an integral character in the narrative in these closing chapters of Job, both in this Elihu section and certainly in the final section of God's speech in the whirlwind, where God chooses to make his case almost wholly on the basis of God's role as Creator of the natural world. Elihu's distinctive contribution to the book is his argument for redemptive suffering—what Calvin calls "the school of the Holy Spirit"—which is also an aspect of providence played out in terms of history and creation. In this chapter we will concentrate on Elihu's theological contributions to the ideas of providence, history, creation, and redemptive suffering.

Elihu: Youth, Anger, and the Spirit of God

Elihu admits to an intense anger that is driving him to speak, especially in the first four chapters. The NRSV does not do justice to the intensity of Elihu's wrath: it is not simply that Elihu "became angry" or "was angry," in the Hebrew it is more precisely that his anger "burned" or "flared up" (*harah af*). Thus in 32:2 Elihu's anger is on fire (*harah af*) because Job "justified himself rather than God." In verse 3 Elihu's anger burns (*harah af*) in the same way, this time at the three friends "because they had found no answer, though they had declared Job to be in the wrong." And in verse 5 once more his "anger flashes" (*af harah*).[3] Not unlike Job, Elihu reaches a point where his patience is too sorely tried to contain himself within the niceties of the wisdom tradition.

Throughout his multichapter monologue, Elihu denies nearly all that Job and the three friends have espoused theologically. He is so frustrated by what he has heard that, purely and simply, theologically Elihu burns with anger. John

> The striking feature of this long monologue of Elihu is that it is conceived with a subtlety to which the three friends of Job had not accustomed us. The latter had confined themselves to the essential points of the thesis: the relation between virtue and happiness, as between sin and misfortune. Elihu tries to discover the meaning of sorrow and trial; he explains the various ways in which the divine justice may manifest itself; he shows how in societies this justice, which is sometimes so little apparent, does in fact operate, and he concludes with an exalted treatise on the action of God in the world of nature. He envisages the case of Job only to a very secondary degree.
>
> Édouard Dhorme, *A Commentary on the Book of Job*, with a prefatory note by H. H. Rowley, trans. Harold Knight (London: Thomas Nelson and Sons, 1967), xiv.

---

3. As Norman C. Habel, *The Book of Job: A Commentary*, Old Testament Library (Philadelphia: Westminster, 1985), 449, points out, it may appear that v. 5 is redundant. But a close inspection of the text discloses four distinct ways in which Elihu's anger is to be understood. In v. 2a the narrator opens by stating that Elihu is angry; anger characterizes this young man.

Calvin, who finds Elihu's understanding of divine providence with-out equal in all of Scripture, consequently also finds his anger to be "righteous indignation."[4]

So, if Elihu is "young in years" and those he speaks to are "aged," where is Elihu's wisdom to be found? In Elihu's case it is from the breath of the spirit of God. More than once Elihu says that his wis-dom, his inspiration, is directly from God, breathed into him—lit-erally inspired—as for a prophet. He says, "But truly it is the spirit [*ruach*] in a mortal, the breath [*nashamah*] of the Almighty [*Shad-dai*], that makes for understanding" (32:8), meaning his own unique understanding, an understanding that supersedes the wisdom of age. Elihu thus announces by whose breath he speaks—the "breath of Shaddai," that "the spirit of God has made me" (33:4a), and that it is the breath of God that gives him life and wisdom (33:4b).

Elihu's self-assessment is not universally upheld. As Habel describes it, "Elihu, who has undergone none of Job's afflictions, claims to be able to interpret them by virtue of a common human spirit, the breath of Shaddai within him."[5] John Calvin's words illus-trate a profound difference between his assessment and those of many contemporary commentators. Habel's Elihu, for instance, is a "hotheaded" "intruder."[6] Habel describes the poet's rendering of Elihu as ironic, humorous, wry, and satirical in a way that causes one to imagine he is talking about a completely different individual than is Calvin. Habel, for instance, sees a wordplay between "word" and "wind" that allows him to speak of Elihu as a "brash fool," "bloated," with "a 'belly' full of 'wind'" (32:17–18), by which "unwittingly Elihu characterizes himself as a windbag and a constipated fool . . . Perhaps the innuendo of this wordplay is captured in the English expression "'to pass wind.'"[7]

On the other hand, for Calvin, Elihu *is* gifted with the Spirit. He is, unlike the friends or Job, modest in his zeal, prudent, and discerning of when to talk and when to keep silent. The Spirit of God for Calvin

---

4. See Sermon 15 title, "Righteous Indignation," and the case Calvin makes for Elihu's warranted and righteous indignation in John Calvin, *Sermons from Job*, trans. Leroy Nixon (Grand Rapids: Eerdmans, 1952), 214–28.

5. Habel, *Job*, 451.

6. Comments on Elihu by ibid., 443, 450.

7. Ibid., 444.

gives grace to "profit those who are younger." In a culture in which wisdom was based on very formal codes and foundations, among the most universally accepted, practiced, and honored being deference to the wisdom of the elders, Elihu's speech is a radical departure from accepted custom. But for Calvin, Elihu's words transcend the formalities of wisdom: Elihu's words, especially Elihu's understanding and "zeal" for divine providence, justice, and power are what matter; for Calvin, wherever one discerns the activity of God in the world, through the work of the Holy Spirit, is an occasion for praise.

FURTHER REFLECTIONS
Concurrence: Calvin and Aquinas on Elihu

Thomas Aquinas is strikingly similar to Calvin in his assessment of Elihu, especially on the Spirit and the Spirit's effect on the clarity and truth of Elihu's speech. Aquinas begins his commentary on the "zeal" of Elihu's speeches by saying something similar to Calvin: "After the debate of Job and his three Friends has been finished, Elihu's debate against Job is added and he, of course, uses sharper arguments against Job than the prior speakers and approaches closer to the truth."[8]

On the issue of Elihu's age and divine inspiration (32:7–8), Aquinas writes

> Next he excuses himself for beginning to speak now, namely, since he has found out by experience that not age but rather divine inspiration is the sufficient cause of wisdom. Hence, he adds *But as I see*, that is, consider by the effect, *the spirit*, namely, God's, *is in men* inasmuch as He works in them. This is the point of adding *and the inspiration of the Almighty*, by which, namely, He breathes into men the Holy Spirit, Who as "the Spirit of wisdom and understanding," *gives understanding*, namely, of the truth, which is the beginning of wisdom for those into whom it is breathed.[9]

8. Thomas Aquinas, *The Literal Exposition on Job: A Scriptural Commentary concerning Providence*, trans. Anthony Damico (Atlanta: Scholars Press, 1989), 365–66.
9. Ibid., 367.

Here Aquinas follows Calvin—or rather, Calvin follows Aquinas—exactly in his assessment of the inner workings of the Holy Spirit on wisdom.

On 33:4 Aquinas continues in the vein of Calvin:

> Now he shows whence he has received such confidence in manifesting the truth, adding *The spirit of God has made me*; therefore, it is no wonder if it moves and perfects its product. This is the point of adding *and the breath of the Almighty has given me life*, namely, it has moved and perfected me for the works of life, among which the understanding of truth is special.[10]

Finally, and of utmost importance for the issue of justice and power as Job perceives it, Aquinas agrees with Calvin that it is by God's benevolent power and justice that God keeps the universe and humanity in existence:

> Elihu shows by experience that there is no violence and iniquity with God. For so great is His power by which He keeps things in being that, if He were to wish to use violence contrary to justice, He could suddenly wipe out all mankind. Hence, he adds *If He*, namely, God, *directs against him*, namely, to crush him, *His heart*, that is, His will, *his spirit*, that is his soul, *and breath*, that is, the bodily life ensuing from the soul, *He will draw to Himself*, namely, separating it from the body by His power, according to Ecclesiastes 12:7: "And let the spirit return to God Who gave it."[11]

Providence, Revelation, and Suggestions of Redemptive Suffering

Providence may or may not be visible immediately to humans (short of an afterlife, which is what moves Aquinas as well as Calvin to find in Job a doctrine of providence inclusive of an afterlife). Revelation is similarly often revealed only in hindsight. Elihu makes three claims about the medium of revelation and how it is delivered that can also be applied to providence. Each claim about revelation (even his "mediator angel") is simultaneously perceptible and imperceptible. In Elihu's case, each type of revelation is through what we might call extraordinary means; that is, none have to do with divine revelation

10. Ibid., 371–72.
11. Ibid., 384.

mediated through creation or history explicitly, or through Scripture or "normal" experience. Yet Elihu believes that he is the recipient of all three means of extraordinary revelation. His warrant for this is his claim that it is possible for God to bring wisdom (and in particular prophetic wisdom) to one as young as he because "God is greater than any mortal. . . . God speaks in one way, and in two, though people do not perceive it" (33:12b, 14), meaning, in effect, that if mortals are listening, God is able to impart wisdom through revelation in any way God might be pleased to do so.

The first form of revelation Elihu mentions is delivered during sleep. "In a dream, in a vision of the night, when deep sleep falls on mortals, while they slumber on their beds, then he opens their ears, and terrifies them with warnings, that he may turn them aside from their deeds, and keep them from pride" (33:15–17). A similar form of revelation occurred to Eliphaz, who claimed a visionary dream, which terrified him but which he took as a valid vision of wisdom given by God (4:12–17).

The second extraordinary means of revelation mentioned by Elihu is a legitimate form for Ambrose, Gregory the Great, and Calvin, but is handled with caution by more recent commentators. This is revelation through the chastening of affliction (33:19–22). With these verses Elihu changes the topic of conversation from divine retribution and litigation to providential suffering. In these short verses, Elihu makes the heretofore unmentioned claim that suffering may chasten an individual or community, that it is salutary, that while we are often not able to see it as such, it is providence working divine pedagogy wherein there is a palliative element that may heal the sufferer at a deeper level. Elihu argues that affliction is medicinal and a testimony to divine love. For many contemporary readers these

> I saw the stars rushing at each other—and thought the lamps of London were gliding through the night into World Collision. . . . Nothing was more notable than the general exaltation of the nerves of sight and hearing, and their power of making colour and sound harmonious as well as intense. . . . But I learned so much about the nature of Phantasy and Phantasm—it would have been totally inconceivable to me without seeing, how the unreal and real could be mixed.
>
> Joan Abse, *John Ruskin: The Passionate Moralist* (London: Quartet Books, 1980), 302.

are deal breakers: it is too much to accept innocent suffering in the context of belief in a loving God, let alone to formulate innocent suffering as divine pedagogy.

To this point this commentary has purposefully avoided mention of suffering as a form of divine healing. One reason is that none of the three friends nor Job understand suffering in this way. A second reason is that contemporary depth psychology and other explorations of the human psyche in turmoil have shown that traumatic suffering is seldom an effective or lasting medium of healing. But beginning in chapter 33 Elihu argues for what has become known as redemptive suffering, suffering that has the overall effect of drawing one closer to God, of enabling one to recognize more clearly one's self and hence one's sin, suffering that has an ultimate effect of drawing the sufferer into deeper faith, more continuous praise, and honest thanksgiving.

Unfortunately, innocent suffering exists in the world, and it would be a ghastly thing, not to mention the antithesis of pastoral care, to suggest to anyone in the midst of suffering that it is in any way "good" for him or her. Lamentation is good for the soul; it is a way of releasing suffering.

But suffering is central to the Christian faith, as it is, in a very different way, to Buddhist practice and religion. The ambiguity of suffering, however, is that, even with Christ, healing had to "travel" through the suffering of the cross. On the other hand, there is a very real sense in which the cross itself is pure love. And so it goes: we attempt to alleviate, cure, eradicate, heal suffering . . . and yet, something of the mystery of redemption resides at the very core of suffering.

FURTHER REFLECTIONS
Suffering as Divine Pedagogy

Gregory the Great generally praises Elihu for his insight into the nature of suffering. Several excerpts give his sense of the close connection between providence and the salutary effect of suffering, and how this sense differs from the three friends' and even from

Job's. For instance, Gregory reminds us how a life of relative virtue and ease can lull us into the false impression that we ourselves are responsible for the good in our lives:

> For if the mind of man has been engaged in virtuous pursuits for ever so short a time, without temptation, it is often in consequence of those very pursuits, in which it is tranquilly engaged, soon elated by those very virtues, which it is endeavoring to multiply within, from being conscious of progress it is making. It is therefore exposed to the assaults of temptations, by the merciful dispensation of our Ruler, that thus pride, at the advance it is making, may be checked.[12]

Following this, referring directly to 33:19, Gregory reminds us that, regardless of our advance in virtue or progress, divine providence brings forth infirmity only to remind us that all virtue, all progress, all that is good, is "divine gift." Gregory also reminds us that any spiritual journey by which we advance toward God is not of our own doing:

> When he chastens us then with pain on our bed, He makes all our bones to waste away; we, who might perhaps have been puffed up by our virtues, are brought low by being sore vexed at the knowledge of our infirmity. For when we are advancing toward God, if no temptation checked our progress, we should believe that we were persons of some strength. But since the Divine dispensation thus deals with us, in order that we may remember our infirmity, we learn when we advance what we are by divine gift.[13]

Finally, we encounter a section in Gregory's *Morals on the Book of Job* that explicitly links suffering to healing; his words sound strange to us today. The commentary is in response to Job 33:18. *For He maketh sore, and bindeth up; he woundeth, and his hands make whole*:

> In two ways the Almighty God wounds those, whom He is minded to bring back to saving health; for sometimes He smites the flesh, and consumes the hardness of the heart by the fear of Him. Thus He recalls to saving health, by dealing wounds, when He afflicts His own Elect outwardly, that

12. Gregory the Great, *Morals on the Book of Job*, vol. 3.1, 23.47, 41.
13. Ibid., 23.48, 41.

they be quickened with inward life. . . . But sometimes, even
if strokes without should seem to have ceased, he inflicts
wounds within; yet in wounding He heals, in that when we
are pierced within with the dart of His dread, he recalls us to
a right sense. . . . But they are "wounded," that they may be
"healed," in that God strikes unfeeling souls with the darts of
His love, and straightway makes them full of feeling, through
the burning heat of charity, hence the spouse saith in the
Song of Songs, *For I am wounded with love* (2:5).[14]

A third and final way of extraordinary revelation that Elihu elabo-
rates is the aid of angels. In 33:23–30 Elihu suggests that, again as
a form and process of self-examination leading to growth in self-
understanding, "Then, if there should be for one of them an angel,
a mediator, one of a thousand, one who declares a person upright"
(v. 23). Through this mediator the person then "prays to God, and is
accepted by him, he comes into his presence with joy" (v. 26a) and
in that prayer of confession will say, "I sinned, and perverted what
was right, and it was not paid back to me" (v. 27b). Elihu even suggests that in the midst of suffering, men and women can recognize
that they have perverted what is right. Of redemption in suffering
through the mediation of the angels, Elihu says, "God indeed does
all these things, twice, three times, with mortals . . . so that they might
see the light of life" (v. 29; 30b). Unlike the friends, Elihu suggests
the consolation of self-examination leading to self-understanding,
virtue, and righteousness, the opportunity for confession and a
reorientation toward what is right and just in the world, a reorientation that turns one toward the light and possibly even a vision of
God's face, a spirit of joy and song, the possibility of salvation rather
than perpetual darkness.

But again, given the radical distancing of Elihu from Job and the
other friends, commentators tend to take vehement positions—
positive or negative—with regard to Elihu. Opinions vary from
the very positive appraisals of John Calvin and William Blake to
the ridicule of Habel to outright dismissal from, for instance, J. C.
L. Gibson,[15] who relegates treatment of Elihu to an appendix, and

14. Ibid., vol. 1, 6.42, 344.
15. J. C. L. Gibson, *Job* (Philadelphia: Westminster, 1985).

to Stephen Mitchell, whose otherwise excellent translation of Job eliminates the chapters in which Elihu appears and speaks.

On the other hand, Susan E. Schreiner makes a clear case that "the sermons on chapters 32–37 [Elihu's speeches] provide a summary of Calvinist theology."[16] The most crucial element of correspondence between Elihu's and Calvin's theology that surfaces in the sermons is the doctrine of providence. Because of the infinite distance between humanity and God, there is an aspect of providence as it plays out in history that is hidden to humanity; it is inscrutable. On the other hand, there is an immanent closeness of the Creator to the creation that allows Elihu, along with Calvin, to emphasize the revelation of God in nature, a revelation that is, in effect, a visible form of providence. Tracing Calvin's doctrine of providence as it is developed in the sermons, Schreiner writes:

> In Elihu's words Calvin finds affirmation of both divine justice and divine hiddenness, of the occasional inexplicableness of suffering as well as the promised judgment of the wicked. . . . In these chapters Calvin reaffirms his earlier teaching that the purpose of affliction is usually to make us sense our sins and to lead us to repentance. [For Calvin] according to Elihu, afflictions are medicinal and testimonies of divine love. . . . In such statements . . . we see, further, Calvin's insistence on the complete inability of even the most righteous person to plead against the purity and justice of God. . . . Calvin finds in Elihu an explicit teaching that providence is often inscrutable and undetectable in the historical realm . . . [and] Calvin goes on to describe the "confusion" that marks the historical sphere during times of divine hiddenness.[17]

Elihu emphasizes that innocent suffering is ambiguous suffering: it takes place more often than not in the context of divine hiddenness; it is transformative and may participate in a redemptive form of divine providence or may just be evil intensified by questions about God.

---

16. Susan E. Schreiner, *Where Shall Wisdom Be Found? Calvin's Exegesis of Job from Medieval and Modern Perspectives* (Chicago: University of Chicago Press, 1994), 133.
17. Ibid., 133–35.

Nature, History and Suffering:
Elihu Sets the Stage for a Whirlwind Speech

In the final chapters of Job, God not only speaks from the midst of creation—a whirlwind—God also speaks almost exclusively about creation. Many writers divide Elihu's speeches into four major sections: 32:6–33:33; 34:1–37; 35:1–16; and 36:1–37:24. Like the speech of God, creation language figures predominately in the first, second, and especially the fourth speech.[18]

Many early Christian commentators also note the connection between Elihu's words and those of God that follow. They assume that Elihu is preparing the reader for the divine answer to Job.

The divine spirit or the divine breath gives life to all creation. It also, as Elihu claims, gives him wisdom that Job and Job's friends all lack. More than wisdom, however, "According to Elihu, the divine breath that gives life to all creation also dwells within human beings, providing insight and understanding to those who would listen to divine instruction."[19] Elihu is not only speaking to Job and his friends of wisdom as it flows, inspired, throughout creation. He is also there to warn Job of the danger of a retribution or punishment resulting from its misuse for anything other than speaking the truth of that same divine breath flowing through creation. In fact, of those who speak falsely, Elihu says:

> There is no gloom or deep darkness
>   where evildoers may hide themselves.
> For he has not appointed a time for anyone
>   to go before God in judgment.
> . . . .
> Thus, knowing their works
>   he overturns them in the night, and they are crushed.
>   (34:22–23, 25)

18. Cf. Leo G. Perdue, *Wisdom Literature: A Theological History* (Louisville, KY: Westminster John Knox, 2007), 128. Perdue also, like most commentators, assumes that the Elihu material is an inserted redaction by a second poet of the earlier poet's rewriting of the Joban folktale.
19. Ibid., 129.

These verses hearken back to chapter 3, where Job pleaded that the night might hide him from God. Meanwhile, Job does not interrupt Elihu's speech or object; he is silent. The poet implies he is listening.

Elihu also begins to use phrases and ask impossible questions about creation ("Do you know how God lays his command upon them, and causes the lightning of his cloud to shine? . . . Can you, like him, spread out the skies, hard as a molten mirror?" [37:15, 18]) that foreshadow the dialogue of God in the whirlwind speeches. However, "unlike the interrogation of Job by YHWH, Elihu's questions are not designed to intimidate Job to move from silence to praise. Rather his examination is designed both to humiliate Job and to contrast the power, justice, and mystery of the Almighty with the weakness and dark ignorance of his mortal antagonist."[20]

Something refreshing emerges with Elihu. Even his burning wrath seems to be tinged with real friendship: friendship for Job, friendship for the friends, companionable friendship with God. Between the friends and Job, different narratives of suffering and the moral imagination have surfaced. Elihu now brings a third. For the friends, the good person who endures suffering will be delivered by God to enjoy a peaceful and prosperous life. The friends would never say suffering is redemptive; it is simply a matter of the will, power, and justice of God. Job also is a good person enduring suffering, regardless of how the three friends interpret his predicament; he is a good person looking not to repentance but to a forensic solution. Until

> After Elihu has recounted many marvels of divine works, at this point he inveighs against Job, who seemed to charge God with injustice even though he was nevertheless unable to comprehend His works, therefore, Elihu says listen, Job!, namely, to what I am saying about the magnitude of divine works; stand, namely through straightforwardness of mind, and consider, namely, by yourself, the marvels of God, namely, which are manifested in His works.
>
> Aquinas, *The Literal Exposition on Job*, chapter 37, trans. Anthony Damico (Atlanta: Scholars Press, 1989), 410.

20. Ibid., 130.

the whirlwind speech Job experiences nothing of the justice of God, only divine will, divine power. Nothing changes, until God shames Job into a new outlook. Only Elihu suggests a fresh perspective on suffering: that it can be transformative, that it can be a kind of prayer.[21] As earlier commentators have said, this attitude—whether one of humility or pride—also impacts suffering as prayer. As Newsom comments, "In Elihu's view the one who cries out in prayer, 'Where is God my maker?' can expect a response that the arrogant cannot (vv. 10–13). . . . Elihu reasserts the traditional values of the lament and thanksgiving traditions of prayer as the appropriate mode of organizing relations with God."[22]

As important as prayer for Elihu is the transformative quality of suffering. Chapter 33 offers poetic affirmation of suffering as pedagogical spiritual journey. But once again, language that implies suffering that transforms or teaches requires careful consideration. In transformative, redemptive suffering, the one who suffers may be redeemed by God. But suffering is never good. What Elihu describes is not so much about suffering as it is about transformative wisdom. Again:

> The spirit of God has made me,
>   and the breath of the Almighty gives me life.
>
> (v. 4)

Elihu comes to Job and the friends not as a self-made sage, but as one transformed, miraculously, in every way by God. Later in the chapter, Elihu recounts Job's false statements (vv. 9–13) as an example of false prayer and a useless effort at change; prayer requires truth to promote transformative grace. The three forms of revelation Elihu describes also are intended to illustrate revelation as transformative rather than human effort as redemptive. All three ways that God "speaks" to mortals are intended to set humans on a new path, a path that will turn their "soul" (*nefesh*) away from the "Pit" (*shahath*

---

21. Cf. Steven Chase, *The Tree of Life: Models of Christian Prayer* (Grand Rapids: Baker Academic, 2005), on the possibility of suffering itself becoming a prayer of lament.
22. Newsom, *Job*, 210, 211.

= Sheol) mentioned by Elihu no fewer than five times: 33:18a, 22a, 24b, 28a, 30a. Thus the most meaningful transformation is that in which the sufferer hears and responds to divine revelation: that transformation turns the soul away from death and back toward life. Each revelation also has its own mode of transformation: the dream turns the soul by filling it with "terrifying warnings"; redemptive suffering has its effect through "continual strife in their bones"; revelation by a mediating angel is much more gentle. The angel will

> let his flesh become fresh with youth;
> > let him return to the days of his youthful vigor;
> then he prays to God, and is accepted by him,
> > he comes into his presence with joy,
> and God repays him for his righteousness.
>
> > > > (vv. 25–26)

Chapter 33 is packed with the transformative power of God. As Elihu emphasizes, "God indeed does all these things" (v. 29a).

Elihu takes revelation in the manner and medium though which God offers it. He speaks what God is (like Job, also from experience): transcendent, utterly, *and* immanent, lovingly. Divine providence is thus *both* potentially visible to men and women *and* perpetually beyond our grasp. Elihu seems to strike a clear, truthful, and kind approach through his own very human wisdom and power and faith.

38:1–42:6

YHWH Appears
with Job's Response

38:1–40:5
From the Whirlwind I:
YHWH Appears, with Questions

God loves to create, finds joy in creation. YHWH's creation can be as terrifying as it is beautiful. Now, in two long speeches, this love of the Creator for creation is given voice in a theophany in which "the LORD answered Job out of the whirlwind" (38:1). The speeches are as gorgeous and as terrifying as their subject. As one commentator writes, "The speeches of YHWH are majestic poems, rich in lyric artistry, literary ambiguity, and theological profundity."[1] They encase Job in mystery and confront him with holy fear. And in the end, Job too will find joy and wonder in creation, and new life in a transformation of mystery.

We have been waiting for YHWH to speak. We have been waiting, but it has been an uncertain waiting: a theophany is rare, even in Scripture. And waiting is fatiguing, especially for a man on a dung-heap, near death. As early as chapter 3 Job cursed the very idea of hope, yet still, at times, he has gathered his courage and dared to expect that YHWH would answer his questions clearly, attentively, and in truth (23:5–7), provide answers to difficult questions for which Job can find no answers (9:13–16; 27–31). Job has been silent since the end of chapter 31. Then, appropriately, from a chaos of wind YHWH appears in the form of wonder and terror, but his speech will leave us finally with more questions than answers.

1. Norman C. Habel, *The Book of Job: A Commentary*, Old Testament Library (Philadelphia: Westminster, 1985), 526.

YHWH's First Speech

What YHWH's questions do not address is as important as their actual content. YHWH's questions do not draw their power or focus from the questions and misconceptions about the book of Job itself. For instance, YHWH's questions do not address the "patience" of Job. They are not meant to force Job to confess or to prove his guilt. They do not directly address the meaning of innocent suffering. They solve nothing of the potential pedagogical complexities of suffering. The divine speeches also are not an opportunity on God's part to goad Job into a higher level of faith. Job does not really "repent," as the NRSV and many other translations would have it, so much as become "comforted" through the divine presence. The theophany as a chaotic whirlwind is not an example of God coming "down to Job's level, [to] meet him where he is," which is pious nonsense; this is still a man covered in oozing soars overpowered by a thunderous

---

Good provides a summary of the diverse responses to the voice from the whirlwind given by other readers and commentators. None of these responses in and of itself provides the definitive reading of the speeches, but each is at least in part feasible. Good writes, for instance, that "Some see Yahweh's speeches as meaningful because Yahweh overwhelms Job with the divine power, some because the speeches bring Job to a proper humility, others because they show Job how to have significant faith, and still others because they imply that 'the universal' has an aesthetic and moral beauty beyond human comprehension."[2] In addition, apart from scholars who would excise all or parts of the speeches as not original to the book, some readers find the Yahweh speeches a meaningful conclusion to the book, whereas others find them irritating and irrelevant. In other words, responses to the Yahweh speeches are as diverse and surprising as the chaotic whirlwind itself. Some kind of falling, what I will soon call "necessary suffering," is programmed into the journey. It is not that suffering or failure *might* happen, or that it will only happen to you if you are bad, or that it will happen to the unfortunate, or to a few in other places, or that you can somehow by cleverness or righteousness avoid it. No, it *will* happen, and to you!

Richard Rohr, *Falling Upward: A Spirituality for the Two Halves of Life* (San Francisco: Jossey-Bass, 2011), xx.

---

2. Edwin M. Good, *In Turns of Tempest: Reading of Job with a Translation* (Stanford, CA: Stanford University Press, 1990), 338–39. Good provides examples of each of these positions, and other positions as well, in his endnotes, 435.

theophany. Neither is Job's "faith too small to cover the contingency of innocent suffering,"[3] which is a perfect and ironic echo of Job's friends and their not-so-friendly advice.

Patristic, medieval, and Reformation writers have found allegorical and moral meanings of the whirlwind speech most appropriate. John Chrysostom, for instance, finds compassion, wisdom, and intelligence in God's speech to Job precisely because Job is a part of that creation God loves: "Since Job was overwhelmed by his dejection, God encourages him with his words. . . . Above all, he shows that he does everything with wisdom and intelligence, and therefore it would have been inconsistent with intelligence, to neglect the human beings for whom he has created everything, even when they are wretched, as in this case."[4]

Ambrose recognizes the potential torment of words, but also that words have the capacity to heal and give solace: "Although they have overcome the torments that were brought to bear against them, many persons have not withstood harsh discourse. Job suffered distress, but he withstood and carried the burden of the words next to that of the wounds. The president of the contest saw him; from out of the cloud and storm (cf. Job 38:1), He gave His hand to him as he struggled . . . proclaimed him the victor and gave him the crown."[5]

Gregory the Great gives a particularly moral interpretation that sees YHWH's response steeped in love: YHWH is taking Job on a journey wherein God's love is transformed to wisdom. "Truly, the fear of the Lord, that is wisdom" (Job 28:28, cf. Prov. 1:7; 9:10; 15:33; Ps. 111:10). Note how Gregory's response to the speech from the whirlwind compares different methods of the moral formation:

> I see it must be observed, that if the speech were said to have
> been addressed to one in health and safety, the Lord would
> not be described as having spoken out of the whirlwind.

3. For these and other interpretations of the whirlwind speech, see David McKenna, "God's Revelation and Job's Repentance," in *Sitting with Job: Selected Studies on the Book of Job*, ed. Roy B. Zuck (Grand Rapids: Baker Book House, 1991), 381–410.

4. Chrysostom, *Commentary on Job*, ed. Ursula Hagedorn and Dieter Hagedorn, PTS 35 (New York: de Gruyter, 1990), 181. In ACCS, 196.

5. Saint Ambrose, "The Prayer of Job and David," in *Seven Exegetical Works*, 327–67 (Washington, DC: Catholic University of America Press, 1972), 357.

But because He speaks to one who has been *scourged*, He is described as having spoken out of the whirlwind. For the Lord speaks to His servants in one way, when He improves them inwardly by compunction, and in another, when he presses on them the severity, lest they be puffed up. For by the gentle address of the Lord is shewn His affectionate sweetness, but by His *terrible* might, is pointed out His *dreadful* power. By the one the soul is persuaded to advance, by the other, that which is advancing is checked. In the one it learns what to desire, in the other what to *fear*. For He in truth is gentle, Who comes to dwell in the midst of us. But when He makes His way by the tempest and whirlwind, he doubtless *disturbs* the hearts which he touches; and puts Himself forth to tame their pride.[6]

For Gregory, Job faces a journey into God's "*terrible* might, [by which] is pointed out His *dreadful* power" that terrifies Job not in order to crush him, but to teach the fear of the Lord that leads to wisdom.

Finally, John Calvin recognizes intentions similar to those of Gregory in the divine method of moral formation: "This is what is now narrated to us: that God seeing that Job was not sufficiently subdued by the propositions and reasons which Elihu had brought forward, causes him to experience his *grandeur* from a whirlwind; in order that being thus *frightened*, he might reform by recognizing his fault, and that he might obey entirely what is set before him . . . we must experience Him as He is; in order that we may learn to *fear* Him, and to hear His Word in all humility and solicitude."[7] Calvin does offer the whirlwind speech as a lesson in moral purity, but for Calvin these are secondary moral results of something much more important: that Job "*experience*" YHWH, that he "*experience Him as He is.*"

Wonder, fear, terror, and beauty in creation and in God illuminate or awaken Job in ways that the "propositions and reasons" of Elihu

---

6. Gregory the Great, *Morals on the Book of Job*, vol. 3.1, part 6, book 28.1, 260–61. Gregory's intention is to convey both moral conformity and the awe, wonder, fear, and mystery of the god speaking out of the whirlwind.

7. Calvin, Sermon 20, "The Lord Answers Job," 287–88. Emphasis added.

and the friends had failed to do. Job enters a certain kind of mutuality or union with God by being present to God through the experience of the whirlwind, which is described nicely by Calvin as Job's "experience of Him as He is." Job's silence during the speech says much, and his very few words at the end tell us more: that, finally, his actions and his way of life have come into a mutual participation with the fullness of this divine presence (see Job 42:10–17).

But as always with the book of Job, there is another dimension of meaning to be addressed. Corrine Patton, for instance, has written, "Part of Job's message is that creation, including many of those elements that constitute its awesome beauty, can be lethal to human beings . . . creation contains a *dangerous* splendor."[8]

FURTHER REFLECTIONS
The Whirlwind as Theophany

A theophany (Greek *theos*, "god," + *phaneia*, "appearance") is a technical term for the perceptible appearance of God to humans. Job has claimed that he wants to meet Yahweh face to face, but who would have expected God's appearance in a whirlwind (*searah*)? A careful reader may have been able to take a lucky guess because Job has already experienced one, although not as an environment for the presence of God:

> If I summoned him and he answered me,
> I do not believe that he would listen to my voice.
> For he crushes me with a tempest
>   [*searah*; in most translations, "whirlwind"],
> and multiplies my wounds without cause.
>
>   (9:16–17)

But God's speaking from the whirlwind is indeed a full-fledged arrival, both audible and visible. Though Job acknowledges a

8. Corrine L. Patton, introduction to *The Whirlwind: Essays on Job, Hermeneutics and Theology in Memory of Jane Morse*, ed. Stephen L. Cook, Corrine L. Patton, and James W. Watts (New York: Sheffield Academic Press, 2001), 15.

whirlwind encounter would be more than dangerous, he is not interested in a mediated (for instance, say, in the form of an angel), secondary, or partial experience of God: he calls for God's unmediated presence. What Job ends up with, though the friends would never have admitted the possibility, is, as Good humorously puts it, a "top-of-the-line theophany."[9] God's appearance supposedly was not something one could experience and survive; God's actual appearance happened only to other ancient heroes such as Abraham and Moses and Elijah. Job thus becomes one of the very few honored by a personal visit from God.

Not only in the Bible, but in Wisdom literature in general, theophanic appearances of the god are rare. YHWH in a whirlwind, speaking in a sustained speech over two chapters, is even more unusual. Perdue writes, "Elsewhere in Wisdom literature, the revelation of God comes through the observation of the cosmos and human experience, formulated into teachings that make their way into the tradition of the sages."[10] Job becomes one of a small group of heroes in the Hebrew Scriptures to experience a theophany and the only one to carry on a sustained conversation with God. The whirlwind itself has been interpreted in eschatological terms[11] and compared to Psalm 29 as a storm in which the "voice of the LORD is over the waters" (Ps. 29:3a), the "voice of the LORD breaks the cedars" (v. 5a), the "voice of the LORD flashes forth flames of fire" (v. 7a), and the "voice of the LORD causes the oaks to whirl" (v. 9a). But these are weak images compared to the speech of YHWH in the whirlwind. Job is unique.

Primarily, the whirlwind theophany is an event of awe and wonder. Through it Job releases himself from the enterprise of retributive justice and in the process learns that "He who speaks to man in the Book of Job is neither a just nor an unjust god but God."[12]

9. Good, *In Turns of Tempest*, 340.

10. Leo G. Perdue, *Wisdom Literature: A Theological History* (Louisville, KY: Westminster John Knox, 2007), 118.

11. Samuel Terrien, *Job: Poet of Existence* (New York: Bobbs-Merrill, 1957), 226.

12. M. Tsevat, "The Meaning of the Book of Job," *Hebrew Union College Annual* 37 (1966): 105, cited in James G. Williams, "The Theophany of Job," in Roy B. Zuck, ed., *Sitting with Job: Selected Studies on the Book of Job* (Grand Rapids: Baker Book House, 1992), 361. For a list of recent interpretations of the theophany, see Williams, "The Theophany of Job," in Zuck, *Sitting with Job*, 359–72.

Regardless of the meaning or context of the voice and vision of God out of the whirlwind, it is unique in Hebrew literature.

38:1–38 *YHWH's First Speech on the Cosmos*

This first long speech of YHWH is divided into two primary sections, the first concerning inanimate cosmic realities emphasizing YHWH's power and mystery in creation, the second focused on YHWH's providential care of animate creatures of earth. In neither section does YHWH address the issues of innocent suffering nor the question of retributive justice thrown back and forth between Job and the friends, nor does God answer directly any of the questions taken up by the friends and Job.

In focusing on his own creation of the cosmos and his knowledge about and control over it, YHWH makes it clear from whence providence originates, is sustained, and is directed. In the tenor of the speeches YHWH's power is unquestionable; YHWH's justice and love may be implied. The questions in the speech directed by God at Job do not seem to ask if Job is a righteous human, but rather if Job is, like YHWH, a god; YHWH asks questions more suited to a rival god than to a human suffering in rotting skin, as if the human were knowledgeable enough to share an intimate conversation with YHWH as co-creator of the universe. The contrast leads to irony and sarcasm in the tone of God's questioning. The immediate answer to all YHWH's questions is simply: YHWH. The implicit answer (which does in an unstated way address some of Job's questions) is that there is a moral order to the universe, but it is beyond human understanding, and it can be accessed, not changed, by faith. Whether this is a sufficient answer to the problem of innocent suffering rests with each reader. Most probably for Job it is not; but in the course of the dialogues Job's questions are transformed and he is illuminated by awe and beauty rather than reason and cognition.

Before beginning the questions whose answer is always YHWH, the Creator, YHWH summons—in a sense, challenges—Job in a sarcastic and adversarial tone that will remain throughout this first speech:

> Who is this that darkens counsel by words
> > without knowledge?
> Gird up your loins like a man,
> > I will question you, and you shall declare to me.
> > > (38:2–3)

YHWH does not say "my" counsel (*etsah*), which suggests to "plan, design, advise," or "debate," and, given the many twists and turns of the story, could refer to a number of things: the original counsel that hatched the plan to test Job in chapters 1–2; the friends' or Job's or Elihu's plans and theories; YHWH's counsel, in which case it could refer to providence, creation, wisdom, or simply YHWH's "plan" for peace and quiet! In chapter 3 Job curses the day "a man-child [*geber*] is conceived" (3:2). Now instead of a curse, YHWH tells Job to become a *geber*, to "gird up your loins like a man [*geber*]." YHWH is drawing a line: YHWH alone will do the questioning and formulate the primary metaphors of this conversation. As we read and listen, the sheer diversity of creation and its qualities, needs, and structures become a radical summation of profound care for every leaf and hippo and nebula. Like a good spiritual director, YHWH is releasing Job from misperception and false self with every question asked and is accompanying Job on a path of transformation or, as Perdue writes, "sapiential pedagogy."[13] God demands that Job demonstrate his own knowledge of primordial "discernment" (*binah*; "understanding" in NRSV). Habel adds that, "'Discernment'" (*bīnā*) is a synonym for the "wisdom" (*hokmā*) acquired by God during the process of creation (28:12, 20–28). As Dhorme observes, 'to know discernment (*bīnā*)' is to know the inner 'truth' of a matter (Prov. 4:1; Isa. 29:24). 'Knowing discernment' (Prov. 4:1) seems to be synonymous with 'gaining wisdom' (Prov. 4:5). Thus God is not merely asking Job if he has understanding, but whether he has acquired that primordial wisdom which would enable him to 'discern' the mysteries of the earth's design."[14]

The first explicit theme of these chapters, formulated through YHWH's questions, is design (*etsah*), the elements of structure,

---

13. Perdue, *Wisdom Literature*, 119.
14. Habel, *Job*, 537. Habel's citation of Édouard Dhorme is without attribution.

function, time, and beauty throughout creation. The questions are intended to prove that Job has neither the power, wisdom, or providential insight to master "the foundation of the earth," "its measurements," "where its foundations ["bases," NRSV] [are] sunk," or how or where or when to lay "its cornerstone" (38:4–6).

YHWH's questioning leads to delightful poetry. Where were you, YHWH asks,

> when the morning stars sang together
> and all the heavenly beings shouted for joy?
>
> (v. 7)

The intentional contrast between the skill and art of design needed to lay a cornerstone is juxtaposed immediately with the highest and most artful of the cosmic creations, both of which sing together playfully and shout joyful celebration.

After using a building metaphor that describes the creation of the earth and emphasizes its orderly design, the poet draws us into something completely different. If Job may have trouble laying "the foundation of the earth," what is he to do with YHWH's depiction of the sea, Yam, the personification of chaos, in the strophe immediately following (38:8–11)? Once again we find irony: design and order followed by an antithesis, chaos. But even within the ironic verses a touch of sarcasm prevails. The birth of the sea or Yam is depicted in metaphorical language that describes the sea as it "burst out from the womb." YHWH then wraps the sea in a "swaddling band" of "clouds" and "darkness." YHWH controls the sea with bars, saying, "Thus far shall you come, and no farther, and here shall your proud waves be stopped?" (v. 11). The question mark after "stopped" is, of

---

> Still, what kind of God is this, who has nothing to say about Job's torture, or the infants of men, maimed and unwanted in peace, dying of cold and horror in war? Job knows that their prayers remain unanswered. Why should he be forced to hear lessons in geology, astronomy, meteorology and zoology, while he is consumed by disease and unrequited love? . . . Is that truly all that God wants to say to a dying man? Is the heart of the matter only a show of omnipotence against the puniness of humans?
>
> Samuel Terrien, *Job: Poet of Existence* (New York: Bobbs-Merrill, 1957), 228, 229.

course, in place because the verse is a continuation of another question to Job. From Job's standpoint the answer has to be no, though he remains silent. "The image," Habel writes, "is deliberately absurd: this violent chaos monster is but an infant, born from a womb, wrapped in baby clothes, placed in a playpen, and told to stay in place."[15] Absurd, yes, but absurd in a way that enhances Job's continuing transformation through awe, terror, and mystery, rather than through understanding. Part of our understanding of what Job is experiencing comes from what he has said previously: again, YHWH alludes to what Job has said in the past. The question returns to chapter 3, where Job used birth imagery, but again this becomes an ironic juxtaposition to YHWH's questions about Job's presence at the creation of the sea, chaos. Job lamented at length (3:1–7) about his own birth, wishing because of his suffering that it had never taken place, that he had never seen the light of his

> Far from offering Job an account of why he has allowed him to suffer, he more or less tells him to go to hell. What can you possibly know about me? is the brunt of his testy intervention. How dare you imagine that you can apply your moral and rational codes to me? Isn't this like a snail trying to second-guess a scientist? Who the hell do you think you are? In the end, Job decides to love God "for naught"—to love him without regard for merits or demerits, reward or retribution, with a love as gratuitous as the scourges he has endured.... Some theologians today, confronted with the problem of evil, more or less take God's line in the Book of Job. To ask after God's reasons for allowing evil, so they claim, is to imagine him as some kind of rational or moral being, which is the last thing he is.
>
> Terry Eagleton, *On Evil* (New Haven, CT: Yale University Press, 2010), 141–42.

birth. Job's lament continues as he cries out that he would prefer to have been stillborn rather than "cared for" by YHWH. YHWH's care Job can do without: YHWH herself, in an ironic, sarcastic reference to chapter 3, says that "when the sea burst from the womb" (38:8) YHWH makes "the clouds the sea's garment, and thick darkness its swaddling band" (v. 9). Throughout verses 8–16 the text provides images of "comfort" by which YHWH cares for her own creation as would a mother. But Job experiences no such comfort; his life

15. Habel, *Job*, 538.

> Moses came down from Mount Sinai. As he came down from the mountain with the two tablets of the covenant in his hand, Moses did not know that the skin of his face shone because he had been talking with God. When Aaron and all the Israelites saw Moses, the skin of his face was shining, and they were afraid to come near him. . . . When Moses had finished speaking with them, he put a veil on his face; but whenever Moses went in before the LORD to speak with him, he would take the veil off, until he came out; and when he came out, and told the Israelites what he had been commanded, the Israelites would see the face of Moses, that the skin of his face was shining.
>
> (Exod. 34:29–30, 33–35)

has unfolded in such a way that he would preferred to have been born dead than to have experienced YHWH's "comfort."

Once again YHWH presents order and design, recalling Job's wish for chaos and death. YHWH throws images from Job's own imagination back at Job, images that may have given Job some comfort in the midst of his hopelessness. Some will say this is sadistic on YHWH's part; others that it forms humility; others that throughout his suffering Job remains a man of faith. The philosopher Terry Eagleton has written that the problem with theodicy is that in pursuing it we have first to imagine a being unimaginable: "Some theologians today, confronted with the problem of evil, more or less take God's line in the Book of Job. To ask after God's reasons for allowing evil, so they claim, is to imagine him as some kind of rational or moral being, which is the last thing he is."[16] Job, also, is finding this to be the case.

The readers, after long acquaintance with Job, hear YHWH's questions addressed to themselves as much as to Job: "Has the rain a father, or who has begotten the drops of dew? From whose womb did the ice come forth, and who has given birth to the hoarfrost of heaven? (38:28–29). Where is the way of the dwelling of the light, and where is the place of darkness, that you may take it to its territory and that you may discern the paths to its home?" (vv. 19–20). "Where were you when I laid the foundation of the earth? Tell me, if you have understanding. Who determined its measurements— surely you know!" (vv. 4–5). All these questions presumably have

---

16. Terry Eagleton, *On Evil* (New Haven, CT: Yale University Press, 2010), 141–42.

answers that a person of wisdom might glimpse; there are also questions that are beyond even wisdom's grasp: "Who has cut a channel for the torrents of rain, and a way for the thunderbolt, to bring rain on a land where no one lives, on the desert, which is empty of human life, to satisfy the waste and desolate land, and to make the ground put forth grass?" (vv. 25–27). In much more imaginative poetical style, the question is similar to asking, "If a tree falls in the woods would anyone hear it?" Yes, just as You bring rain to the desert where no one dwells, so the flowers bloom in profusion where no eyes see.

In another theophany, YHWH gave Moses straightforward, reasoned, easy-to-interpret laws and moral regulations. YHWH gives Job a nearly absurd, crazy-quilt series of questions that one suspects begin to cause Job to see in a new way, to see a shine in the roaring God as the whirlwind spins.

But what of the suffering! The box quotes by Terrien and Eagleton both remind us that in the midst of the grandeur of the whirlwind theophany is a question that in itself is awesome, terrifying, the ground of fear, and may in itself be powerful enough to destroy all creation: but what of the suffering?

38:39–40:2 *YHWH's First Speech on the Animals*

The theophany and the questions continue; the great storm whirls in from the east. Once again glorious poetry, but as Gordis so aptly puts it, "Their purpose, however, is not the glorification of nature, but the vindication of God's nature."[17] Whether it vindicates God's nature or not, the poetry does open our eyes to the grace, diversity, and beauty of nature. The unusual content of the words that come from the mouth of God seems at first glance not to answer in a direct way any of Job's questions of recompense or retributory justice or innocent suffering. They glorify nature and on the surface may vindicate God. But there is a deeper analysis of the world nestled in the curious speech that is guiding Job (and the reader) to a new form of awareness, a new consciousness, an ongoing process of transformation that sweeps in the glory of divine creation as a form of

17. Robert Gordis, *The Book of God and Man: A Study of Job* (Chicago: The University of Chicago Press, 1965), 117.

healing, and in a sense internalizes it as a form of renewal. The celebration with which YHWH describes the creation is a part of this transformation, as is YHWH's mode of questioning Job: each question is in some sense its own answer, as YHWH the creative artist reveals the spectacular character of creation. But the reader remains uneasy. Something in addition to the revelation of creation is on the agenda.

In this section YHWH is shown as the one who providentially cares for animals, especially the wild beasts untamed by humans. The animals are paired, with YHWH showing how he cares for each animal's instinct, reproduction, and need for food. These pairings include the lion and the raven, the mountain goat and the deer, the wild ass and the wild ox, the ostrich and the horse, and the hawk and the eagle. As with the rain that falls on the deserts no human inhabits, all these animals exist without the domestication or aid of humanity; they dwell in regions beyond human beings, and in many cases completely beyond humanity's reach. They are then not a part of creation over which humanity has dominion or control (Gen. 1:26). Nor are they the kind of animals that, in YHWH's covenant with Noah, would be prone to fear in the presence of humans ("The fear and dread of you shall rest on every animal of the earth, and on every bird of the air, on everything that creeps on the ground, and on all the fish of the sea; into your hand they are delivered"; Gen. 9:2). They are animals who live generally unaffected by humans and who

> Instead of imitating these philosophers who with analysis and syntheses worry over the goal of life and the justification of the world, and the meaning of the strange and painful phenomenon called Existence, the artist takes up some fragment of that existence, transfigures it, shows it: There! And therewith the spectator is filled with enthusiastic joy, and the transcendent Adventure of Existence is justified. All the pain and the madness, even the ugliness and common place of the world, he converts into shining jewels. By revealing the spectacular character of reality he restores the serenity of its innocence. We see the face of the world as of a lovely woman smiling through her tears.
>
> Havelock Ellis, *The Dance of Life* (New York: Houghton Mifflin Company, 1923), 333.

would thrive without their presence. The one exception to this is the horse, which is both difficult to tame and described by the poet as a fierce and majestic fighter who "laughs at fear" (39:22), and which in the midst of battles that would cow even the bravest soldier functions as though human fighting only rouses the blood and brings out the horse's natural wildness (vv. 19–25).

As for the ostrich (39:13–18) it is, in a word, stupid. As a nurturer of its young it fails utterly, leaving its eggs on the ground unattended where any "foot may crush them" or "sharp teeth crack them open."[18] Later the ostrich "deals cruelly with its young, as if they were not its own." Of the ostrich it is said that its maker forgot to give it wisdom, and has "given it no share in understanding." And "when she spreads her wings to run, she laughs at the horse and rider."[19] In short it is a bird that cannot fly, a comic intruder in the list of other animals, and a "laughing, rejoicing anomaly of bird that is a mystery of gay absurdity."[20] It seems that in YHWH's ordered design, for apparently no reason that humans might understand, there is room for the wild and fearless as well as the absurd and incongruous.

Job in the presence of YHWH hears the story of creation as at once ambiguous, ironic, joyful, beautiful, and paradoxical. How does Job hear and understand these words? Is something of the grandeur and even transcendence of God being absorbed? Is wisdom, understanding, discernment, and fear of the Lord causing his own face to shine? Job is about to respond to the divine narrative; perhaps in Job's answer there is evidence of the effect of the theophany on his discernment and self-understanding.

40:3–5 *A Second Summons and Job's Response*

In verses 1 and 2 God summons Job for the second time to respond. Balentine finds in the words of God's summons a subtle clue to a common language between God and Job:

18. This text is especially corrupt; the translation here is from Stephen Mitchell, *The Book of Job* (New York: HarperCollins, 2002), 83.
19. Ibid.
20. Habel, *Job*, 546.

Because he knows that God is no ordinary defendant, Job has sought but despaired of finding an "umpire" (*môkîaḥ*; 9:33), who can mediate the differences between these two unevenly matched litigants. Now God addresses Job as the *môkîaḥ* (v. 2b; NRSV: "who argues with God") who must speak if this "case" is to proceed any further. S. Mitchell has captured nicely the general sense of God's words: "Has God's accuser resigned? Has my critic swallowed his tongue?"[21]

Balentine then suggests that God's tone may convey to Job a genuine invitation to respond. And YHWH does invite Job to respond. But the tone of the invitation has by now become nearly cognate to Job's sarcasm, irony, anger, and even wrath toward the God of his suffering. Still, we can sense that the real summons to Job in the language of the theophany is toward wisdom, knowledge, and fullness of life. It remains to be seen if Job will follow that path to wisdom.

Thus in a kind of whirlwind of his own in which Job swirls with creation images depicting providence, power, and beauty, Job is invited to respond. Job's first, short response can be summed up in one word in Hebrew, *qallotî*, "I am small" (v. 4a). The NRSV captures it nicely, "See, I am of small account; what shall I answer you?" (v. 4a). Job does not say he is innocent, as he knows he is. He does not say he has sinned, as his friends have claimed he has. He does not say he is terrified, as he thought he would be and no doubt is. He does not comment on injustice or praise the mysterious permeating the universe, as Elihu would have wanted him to. Job does not praise God's power or beauty or truth or goodness. He does not litigate; he does not run or try to hide; he does not complain. He simply says "I am small," an answer that in itself says there is nothing more he can say. A journey into smallness and silence: nothing else is real.

But as Jack Miles writes, "A refusal to speak can be wondrously inscrutable."[22] While Job's silence may be deferential, it may also be defiant. Sheer silence on Job's part would be, for dramatic purposes, perhaps a bit too ambiguous. And so to his silence Job adds a gesture: "I lay my hand on my mouth" (v. 4b). His silence is embodied;

---

21. Samuel E. Balentine, *Job*, Smyth & Helwys Bible Commentary (Macon, GA: Smyth & Helwys, 2006), 667.
22. Jack Miles, *God: A Biography* (New York: Alfred A. Knopf, 1995), 317–18; quoted in Balentine, *Job*, 669.

the hand that had built so much, along with his mouth, will participate in the silence. And Job can "proceed no further" (v. 5b). He
touches his hand to his silent mouth: his own answer to God's questions is to cover his silence with silence.

But YHWH has more to say.

40:6–41:34

From the Whirlwind II:
Beasts and Evil All Around

For the word of the LORD is upright,
  and all his work is done in faithfulness.
He loves righteousness and justice;
  the earth is full of the steadfast love of the LORD.

By the word of the LORD the heavens were made,
  and all their host by the breath of his mouth.
He gathered the waters of the sea as in a bottle;
  he put the deeps in storehouses.

Let all the earth fear the LORD;
  let all the inhabitants of the world stand in awe of him.
                                                    (Ps. 33:4–8)

The Master Craftsman, the Artist of perfection, has come in a
whirlwind. God has chosen questions as the implements of his craft,
and the words and the breath of his mouth to chisel and paint, to
sculpt and to compose creation. The breath of God's mouth from the
whirlwind has left Job small and silent. The voice from the theophany has emphasized the harmony and beauty of the natural world.
And all the earth fears the Lord. The Creator has put the sea in a
bottle, the weather in distant storehouses.

In all that YHWH has spoken rests an implication: there is moral
meaning in the universe that is beyond the capacity of human understanding. As if that were not enough to display YHWH's Absolute
Being as the ground of all being and the essence of existence, Job is
about to meet two new creatures. YHWH brings to Job's attention

two chaos monsters that appear to have broken free of the bottle and crushed the walls of the storehouses: Behemoth and Leviathan. Together they transcend even the moral and theological realities YHWH has already presented through the providential foundation, creation, and sustaining of the universe. YHWH has as yet said nothing about the existence of evil in the world. Behemoth and Leviathan might suggest its existence, indeed might imply that evil itself is part of the creation of this monotheistic Master Craftsman. Yet the psalm says, "For the word of the LORD is upright, and all his work is done in faithfulness. He loves righteousness and justice." Does he indeed? Where in these works do evil and suffering find a place, or the righteousness and justice experienced by Job? Somehow, still, "the earth is full of the steadfast love of the LORD." That may be true, but still something is amiss, something is out of balance: there is chaos, there is evil, there is innocent suffering, there are Behemoth and Leviathan.

40:6–14 *A Second Summons*

The opening of the second summons begins identically to the first (38:1). The subject of the challenge, however, moves from YHWH's cosmic design to the relation between chaos and creation and the justice involved in controlling chaos and maintaining the cosmos.

FURTHER REFLECTIONS
Guilty? Innocent? Just?

It is translated in the NRSV as:

> Will you even put me in the wrong?
> Will you condemn me that you may be justified?
> (40:8)

Verse 8 of Job 40 has been called both the pivot on which the whole book turns and, at the same time, impossible to translate. As it is translated in the NRSV, the question posed by YHWH asks if

Job condemns and puts God in the wrong in order that Job himself might be justified in railing against his suffering, that he may be in the right.

An interesting thought experiment is to take the verse as it is rendered in the NRSV and imagine the question asked by different people to different subjects. For instance, if Job is asking this question of God, Job is asking, "Are you, YHWH, claiming that I am wrong, do you condemn me in order to justify yourself?" What is Job to think, being innocent—that his guilt nonetheless justifies God? Or the friends may say, "Job, are you claiming we are wrong and do you condemn us simply to justify yourself?" Or YHWH might be asking the friends, "Are you condemning and placing Job in the wrong, to justify yourselves?" Of course they are. Or YHWH might ask the reader, "Are you, reader, claiming that I am wrong, do you condemn me in order to justify yourself?" Or the reader might reverse the key words and ask, "Am I claiming to be right, do I extol myself in order to justify God?" The possible combinations are many.

Righteousness and justification are slippery; as the poet has presented the story, a theological interrogation of right versus wrong would never corner or capture righteousness or justification as absolute categories. Compare the "Gods" of chapters 1 and 2, the silent God of the many dialogue chapters, and this God of the whirlwind: is the God of the divine council who is manipulated by the *satan* this same God of the whirlwind? The book of Job stripped to its barest, most severe narrative is about suffering: there is no absolute answer to suffering. There is no absolute answer as to the identity of the Gods that show up in the narrative. That which is absolute (for instance, the God of the whirlwind) is of a different moral and spiritual category than that which is suffering (for instance, the God of the divine council). Cosmic justice includes innocent suffering.

The many possible combinations are complicated by the difficulty in translating. Good notes that possibilities for translating what NRSV renders as "justice" (*mishpat*) include both "order" and "custom" as well as "justice":

> The supposition that that is the word's [justice] "meaning" has determined many an interpretation: "Would you impugn My justice?" (JPS); "Would you pervert my justice?" (Habel);

"Will you deny my justice?" (Gordis). A fourth is "judgment"
…:"Would you annul my judgment?" (Pope);"Do you dare to
deny my judgment?" (Mitchell);"Do you really wish to cancel
my just verdict?" (Fohrer).[23]

There are many more nuances to this crucial verse. But the critical issue is one of balance and how YHWH's speeches, whether in
legal or moral or theological terms, upset that balance. What YHWH
is saying and what Job is hearing is that the world does not function
in neat moral categories: why or how, even in a perfect world, could
everything come out even?

YHWH is about to describe the fearsome power of two monsters of
chaos who would be right at home in the world of Kafka's through-
the-looking-glass court and many, contradictory bases for acquittal
(see Kafka quote in text box on p. 19). These monsters of confusion
are the enemy combatants of a monotheistic God. Their presence
disrupts Job's balance in every area: moral, theological, imagina-
tional, cosmological. What is Job to do, for instance, with the first,
Behemoth?

40:15–41:34 *Behemoth and Leviathan*

With Behemoth and Leviathan, we (and Job) confront two strange,
ferocious, and powerful creatures that also claim a certain compelling beauty. Since this pair is so very strange, we will begin with some
of the more popular interpretive claims about the nature of these
beasts. We will then look at YHWH's relation to them and what that
relation says about creation and chaos. Important details about each
particular beast will then be given, followed by a look at the beast in
a theological framework that includes suffering. Finally, in keeping
with our thesis that the theophany has a profound, transformative
effect on Job, we will comment on Job's experience of these beasts
described by God, especially in relation to Job's own suffering.

After first registering his usual dissatisfaction with theories other

---

23. Good, *In Turns of Tempest*, 353.

than his own—in this case "two almost equally mistaken theories" that the beasts are either mythical monsters of pagan origin or real creatures, "with favorites" for the past 350 years being hippopotamus and crocodile[24]—David Wolfers takes us on an elaborate, idiosyncratic journey leading to a possible partial answer about the identity of these beasts. In the end Wolfers concludes, "with little doubt," that the two beasts are what he calls symbolic allegories that he has worked out in the following way:[25]

Behemoth = Judah   = Jordan   = pride   = identification with Job
Leviathan = Assyria = Euphrates = the wicked = chaos monster

This is interesting, but it cuts too many corners and stuffs some ideas and allegories into categories where the fit is questionable.

The word *behemoth* means "super beast," and outside 40:15–24 it occurs nowhere else in the Hebrew Bible.[26] But as Newsom has noted, the debate about whether either of these two animals is real is probably misplaced. The descriptions in Job suggest that both Behemoth and Leviathan are better understood as liminal creatures whose characteristics place them somewhere between earthly animals and supernatural figures that belong to the world of myth and legend.[27]

> It's the Black Sea in a midnight gale.—It's the unnatural combat of the four primal elements.—It's a blasted heath.—It's a Hyperborean winter scene.—It's the breaking-up of the ice-bound stream of Time.
>
> Herman Melville, *Moby Dick*, Norton Critical Editions, 2nd ed., ed. Hershel Parker and Harrison Hayford (New York: W. W. Norton, 2002), 26.

Elmer Smick has given an evenhanded summary of the most common contemporary options for both Behemoth and Leviathan: either (1) Behemoth and Leviathan are natural creatures, animals

24. David Wolfers, *Deep Things Out of Darkness: The Book of Job* (Grand Rapids: Eerdmans, 1995), 161–62.
25. Ibid., 163–93.
26. Samuel E. Balentine, *Job*, Smyth & Helwys Bible Commentary (Macon, GA: Smyth & Helwys, 2006), 683.
27. Newsom, *Job*, 248.

such as the hippopotamus and the crocodile described in mythic language, or (2) they are symbols of political enemies, or (3) they represent the Red Sea, as seen in Psalm 74, or (4) they are symbols of some eschatological evil, as in Isaiah 27.[28] Corrine Patton adds that more recent scholars "such as Pope, Perdue, and [Tryggve] Mettinger would see these figures as the primordial monsters of chaos whom the deity defeats in the course of creation. As such, then these figures would symbolize chaos, which, although defeated, remain to threaten creation at any moment."[29]

But whether YHWH remains in control of the two beasts is also a question. One can even ask whether God may have created them. Certainly there is something threatening in these animals, perhaps even to their creator. One way of looking into the chaotic nature of these two beasts is to look at them in terms of revelation. Typically, creation is something humans can observe and in doing so discern something of God's plan or providence; in that sense creation can be revelatory.

Creation as chaos darkens the clarity of creation as revelation. Corrine Patton lists several logical conclusions to the doctrine of revelation from creation that bear on the relation of Leviathan and Behemoth to God:

> First, [revelation] presumes that God controls what humans observe, and therefore that God controls creation. . . . Second, the idea that humans should act as God intended them to act implies this creation has a certain divine order or hierarchy, and that each human has a discernable place within that order. . . . Third, wisdom literature envisions the effects of opposition to God's order as punishments such as Job suffers: shame, disease, separation from the community, childlessness, poverty. . . . Fourth, the presumption of a divine order implies that any deviation in that order is either an action opposed to God's activity or evidence that God is losing control and chaos is triumphing.[30]

28. Elmer Smick, "Another Look at the Mythological Elements in the Book of Job," *Westminster Theological Journal* 40 (1978): 213–28.

29. Corrine L. Patton, "The Beauty of the Beast: Leviathan and Behemoth in Light of Catholic Theology," in Cook et al., *Whirlwind*, 149.

30. Ibid., 153–54.

From any perspective, the monsters are intentionally ambiguous. Do the beasts have a discernible place in the cosmic order? If they do, it is as instruments deliberately placed to interfere with that order. Is it likely that Behemoth or Leviathan experience any punishment? YHWH is clear in declaring that there is nothing that can harm them; it is hard to see them suffering in any way; it is even probable that, as described, they do not die. Does God control these creatures? It is not clear that God does. By now the reader is well versed in options for understanding Job's suffering. The two monsters present yet another option for that suffering: chaos. In Genesis chaos is that which God tames, bounds, and enlightens. From the perspective of Genesis, God can control chaos; but by its very nature chaos exists, but it exists outside divine order (if not outside divine control) and operates exclusive of moral order. Is chaos, then, personified in Behemoth and Leviathan, causing and maintaining Job's suffering even beyond the divine intention?

The reader knows that Job's suffering does not reflect on God's creative power. Job's suffering may impact divine justice or goodness, or it may present a God who has little empathy for suffering in general. But in the context of the theophany and Job's spiritual and theological awakening in the midst of the whirlwind's own chaos, Job perceives chaos and evil in the monsters. Certainly what he does not see is some orderly, sanitized mechanism of retributive justice. Job has his encounter with the Creator; in the theophany Job enters

---

Many earlier commentators associate Behemoth with Satan. An example is Isho'dad of Merv, a ninth-century Syriac commentator:

"The Behemoth is a dragon without equal. . . . In the whole creation . . . there is no animal that is unique and not male or female, because all animals have been created in pairs. On the other hand, those who assert that this book was written by the divine Moses maintain the reality of the Behemoth. It is a figure of Satan, they say, and as this animal destroys everything it sees, so Satan does the same thing secretly, and therefore it has been made Satan's accomplice in crime. Both in its name and in its action it is the figure of Satan, because according to the sense of the word, Behemoth means 'through it death,' that is, death has entered among people through it."

Isho'dad of Merv, *Commentary on Job* 40.10 (15), Corpus scriptorum christianorum orientalium (Leuven, 1903–), 229:265. In ACCS, 209.

the divine presence, and as that presence evokes two creatures of chaos Job "sees" the cause, perhaps the effect, perhaps the existential reality and experience of his own suffering.

FURTHER REFLECTIONS
Behemoth and Leviathan: Did God Create Evil?

Within this second speech are some intriguing phrases and hints about the place of Behemoth and Leviathan in created order and therefore implications about the place of evil, inside or outside creation.

The description of Behemoth begins:

> Look at Behemoth,
> Which I made [asah] just as I made you.
> (40:15a,b)

Habel translates:

> Behold, now, Behemoth, whom I made [asah] along with you.

In both translations the "you" of course is Job. The NRSV translation accentuates equality of substance, essence, or quality in making Behemoth and Job. The Habel translation accentuates timing; Job and Behemoth were made together at the same time and thus in the hierarchy of beings they are in some sense equal. In either case, God makes and relates chaos/evil and Job.

In focusing on the relation of order, chaos, and evil, the second speech does not deny the existence of chaos, or its harmful effects, nor does it deny the beasts as frequently beyond control or inherently evil. With regard to the nature and creation of chaos, Patton writes, "the poem implies three things: (1) that chaos is created by God, (2) that chaos is created for God's enjoyment, and (3) that chaos is beautiful."[31]

Behemoth, then, is not an eternal creature; it was created, but created primordially, first among all God's creations. YHWH wants

---

31. Ibid., 156.

to make clear that Behemoth is a special creation. We need not be overly impressed by the primordial originality of the creation (as others hold the same privilege in other parts of Scripture: Wisdom is first of God's creations in Prov. 8:22, the "heavens and the earth" are first in Gen. 1:1, and in Gen. 2:4b, 7 "the earth and the heavens" again are first and as the first living being "God formed man from the dust of the ground, and breathed into his nostrils the breath of life). But what we can learn of importance from Behemoth is two-fold: first, that there is a strong identity between Behemoth and Job (40:15), and second, that in whatever order the beast was cre-ated, it *was* made, God *created* Behemoth. Based on the Hebrew of 41:25, J.D. Levenson does claim that the text makes no explicit claim that Leviathan was created, and so concludes that in Leviathan is an eternal quality of chaos that opposes creation.[32] The Hebrew of 41:25 can, however, be translated as an assertion that Leviathan is also created. But as Patton adds, "even if one rejects the notion of Leviathan's creation in this verse, God does not explicitly assert in the first divine speech that each animal was created."[33] Thus given the explicit passage that says Behe-moth was created and the implica-tions that Leviathan was likewise created, against the conclusion of most commentators, evil and chaos seem to be caught up in the divine activity, and a part of YHWH's answer to Job is that evil and chaos as a part of creation are com-plicit in Job's suffering.

> Are all your tricks a test? If so, I
>   hope you find, next time,
>   Someone in whom you
>   cannot spot the weakness
> Through which you will
>   corrupt him with your
>   charm. Mine you did
> And me you have: thanks to
>   us both, I have broken
> Both of the promises I made as
>   an apprentice;—
>   To hate nothing and to ask
>   nothing for its love.
>
> W. H. Auden, *The Sea and the Mirror: A Commentary on Shakespeare's "The Tempest"* (Princeton, NJ: Princeton University Press, 2003), 8.

What this means for humans is that God created evil or some-thing very close to it, and that this evil is active in the world. That

---

32. J. D. Levenson, *Creation and the Persistence of Evil: The Jewish Drama of Divine Omnipotence* (San Francisco: Harper & Row, 1998), 49. Cited in Patton, "Beauty of the Beast," 156.
33. Patton, "Beauty of the Beast," 157.

is a hard sentence to write. The strange beauty and fascination of
Behemoth and Leviathian, of chaos and evil, make the sentence all
the more chilling.

The relation of the Creator to evil and the implication of that relation
for Job's own suffering continue to haunt the chapters. In 40:11–14,
YHWH invites Job, if he can, to "tread down the wicked where they
stand. Hide them all in the dust together; bind their faces in the
world below" (vv. 12b–13). Of course Job is incapable of perform-
ing this act; the implication is that YHWH is capable. But implicit in
the challenge is the concession by God that the world order is not
perfect, that the wicked need treading down. For whatever reason
YHWH does maintain complete control over evil but cannot, did
not yet, or will not annihilate evil. The reasons are as inscrutable as
is Job's suffering, but they do point to the tantalizing possibility of
divine suffering: the reasons, given the very strange and even mystical animals Leviathan and Behemoth, imply that evil maintains
something of its own control, with the further implication that both
symbolize, along with humanity, process theology's premise of co-
creation. If this is the case, in the very act of creation God risks and
encounters suffering for the suffering world.

42:1–17
Epilogue: Job's Second Answer . . .
Wonder and Comfort

Job's Second Answer and Surrender
Job's second and final answer to God has been a subject of debate
among readers of Job from the earliest times. This is the case especially for verse 6, which the NRSV renders, "therefore I despise
myself, and repent in dust and ashes." With other commentators, I
believe that this interpretation is incorrect: all Job's loss, grief, and
suffering, his deep speeches from dark places, his theophanic vision
more detailed than any other in the Hebrew Bible, including that of
Moses, does not lead to an emotional, psychological, and spiritual

state of contrition, abject humbling, self-hate, surrender, or for-saking his position of lamentation in exchange for a feeble form of repentance "in dust and ashes."

Such interpretations, though common over the centuries, are in themselves monstrous, inhuman, and impious, and have caused more shame, blame, and uncalled-for guilt than any healing or good. Job has been a righteous man, a just man, an honest man of lam-entation, an adversary, a fighter, someone YHWH, *YHWH*, appears before and speaks. The book of Job is a spiritual journey, both for its reader and for Job. It is a journey through deep, innocent, seem-ingly random pain and suffering, the kind of suffering every human experiences in one way or another, yet not all arrive enlightened and transformed to a beatific vision out of which Job can say, "but now my eye sees you" (42:5). Or perhaps all who suffer do, in one way or another, arrive at such a place. Who am I to say? I think of holocausts and Hiroshimas and, like Aquinas, I must move to an afterlife to par-don God. And who am I to pardon?

Job's response to the divine theophany is very brief, using the rhetorical device of repeating phrases of YHWH's, then responding to them in a contrastive way that admits of YHWH's wisdom com-pared to Job's relative ignorance. The epilogue, like the prologue, is frustratingly complex in its simplicity: both invite us in their simplic-ity to complexify the narrative by forcing us to project something of our own lives into the story. But perhaps that is a part of their beauty as well. From the prologue we know of a man who with the approval of YHWH suffers innocently; from the poetic dialogue we know of a man who continues to suffer but who maintains the integrity of his innocence against unsympathetic friends and a silent God; from the whirlwind we learn of an angry God who created a universe of beauty yet is willing, in a sense, to crush Job further; in the epilogue we see a man who, with few questions answered, walks away and back to his possessions, his family, his standing in the community, and his wisdom. It appears at first reading as though he simply turns his back to his readers and friends and is gone. Answers to many questions remain unsaid.

The epilogue tells us so much less about Job than does the pro-logue. We are told that Job prays for the friends, which tells us something of his piety, but this is nothing new: Job had done the same for his sons in the prologue.

Only one other thing that Job does before he dies in the epilogue, "old and full of days," is mentioned. This one detail is a kind of surrender to the understanding that *all* things created by God are precious. The detail is naming his three daughters and giving them an inheritance. In the prologue, the emphasis had been on the sons. In the epilogue it is on the daughters: the sons are not named, but the daughters are; the daughters receive an inheritance "along with their brothers," which was unheard of in Job's time and culture. But to Job, *all* things are precious. The daughter's names are Jemimah, which means "affectionate dove," a symbol of peace; Keziah, which means "cinnamon," the most fragrant of spices; and Keren-happuch, which has the allegorical meaning of "horn of adornment" and the literal meaning of an outward feminine grace derived from inward virtue. Given the fact that this surrender is focused on Job's daughters, Stephen Mitchell writes, "It is as if, once he has learned to surrender, his world too gives up the male compulsion to control."[34] Beyond a first reading, the incident with his daughters does tell us much about the man from Uz. In naming his daughters and giving them a portion of his inheritance, he shows that he has engaged and embodied something of the feminine. In this act of naming we can intuit much: Job is thoughtful, sensitive, kind, at peace, gentle, calm, generous, faithful, and because of all of these, wise. These are of course not exclusively feminine traits; they are instead traits inferred from a man who has surrendered self to the greater reality that *all* things are precious, *all* things are to be loved.

The epilogue suggests something of God's character as well. God changes. In a guilt-and-blame culture, God is willing to forgive.

Precritical Interpretations

In the writings of the church fathers and mothers, there is disagreement concerning the function and meaning of Job's final speech. Not all assume that YHWH has just crushed Job and that therefore Job "despises" himself, as the NRSV would have it, nor do all assume that he "repents," also as in the NRSV, nor do they see Job in the end

---

34. Mitchell, *Job*, xxx.

sitting abjectly like a worm in and no better than "dust and ashes" (NRSV).

John Calvin, for instance, believes Job is a bit rash and perhaps foolish but focuses on God's method of interrogation, suggesting from it an incisive method of meditation that perhaps Job would have been wise to follow:

> What is the cause, then that men are so rash as to advance themselves so foolishly against God? It is because they give themselves license to speak and it seems to them that God has no reply. Now here is the remedy that God gives us to put down the foolish temerity that is in us: it is, that we think of that which He will be able to ask of us. If God begins to interrogate us, what shall we answer?[35]

Calvin is suggesting an ancient spiritual, meditative practice of prayer in which we imagine conversation with God, what God might ask us about ourselves, and what our responses might be.

Gregory the Great, Ambrose, and Maimonides also give compelling analysis of the final chapter. Gregory sees a kind of moral illumination in Job. Commenting on verse 6, Gregory notes that the more one sees of one's self clearly, the more one "discerns the light of greater grace ... [f]or when he is elevated within, by all that he is, he endeavors to agree with that standard which he beholds above him."[36] Gregory taps into a Platonic spiritual tradition in which true self-knowledge elevates the soul ever "upward" to "behold [that which is] above him." For Gregory, Job is purified, so self-aware that he ascends to the height of which there is no greater: "but now my eye sees you" (42:5b).

Ambrose interprets God's words to Job as a "third trial," those of the wounds of words. God's words, for Ambrose, are more penetrating than any of Job's previous suffering, yet it is through these words that God gives God's hand to Job and lifts him from the "way" of penitence and purgation to the "way" of light. Words penetrate the soul, and if properly given and received, enlighten the soul rather than create self-hatred or cause "despising" of one's self: "A third contest was in store for Job. He had lost all that was his, that is, his

---

35. Calvin, Sermon 20, 299.
36. Gregory, *Morals on the Book of Job*, vol. 3.2, 42:6, 665.

inheritance along with his children, and his flesh suffering wounds; it remained for him to overcome the trials posed by words. The combat was not a trivial one. Adam was beguiled by speech, and Samson was overcome by a word; in truth nothing penetrates the soul so much as a polished discourse and, on the other hand nothing is so biting as a discourse of a harsher tenor. . . . Job suffered distress, but he withstood and carried the burden of the words next to that of the wounds."[37]

Maimonides, the great medieval philosopher and exegete, adds a new interpretive dimension that also becomes a spiritual practice. He writes that Job's experience teaches him that his ways are not God's ways and thus to take all things "lightly," and to *accept* all things that come his way with "love":

> This is the object of the Book of Job as a whole; . . . so that you should not fall into error and seek to affirm in your imagination that His knowledge is like our knowledge or that His purpose and His providence and His governance are like our purpose and our providence and our governance. If man knows this, every misfortune will be borne lightly by him. And misfortunes will not add to his doubts regarding the deity [but] . . . add to his love.[38]

Acceptance—of suffering, of the moment, of providence—may be the highest form of self-abandonment to Divine Love.

Surrender and Comfort

Based on Job's final words—"therefore I despise myself, and repent in dust and ashes" (v. 6)—just following YHWH's speech in the whirlwind and just before all that had been lost to him is returned, many contemporary readers of Job also end with a presumed recognition of Job's guilt. But, more accurately, we can say that Job ends with a sense of wonder, serenity, acceptance, and comfort.

As some of the more ancient commentators suggest, Job's trials are best seen as part of a spiritual journey. James Williams writes, "I see the intention of the book as one of relating how Job experiences a 'spiritual journey.'"[39] The spiritual journey can mean many things

37. Ambrose, "Prayer of Job and David," 357.
38. Maimonides, *The Guide of the Perplexed* 3.23, 497.
39. Williams, "Theophany of Job," 363.

and is described in many ways. For Job, of primary importance is that it is a "way" or "path" along which a "soul journey" occurs. A part of Job's way, for instance, is the path of suffering. Change occurs along the way; there is movement as well as transformation leading, hopefully, to a place more integrative, healing, and compassionate.

The spiritual journey is archetypical and can be complex, something at times of hell, something at times of paradise. Dante Alighieri's *Divine Comedy* is a story of the spiritual journey of Dante himself, detailed and complex, colorful and imaginative, holistic and integrating. The spiritual journey can also be as simple as Thérèse of Lisieux's "little way." At its least complicated it is no more than a simple acceptance and turn toward God, a conversion. But acceptance and turning is never the end of the spiritual journey: driven by internal longing and desire, there is always another turning to be made. And yet there is always something provocative, even dangerous, in acceptance and turning. Moses knew of that danger; one can scorch one's face until it glows or with Peter one can walk on water, forget where one is, and nearly drown. Job too is aware of the danger: Job's way is one of painfulness that burns throughout the book. Yet from beginning to end he turns, lamenting surely, in anger surely, hopeless surely, but toward God.

Wonder and attentiveness are attributes, capacities that likewise turn us toward the sacred. A strange fascination, terror, mystery, and fear also draw us to what is holy, a wonder that draws attentiveness and turns us toward God. The same is true of the monsters Behemoth and Leviathan. Like Melville's Moby Dick, there is something attractive and fascinating about them, even in their destructive, chaotic powers.

A theophany in a whirlwind: wonder and attentiveness. If one were limited to just two words to describe the holy in YHWH, *wonder* and *attentiveness* would do quite well. This is what holy Job is seeing, is drawn toward in the theophany, and also what God is intent on teaching Job: acceptance tending to the mysteries of wonder. As Stephen Mitchell writes, "Each verse [of YHWH's speech] presents Job with an image so intense that, as Job later acknowledges, he doesn't hear but *sees* the Voice."[40]

40. Mitchell, *Job*, xx.

Of course this is not just a nice, tidy little wrap-up to the story offered in a suitably packaged little bundle. Job suffered ferociously. At least as unpalatable as Job's suffering are the death of his children and the supposed replacement of those children with ten new children. As any parent knows, this is preposterous: no child takes the place of a lost child.

Job's first response, then, is wonder and awe. He puts his hand over his mouth and speaks nothing, remains silent. In the form of the Beast and the Serpent, YHWH then begins to speak of good and evil. Speaking from the whirlwind, YHWH seems not to envision a moral universe in which good and evil battle relentlessly to some eschatological resolution of good over evil. He is speaking rather in criticism of what some would call theological dualism. YHWH points rather toward a theology imaged as an infinite sphere that includes these monsters of chaos and evil as well as ruby-throated hummingbirds and stars and redwood trees and history and afterlife. The grandeur of the book of Job is that, presumably, the sphere would also include YHWH, YHWH neither higher nor lower, neither grander nor more beautiful, simply seen, attended to, a mutual participant in wonder. Such a sphere needs the dark to know the light, the light to recognize the dark, and both to hear with our ears and see with our eyes. Evil breeds its devils only in the neighborhood of good. But the more one accepts the suffering, the more one attends to the good, living within the tension of their coinciding opposition.

The Beast and the Serpent are God's playthings and are a part of the infinite sphere running from angel to beast and from God to his wager with the *satan,* a wager that also happened to deepen divine wisdom and perhaps is having its way with what we call Satan today.

Job's final words in 42:6 are not about self-abasement. Self-loathing is not what God has been showing Job or speaking about. The friends try to hold up a tired and no longer feasible theology of justice, righteousness, providence, and self-abasement. Self-abnegation is not the lesson God gives Job in its grammar of wonder and attention. As a part of his journey Job surrenders to this divine wisdom; he submits to a relationship spherical in shape. Job surrenders and enters the sphere that includes family, YHWH, the *satan,* friends, creation, Behemoth, and daughters. Such a sphere carries with it no purely human-centered answers.

Job's final speech is another masterpiece within this masterful poem. It is a miracle of tact, of acceptance and serenity toward God and toward his suffering. It is a wonder of the unspoken that manages to say much about Job's dynamic transformation. What we need to know about the transformation is spoken, but not a word more. The theophany itself is like a sphere inside a sphere inside a radiant, spiraling sphere.

Is this a moral God? No, not in the traditional sense. There are no scales to balance sin against blessing; no scales of righteousness against which punishment might be measured, and as the Lord accepts Job's prayer for his friends the movement is from morality to beauty. The God we find at the end of the book of Job is close to that God found in Second Isaiah: "I form light and create darkness; I make weal and create woe; I the LORD do all these things" (Isa. 45:7), which is about as close as any passage in Scripture gets to the highly charged picture of YHWH we find in Job. But morally, the blindfold is off. Job's final words come from acceptance, not from submission. They do not represent a gesture of transaction as between a slave and a master—"therefore I despise myself, and repent in dust and ashes," as in the NRSV—but more "therefore I will be quiet, comforted that I am dust." This is acceptance in which Job gives himself completely to God, having faced evil in the form of Leviathan and Behemoth, in the only way possible: in wonder and in love. Complete acceptance. Complete surrender. He surrenders into dust, into the earth of his creation.

> Therefore I will be quiet,
> Comforted that I am dust.[41]
>
> (v. 6)

---

41. Translation from Mitchell, *Job*. See Mitchell, xxxii; Mitchell makes a convincing case for the verb *nhm* to be read as "comforted" rather than "changed mind" or "repented"; cf. xxxii, 128.

Conclusion:
Entertaining Suffering

After spending many, many hours with Job, I have come to think of Job's experience as "entertainment" or "entertaining" suffering, which at first glance may seem a little odd. In researching, thinking about, writing, and *experiencing* Job, I have come to see that, ironically, "entertaining" is Job's most enlightened response to suffering. As with death, we have ambiguous responses to suffering, and perhaps that is why Job—and hence the Joban reader—ends with many more questions than answers. Another name for the book of Job might be "The Book of Why?"

Setting aside the ambiguity for now, one of the things that Job does well is "entertain" suffering, much as a host would entertain a guest in an act of hospitality, an act of courtesy in which the host may discover as much about himself or herself as about the guest, in this case, suffering. At the same time the guest can be transformed by the host, in this case, Job or the reader. One does not go out in search of suffering as a guest; but if suffering knocks on one's door, it does no good, as Job found, to attempt to shut suffering out; to make such an attempt can only make it worse. A certain loss of ego or self is required to entertain suffering, but as with a guest like death, the self can begin to bury suffering in a way that leaves the ego intact.

Jacques Lacan remembers that Freud said that neurotic persons suffer mainly from reminiscences, that is, "from a past that has not reached its term, from the unburied dead."[1]

---

1. Stuart Schneiderman, *Jacques Lacan: The Death of an Intellectual Hero* (Cambridge, MA: Harvard University Press, 1983), 146.

As is common with Freud, within this short phrase is contained images of both birth and death. I believe that in the book of Job it is the YHWH figure that gives birth to suffering, then turns the suffering to death of the self, then helps Job to bury the dead. That the birth of Job's suffering is initiated by YHWH is obvious from the narrative. That the same YHWH helps Job to first entertain, then to bury, suffering is perhaps not so obvious. But I believe this occurs during the whirlwind speech as YHWH reminds Job that, on the one hand, creation with its suffering is not Job's doing, while on the other hand, the chaos monsters, Leviathan and Behemoth, are aspects of Job's self which YHWH helps bring to consciousness, then to bury. The burial is contained in the prose epilogue as Job "remembers" his healed self by receiving exactly what he had lost. This remembering is given further transformational emphasis through the focus on the feminine as Job names his three lovely daughters (and does not name his sons) and gives them each a portion of his inheritance. As George Steiner has remarked, "the master translator is the perfect host."[2] Job is a master translator of suffering: he entertains and transforms suffering as would the perfect host.

This is not to say that the book of Job is not the most painful book in all of Scripture: it is. But in his long and ambiguous struggle, Job manages to host, to entertain, suffering. In the remainder of this postscript I will turn to "entertainment" as a way of hosting suffering, allowing it to remain the experiential, existential reality it is, rather than allowing it to slip into an academic, scholarly, or overly rational enterprise. The "entertainment" provided is from Job and from other writers and poets. Most of the "entertainments" are also found in the text of this book; "entertaining" suffering, translating it, hosting it, is a practiced art.

As a verb, *entertaining* means holding suffering attentively in a pleasant, agreeable, diverting, or amusing way; entertaining suffering means holding, maintaining, and keeping suffering as a guest with a certain amount of hospitality; entertaining suffering means admitting suffering into the mind and body and soul, harboring it, even cherishing it. As a gerundive adjective, entertaining suffering

---

2. George Steiner, *Real Presences* (Chicago: University of Chicago Press, 1989), 146.

is not a species of masochism but rather a way of giving suffering its due, which is in part, I believe, the capacity to invert and inflict mayhem on any of the above verbal meanings of the word. Etymologically *entertaining* is from the Latin *inter*, meaning "in the midst of, in between, betwixt, among, amid," or "surrounded by," and *tenere*, meaning "to hold, to keep, to have, to maintain," or, with an accessory idea of firmness or persistence, "to hold fast to, to occupy, to watch, to guard, to defend." But since remaining "in the midst of holding fast to" suffering is difficult, uncomfortable, and intuitively not an unalienable right, I will from time to time turn to "entertainment" as a means of helping us remain "in the midst of holding fast to suffering."

Entertainment. This first "entertainment" is from Job himself.

> If I look for Sheol as my house,
>   if I spread my couch in darkness,
> if I say to the Pit, "You are my father,"
>   and to the worm, "My mother," or "My sister,"
> where then is my hope?
>   Who will see my hope?
> Will it go down to the bars of Sheol?
>   Shall we descend together into the dust?
> (Job 17:13–16)

Suffering Questions

In her book on the history of exegesis of the book of Job, Susan E. Schreiner writes, "The man on the dungheap repeatedly raised questions that would haunt the ages that followed him. . . . [Job's story] has forced its readers to wrestle with the most painful realities of human existence."[3]

Job's endless questions are the substance of Job's response to "the painful realities of human existence." Using an image from nature, Job has, for instance, many questions about hope. He asks at one point:

---

3. Susan E. Schreiner, *Where Shall Wisdom Be Found? Calvin's Exegesis of Job from Medieval and Modern Perspectives* (Chicago: University of Chicago Press, 1994), 11.

> For there is hope for a tree,
>> if it is cut down, that it will sprout again,
>> and that its shoots will not cease.
> Though its root grows old in the earth,
>> and its stump dies in the ground,
> yet at the scent of water it will bud
>> and put forth branches like a young plant.
> But mortals die, and are laid low;
>> humans expire, and where are they?
>>> (Job 14:7–10)

The point here is contrast: a tree has hope; Job does not.

The most influential writer on the book of Job in the Christian spiritual and theological traditions is Gregory the Great. But he does not much like questions. According to Gregory, one may ask questions in order to learn, but one does not ask questions about God: asking questions about God only displays one's ignorance. Of course asking such questions about divine power and righteousness is exactly what Job *does*; but for Gregory such inquisitiveness is ignorance. Still, Gregory's book, *Morals on the Book of Job*, is an astonishing and serpentine and endlessly fascinating piece of work. But it is also a demon of a book from which Gregory himself seems never quite able to escape. One comes away from this book with the sense that Gregory was never able to entertain or host or bury suffering. For instance, about questions, Gregory writes, "And because a person asks a *question* in order to be able to learn that of which that person is ignorant, for a person to *question God*, is for that person to acknowledge that he or she is ignorant in God's sight."[4]

Entertainment. From Austrian composer, Hugo Wolf:

> I would like most to hang myself on the nearest branch of the cherry trees standing now in full bloom. This wonderful spring with its secret life and movement troubles me unspeakably. These eternal blue skies, lasting for weeks, this continuous sprouting and budding in nature, these coaxing breezes impregnated with spring sunlight and fragrance of flowers . . .

4. Gregory the Great, *Morals on the Book of Job*, vol. 3.2, 35.3.4, trans. J. Bliss (Oxford: John Henry Parker; F. & J. Rivington, London, 1850), 664.

make me frantic. Everywhere this bewildering urge for life, fruitfulness, creation—and only I, although like the humblest grass of the fields one of God's creatures, may not take part in this festival of resurrection, at any rate not except as a spectator with grief and envy.[5]

Suffering Comfort

One of the most famous attempts to give answer to the question of suffering is the philosophical approach known as theodicy. Theodicy is a post-Enlightenment endeavor that proposes to find a "solution" to the "problem of evil" and suffering. The term was introduced into philosophy by Gottfried Wilhelm Leibniz, who in 1710 published an essay to show philosophically that the evil in the world does not conflict with the goodness of God. Many people have called the book of Job itself a theodicy. It definitely is not. The book is anything but a solution to the problem of evil; Job's friends are budding theodicists, but neither Job himself nor the book in total is anything like a theodicy. Job does *not* answer; he *only* questions.

Entertainment. William Styron, in *Darkness Visible*, writes:

> The pain is unrelenting, and what makes the condition intolerable is the foreknowledge that no remedy will come—not in a day, an hour, a month, or a minute. If there is mild relief, one knows that it is only temporary; more pain will follow. It is hopelessness even more than pain that crushes the soul.[6]

This is harsh, to be sure; but entertaining suffering, as Robert Burns writes, is a desolate brother of comfort.

Entertainment. Robert Burns, the Scottish poet and lyricist, in a letter writes:

> Lord, what is Man! Day follows night, and night comes after day, only to curse him with life which gives him no pleasure. Today, in the luxuriance of health, exulting in the enjoyment

5. F. Walker, *Hugo Wolf: A Biography* (London: J. M. Dent & Sons, 1968), 322.
6. William Styron, *Darkness Visible: A Memoir of Madness* (New York: W. W. Norton, 1983), 62.

of existence; in a few days, perhaps in a few hours, loaded with conscious painful being, counting the tardy pace of the lingering moments and refusing or denied a Comforter.[7]

Suffering Faith, Suffering Hope, Suffering Love

Robert Ellsberg has written something that I think Freud and Jung are trying to get at: "The saints do not teach us how to avoid suffering; they teach us how to suffer."[8]

This next, wonderful quotation is from the saintly Cyril of Jerusalem, instructing catechumens: "The dragon is at the side of the road watching those who pass. Take care lest he devour you! You are going to the Father of souls, but it is necessary to pass by the dragon."[9] The entertaining of suffering has, I believe, something to do with that dragon, necessary to pass. It is necessary because our journey to the Father of souls takes us just there where the dragon is watching; to get there we *must* entertain and host the dragon in order to pass.

Job is set on a journey. That path, his journey, is suffering. The word "love" is used only three times in Job, in each case it is a perverse, lamentable kind of love (cf. 10:12; 19:19; 37:13).[10] This poem is not about a journey of love. It is about dragons. Job is on the road to the Mother of souls where he discovers, centuries before the fact,

---

7. Robert Burns, letter 374, December 3, 1789, in *The Letters of Robert Burns*, vol. 1, *1780–1789*, 2nd ed., ed. G. Ross Roy (Oxford: Oxford University Press, 1985), 457.

8. Robert Ellsberg, *The Saint's Guide to Happiness* (New York: North Point Press, 2003), 104.

9. Cited without attribution in Flannery O'Conner, "Letter to A," January 1, 1956, in Flannery O'Conner, *Collected Works*, ed. Sally Fitzgerald (New York: Library of America, 1988), 979.

10. The first use of the word "love" is at 10:12, in the midst of a chapter when Job's sanity is an issue: the chaper begins, "I loathe my life . . ." (10:1a) and Job's use of the word is a plea to God for God to remember how Job once was treated. The second use of the word "love" at 19:19 needs no commentary: "All my intimate friends abhor me, and those whom I loved have turned against me." Elihu uses the word "love" in 37:13 only after he is told of the power and might of the divinity: the thunder of his voice, lightening, a roaring voice, storms and winds and cold, from "the breath of God ice" is given (v. 10a). All these have the effect of terrifying, traumatizing, cowering both animals and humans in order to, as Elihu says, ". . . for correction, or for his land, or for love, he [God] causes this to happen" (v. 13). Love is mentioned in Job, but only as a means to intensify Job's suffering.

that there is a point where suffering and love converge, on a cross. It takes a saint, I suppose, to find, accept, and live into this convergence; Job does not actually find the convergence because he has not found love. Holy Job instead sets up the psychic, somatic, and spiritual *necessity* for this cross, this convergence, this hosting and "entertainment"; the necessity for love to converge with suffering. But for Job himself, though we can say that Job points to where love *might* be, love is simply not yet on the road he travels.

Job is in a dark night. Through complaint (constant prayer), questioning, and chaos he finds a way into entertaining suffering to the point where suffering itself becomes the host. An analogy to Job's dark night is today's dark night of the planet.

Entertainment. Cormac McCarthy writes of a darkening night of the planet in the novel *The Road.*

> [The father had] had this feeling before, beyond the numbness and the dull despair. The world shrinking down about a raw core of parsible entities. The names of things slowly following those things into oblivion. Colors. The names of birds. Things to eat. Finally the names of things one believed to be true. More fragile than he would have thought. How much was gone already? The sacred idiom shorn of its referents and so of its reality. Drawing down like something trying to preserve heat. In time to wink out forever.[11]

Given McCarthy's metaphor, in which "wink out forever" is synonymous with death, is it too coy to say that by the end of the book of Job, Job learns to entertain suffering to the point where suffering in his life becomes a laser-focused light which then "winks out forever"? Only if we believe Job has not become the master translator, the perfect host in the art of entertaining suffering.

11. Cormac McCarthy, *The Road* (New York: Alfred A. Knopf, 2006), 75.

Suggestions for Further Reading

Balentine, Samuel, E. *Job*. Smyth & Helwys Bible Commentary. Macon, GA: Smyth & Helwys, 2006. Part of a helpful series with sidebars, visual art, commentary, and theological reflection, this volume on Job provides historical setting, literary design, and details of language, culture, and context. Accessible to interested laypersons and students, teachers, and those planning sermons and preaching.

Dhorme, Édouard. *A Commentary on the Book of Job*. With a prefatory note by H. H. Rowley. Translated by Harold Knight. London: Thomas Nelson and Sons, 1967. Scholarly historical-critical study, a careful, encyclopedic commentary on the book of Job. Attention to historical context, linguistic issues involving syntax, grammar, and vocabulary, and prehistory of the book of Job using form criticism and poetic analysis.

Good, Edwin M. *In Turns of Tempest: A Reading of Job with a Translation*. Stanford, CA: Stanford University Press, 1990. Commentary accessible to students, teachers, and scholars. Some theological interpretation with focus on literary analysis. Uses literary theory of deconstruction emphasizing "play" and indeterminancy of the text. Good is not afraid to show a change in his thinking as the book progresses. Very good on the function and language of the legal metaphor in Job.

Gordis, Robert. *The Book of God and Man: A Story of Job*. Chicago: University of Chicago Press, 1965. An approachable commentary, using primarily literary approach to argue for a unified and unifying "inner unity and architectonic structure" to Job. In this Gordis is not unlike some premodern writers on Job.

———. *The Book of Job: Commentary, New Translation, and Special Studies*. New York: Jewish Theological Seminary of America, 1978. Of value primarily to scholars.

Habel, Norman C. *The Book of Job: A Commentary*. Old Testament Library. Philadelphia: Westminster, 1985. Readable and nicely designed translation and commentary intended for students, teachers, and laypersons interested in Job, as well as scholars and literary critics. Habel is most concerned with the literary aspects of Job, its inner integrity, and the meaning of the book as a whole, which allows for some theological speculation.

Janzen, Gerald J. *At the Scent of Water: The Ground of Hope in the Book of Job*. Grand Rapids: Eerdmans, 2009. A short but thought-provoking book. Janzen wrote an earlier commentary on Job; this book shows twenty-five years of added maturity. It is experiential, relational, and self-consciously autobiographical without ignoring his deep knowledge of language, literary style, theology, and hermeneutics. Good for first-time readers of Job as well as teachers, preachers, and scholars.

Newsom, Carol A. *The Book of Job: A Contest of Moral Imaginations*. Oxford: Oxford University Press, 2003. Well-argued and accessible book using Job as a "polyphonic" text and as an illustration of the means by which ethics and moral behavior can be linked and influenced by genre, language, and imagination.

Perdue, Leo G. *Wisdom Literature: A Theological History*. Louisville, KY: Westminster John Knox, 2007. Provides insight on an important but often neglected aspect of the book of Job, its place within the larger tradition of Wisdom literature. Excellent overview of the content, purposes, and genres of Wisdom literature with pertinent examples from the tradition, including Job. Excellent chapter on the historical theology of Wisdom literature.

Premodern commentators: John Chrysostom, Ephrem the Syrian, Gregory the Great, Ambrose, Maimonides, Thomas Aquinas, John Calvin. Many premodern commentaries are available; these are some of the most important and most cited today. Gregory's commentary is labyrinthine, utilizing literal, allegorical, tropological (moral), and anagogical interpretations. John Calvin wrote no commentary but composed 159 sermons on Job that are very readable for layperson, student, teacher, and scholar. Ambrose's short study compares Job and David on the issue of prayer. With regard to the purpose of suffering, Maimonides, Aquinas, and Calvin see suffering as a means to deeper understanding of self, creation, and God, while for Gregory suffering is a moral lesson: it is medicinal, purgative, and pedagogical.

Schreiner, Susan E. *Where Shall Wisdom Be Found? Calvin's Exegesis of Job from Medieval and Modern Perspectives*. Chicago: University of Chicago Press, 1994. Excellent writer, good at providing key connections, especially between medieval commentators—Gregory the Great, Maimonides, and Aquinas—and Calvin. Good historical work with strong and compelling emphasis on theology.

Terrien, Samuel. *The Iconography of Job through the Centuries: Artists as Biblical Interpreters*. University Park: Pennsylvania State University Press, 1996. Wonderful comprehensive, easy-to-read collection of visual art inspired by the book of Job from mid-third century through twentieth century, showing how artists "exegete" Job. Excellent commentary by an accomplished Joban scholar and art historian.

Modern Commentaries

Balentine, Samuel E. *Job*. Smyth & Helwys Bible Commentary. Macon, GA: Smyth &Helwys, 2006.

Bergant, Dianne, CSA. *Job, Ecclesiastes*. Old Testament Message. Wilmington, DE: Michael Glazier, 1982.

Dhorme, Édouard. *A Commentary on the Book of Job*. With a prefatory note by H. H. Rowley. Translated by Harold Knight. London: Thomas Nelson and Sons, 1967.

Driver, S. R., and G. B. Gray. *A Critical and Exegetical Commentary on the Book of Job*. International Critical Commentary. Edinburgh: T & T Clark, 1977.

Good, Edwin M. *In Turns of Tempest: A Reading of Job with a Translation*. Stanford, CA: Stanford University Press, 1990.

Gordis, Robert. *The Book of God and Man: A Study of Job*. Chicago: University of Chicago Press, 1965.

————. *The Book of Job: Commentary, New Translation, and Special Studies*. New York: Jewish Theological Seminary of America, 1978.

Habel, Norman C. *The Book of Job: A Commentary*. Old Testament Library. Philadelphia: Westminster, 1985.

Hartley, John E. *The Book of Job*. Grand Rapids: Eerdmans, 1988.

Janzen, Gerald J. *Job*. Interpretation. Atlanta: John Knox, 1985.

Newsom, Carol A. "The Book of Job: Introduction, Commentary, and Reflections." *NIB* 4:317–637. Nashville: Abingdon, 1996.

Pope, Marvin. *Job*. Anchor Bible. Garden City, NY: Doubleday, 1965.

Rowley, H. H. *Job*. New Century Bible. Greenwood, SC: Attic Press, 1976.

Terrien, Samuel. *Job: Poet of Existence*. New York: Bobbs-Merrill, 1957.

Wharton, James A. *Job*. Westminster Bible Companion. Louisville, KY: Westminster John Knox, 1999.

Wolfers, David. *Deep Things Out of Darkness: The Book of Job, Essays and a New English Translation*. Grand Rapids: Eerdmans, 1995.

Premodern Commentaries

Ambrose. "The Prayer of Job and David." In *Saint Ambrose: Seven Exegetical Works*, translated by Michael P. McHugh, 327–67. Washington, DC: Catholic University of America Press, 1972.

Aquinas, Thomas. *The Literal Exposition on Job: A Scriptural Commentary concerning Providence*. Translated by Anthony Damico. Atlanta: Scholars Press, 1989.

Calvin, John. *Sermons from Job*. Translated by Leroy Nixon. Grand Rapids: Eerdmans, 1952.

Chrysostom, John. *Commentary on Job*. Edited by Ursula Hagedorn and Dieter Hagedorn. PTS 35. New York: de Gruyter, 1990. In ACCS.

———. *Commentaries on the Sages*. Vol. 1, *Commentary on Job*. Translated by Robert Charles Hill. Brookline, MA: Holy Cross Orthodox Press, 2006.

Ephrem the Syrian. *Commentary on Job*. *Sancti Patris nostri Ephraem Syri opera omnia*. Rome, 1737. In ACCS.

Gregory the Great. *Morals on the Book of Job*. Translated by Members of the English Church. 3 vols. Library of the Fathers of the Holy Catholic Church. Oxford: John Henry Parker, 1845.

Isho'dad of Merv. *Commentary on Job*. Corpus scriptorum christianorum orientalium. Leuven, 1903–. In ACCS.

Julian of Eclanum. *Exposition on the Book of Job*. Corpus Christianorum: Series latina 88. Turnhout, Belgium: Brepols, 1991. In ACCS.

Maimonides, Moses. *The Guide of the Perplexed*. Translated by Shlomo Pines. Chicago: University of Chicago Press, 1963.

Olympiodorus. *Commentary on Job*. Edited by Ursula Hagedorn. PTS 24. New York: de Gruyter, 1984. In ACCS.

Philip the Priest. *Commentary on the Book of Job*. Patrologiae cursus completus: Series latina 26. Paris: Migne, 1844–64. In ACCS.

Simonetti, Manlio, and Marco Conti, eds. *Job*. ACCS Old Testament 6. Downers Grove, IL: InterVarsity Press, 2006.

Additional Sources

Astell, Ann W. *Job, Boethius, and Epic Truth*. Ithaca, NY: Cornell University Press, 1994.

Barnes, Albert. "Job 19:25–29." In Zuck, *Sitting with Job*, 283–97.

Barth, Karl. *Church Dogmatics*, IV/3.1. Edited by G. W. Bromiley and T. F. Torrance. Edinburgh: T & T Clark, 1961.

Besserman, Lawrence L. *The Legend of Job in the Middle Ages*. Cambridge, MA: Harvard University Press, 1979.

Bloom, Harold, ed. *The Book of Job*. New York: Chelsea House, 1988.

Burns, Robert. *The Letters of Robert Burns*. 2 vols. 2nd ed. Edited by G. Ross Roy. Oxford: Oxford University Press, 1990.

Byron, Lord George Gordon. "Darkness." In *The Last Man*. Mary Shelley. Vol. 1. London, 1826. Romantic Circles. http:// www.rc.umd.edu/editions/mws/lastman/bydark.htm.

———. "Letter to Francis Hodgson, October 13, 1811." In *Letters and Journals of Lord Byron*, edited by Thomas Moore. Vol. 2. Frankfurt, 1830. *Literary Journals*. http://lordbyron.cath .lib.vt.edu/monograph.php?doc=ThMoore.1830&select= AD1811.27.

Carlyle, Thomas. "The Hero as a Prophet." In *On Heroes, Hero Worship, and the Heroic in History*, edited by Archibald MacMechan. Boston: Ginn, 1901.

Chase, Steven. *Tree of Life: Models of Christian Prayer*. Grand Rapids: Baker Academic, 2005.

Childs, Brevard S. *Introduction to the Old Testament as Scripture*. Philadelphia: Fortress, 1979.

Chödrön, Pema. *When Things Fall Apart: Heart Advice for Difficult Times*. Boston: Shambhala Classics, 2000.

Clines, David J. A. "The Arguments of Job's Three Friends." In *Art and Meaning: Rhetoric in Biblical Literature*, edited by D. J. A. Clines, D. M. Gunn, and A. J. Houser, 199–214. JSOTSup 19. Sheffield: Sheffield Academic Press, 1982.

———. "A Brief Explanation of Job 12–14." In Zuck, *Sitting with Job*, 125–40.

Cook, Stephen L., Corrine L. Patton, and James W. Watts, eds. *The Whirlwind: Essays on Job, Hermeneutics and Theology in Memory of Jane Morse*. JSOTSup 336. New York: Sheffield Academic Press, 2001.

Cross, Frank Moore. *From Epic to Canon: History and Literature in Ancient Israel*. Baltimore: Johns Hopkins University Press, 1998.

Daiches, David. "God Under Attack." In *The Book of Job*, edited by Harold Bloom, 37–62. New York: Chelsea House, 1988.

Dante Alighieri. *The Divine Comedy, The Inferno*, 1.1–9. Translated by Henry Wadsworth Longfellow and Gustave Doré. New York: Barnes & Noble, 2003.

Dickinson, Emily. *The Complete Poems of Emily Dickinson*. Edited by Thomas H. Johnson. Boston: Little, Brown, 1960.

Dostoevsky, Fyodor. *The Brothers Karamazov*. Translation by Constance Garnett. New York: Barnes & Noble Classics, 2004.

Douglass, Frederick. *Narrative of the Life of Frederick Douglass, An American Slave*. New York: Barnes & Noble Classics, 2003.

Eagleton, Terry. *On Evil*. New Haven, CT: Yale University Press, 2010.

Eisen, Robert. *The Book of Job in Medieval Jewish Philosophy*. Oxford: Oxford University Press, 2004.

Evans, Richard J. *The Third Reich at War*. New York: Penguin Press, 2009.

Fontaine, Carole R. "Wounded Hero on a Shaman's Quest: Job in the Context of Folk Literature." In Perdue and Gilpin, *Voice from the Whirlwind*, 70–85.

Foucault, Michel. *Discipline and Punishment: The Birth of the Prison*. Translated by Alan Sheridan. New York: Vintage Books, 1995.

———. *Madness and Civilization: A History of Insanity in the Age of Reason*. Translated by Jean Khalfa. New York: Vantage Books, 1965.

Frost, Robert. *Collected Poems, Prose, and Plays*. New York: Library of America, 1995.

Frye, Northrop. *Anatomy of Criticism: Four Essays*. Princeton, NJ: Princeton University Press, 1957.

Fullerton, Kemper. "Double Entendre in the First Speech of Eliphaz." *Journal of Biblical Literature* 49 (1930): 320–74.

Gabirol, Solomon ibn. "The Royal Crown." In *Selected Religious Poems of Solomon ibn Gabirol*, translated by Israel Zangwill. Philadelphia: Jewish Publication Society of America, 1923.

Gilkey, Langdon. "Power, Order, Justice, and Redemption: Theological Comments on the Book of Job." In Perdue and Gilpin, *Voice from the Whirlwind*, 159–71.

Girard, René. *Job: The Victim of His People*. Translated by Yvonne Freccero. Stanford, CA: Stanford University Press, 1987.

Goetz, Ronald. "The Suffering of God: The Rise of a New Orthodoxy." *The Christian Century* 103, no. 13 (April 1986): 385–89.

Gutiérrez, Gustavo. *On Job: God-Talk and the Suffering of the Innocent.* Translated by Matthew J. O'Connell. New York: Orbis, 2003.

Habel, Norman C. "In Defense of God the Sage." In Perdue and Gilpin, *Voice from the Whirlwind*, 21–38.

Hoffman, Yair. *A Blemished Perfection: The Book of Job in Context.* Sheffield: Sheffield Academic Press, 1996.

Hopkins, Gerard Manley. "No Worst, There Is None." In *The Poetical Works of Gerard Manley Hopkins*, edited by Norman Mackenzie. Oxford: Oxford University Press, 1990.

Janzen, Gerald J. *At the Scent of Water: The Ground of Hope in the Book of Job.* Grand Rapids: Eerdmans, 2009.

Jarrell, Randall. "90 North." In *Randall Jarrell: The Complete Poems.* New York: Farrar, Straus & Giroux, 1969.

Jung, C. G. *Answer to Job.* Translated by R. F. C. Hull. Princeton, NJ: Princeton University Press, 1958.

Kafka, Franz. *The Trial.* Translated by Willa and Edwin Muir. New York: Alfred A. Knopf, 1948.

Levenson, J. D. *Creation and the Persistence of Evil: The Jewish Drama of Divine Omnipotence.* San Francisco: Harper & Row, 1998.

Macleish, Archibald. *J.B.: A Play in Verse.* Boston: Houghton Mifflin, 1961.

May, Gerald G. *The Dark Night of the Soul: A Psychiatrist Explores the Connection between Darkness and Spiritual Growth.* San Francisco: HarperSanFrancisco, 2004.

McCarthy, Cormac. *The Road.* New York: Alfred A. Knopf, 2006.

McKenna, David. "God's Revelation and Job's Repentance." In Zuck, *Sitting with Job*, 381–410.

Melville, Herman. *Moby Dick.* Edited by Hershel Parker and Harrison Hayford. Norton Critical Editions. 2nd ed. New York: W. W. Norton, 2002.

Miles, Jack. *God: A Biography.* New York: Alfred A. Knopf, 1995.

Mitchell, Stephen. *The Book of Job.* New York: HarperCollins, 2002.

Newsom, Carol A. *The Book of Job: A Contest of Moral Imaginations.* Oxford: Oxford University Press, 2003.

Norris, Kathleen. *Acedia and Me: A Marriage, Monks, and A Writer's Life.* New York: Riverhead Books, 2008.

O'Conner, Flannery. "Letter to A, January 1, 1956." In *Collected Works*, edited by Sally Fitzgerald. New York: Library of America, 1988.

Patton, Corrine L. "The Beauty of the Beast: Leviathan and Behemoth in Light of Catholic Theology." In Cook et al., *The Whirlwind*, 142–67.

Penington, Issac. "Letter to Bridget Atley, 1665." In *Quaker Spirituality: Selected Writings*, edited by Douglas V. Steere. New York: Paulist Press, 1984.

Perdue, Leo G. *Wisdom Literature: A Theological History.* Louisville, KY: Westminster John Knox, 2007.

Perdue, Leo G., and W. Clark Gilpin, eds. *The Voice from the Whirlwind: Interpreting the Book of Job.* Nashville: Abingdon, 1992.

Placher, William C. *Mark.* Belief. Louisville, KY: Westminster John Knox, 2010.

Poe, Edgar Allan. Letter to John P. Kennedy, September 11, 1835. In *The Letters of Edgar Allan Poe*, edited by John Wand Ostrom. Vol. 1. Cambridge, MA: Harvard University Press, 1948.

Rankin, Oliver Shaw. *Israel's Wisdom Literature: Its Bearing on Theology and the History of Religion.* New York: Schocken, 1969.

Ricoeur, Paul. "A Reaffirmation of the Tragic." In *The Book of Job*, edited by Harold Bloom. New York: Chelsea House, 1988.

Rilke, Rainer Maria. "Little Tear-Vase." In *Ahead of All Parting: The Selected Poetry and Prose of Rainer Maria Rilke,* translated by Stephen Mitchell. New York: Modern Library, 1995.

Roethke, Theodore. "In a Dark Time." In *The Collected Poems of Theodore Roethke.* New York: Doubleday, 1975.

Rohr, Richard. *Falling Upward: A Spirituality for the Two Halves of Life.* San Francisco: Jossey-Bass, 2011.

———. *Job and the Mystery of Suffering: Spiritual Reflections*. New York: Crossroad, 1998.

Scheindlin, Raymond P. *The Book of Job: Translation, Introduction, and Notes*. New York: W. W. Norton, 1998.

Schreiner, Susan E. *Where Shall Wisdom Be Found? Calvin's Exegesis of Job from Medieval and Modern Perspectives*. Chicago: University of Chicago Press, 1994.

———. "'Why Do the Wicked Live?' Job and David in Calvin's *Sermons on Job*." In Perdue, Leo G. and W. Clark Gilpin, eds. *The Voice from the Whirlwind: Interpreting the Book of Job*. Nashville: Abingdon Press 1992.

Styron, William. *Darkness Visible: A Memoir of Madness*. New York: W. W. Norton, 1983.

Terrien, Samuel. *The Iconography of Job through the Centuries: Artists as Biblical Interpreters*. University Park: Pennsylvania State University Press, 1996.

———. "Job." In *The Interpreter's Dictionary of the Bible*, edited by G. A. Buttrick et al. Vol. 3. Nashville: Abingdon, 1962.

Thiel, John E. *God, Evil, and Innocent Suffering: A Theological Reflection*. New York: Crossroad, 2002.

Tilley, Terrence W. *The Evils of Theodicy*. Eugene, OR: Wipf & Stock, 2000.

Tromp, Nicholas J. *Primitive Conceptions of Death and the Nether World in the Old Testament*. Rome: Pontifical Biblical Institute, 1969.

Wells, H. G. *The Undying Fire*. New York: Macmillan, 1919.

Wiesel, Elie. *The Trial of God: A Play in Three Acts*. Translation by Marion Wiesel. New York: Random House, 1979.

Wilcox, John T. *The Bitterness of Job: A Philosophical Reading*. Ann Arbor: University of Michigan Press, 1994.

Williams, James G. "Theophany of Job." In Zuck, *Sitting with Job*, 359–72.

Zuck, Roy B., ed. *Sitting with Job: Selected Studies on the Book of Job*. Grand Rapids: Baker Book House, 1992.

Index of Scripture

Index of Subjects

Abaddon, 191, 212–13. *See also* Sheol
Abraham, 23, 42, 255
Abse, Joan, 241
absence of God. *See* God
Acedia & Me (Norris), 156
Adam and Eve, 18–19, 166, 224
afterlife. *See* immortality
Alighieri, Dante. *See* Dante
All Things Shining (Dreyfus and Kelly), 162
Ambrose, 16, 64, 139, 241, 252, 277–78
angels, 244, 249
anger
    of Elihu, 237–38, 247
    of God, 39, 69, 112, 125, 146, 156
    of God against Job's friends, 125, 139
    of Job at God, 52–54, 82, 85
    of Job at his friends, 128–29, 141–42
animals, 8, 46–47, 87–88, 104, 112, 118, 120–21, 256, 261–63
Answer to Job (Jung), 45
anthropology. *See* theological anthropology
Aquinas, Thomas
    on Elihu, 239–40, 247
    on immortality and afterlife, 64–65, 139, 275
    on Job as prefigurement of Jesus, 224
    on providence, 56
    on reasons for suffering, 11
    on redeemer passage, 140
Aramaic Targum of Job, 187
Aristotle, 55
Ash'arite school of Islamic theology, 55
Astell, Ann W., 235n2

Auden, W. H., 273
Augustine, 166
authorship of book of Job, 6–9, 185

Babylonian exile, 5, 83
Balentine, Samuel E.
    on Eliphaz, 170
    on fate of the wicked, 204
    on innocent suffering, 26
    on *mashal* (discourse), 196–97
    on third set of dialogues, 161, 186–87
    on whirlwind theophany, 194, 263–64
Barnes, Albert, 137
Barth, Karl, 182, 200
Baudelaire, Charles, 21, 70
beatitudes
    of Jesus Christ, 224
    of Job, 221–26
Behemoth, 57, 115, 204, 266, 268–74, 279–81
Berlioz, Hector, 53
Besserman, Lawrence L., 4n7
Bildad the Shuhite
    complaint of, against Job, 117–19
    on creation images, 61–63
    on fate of the wicked, 117–23, 149, 150
    on God's sovereignty, 188–89
    on hope, 60, 62
    on Job's lack of knowledge of God, 123–24
    Job's responses to, 67–77, 126–42, 190